Published in 1985 by Grisewood & Dempsey Ltd.,
Elsley Court, 20–22 Great Titchfield Street, London W1P 7AD.

© Grisewood & Dempsey Ltd 1985

Phototypeset by Southern Positives and Negatives (SPAN), Lingfield, Surrey

Printed and bound in Spain.

ISBN 0–906279–33–X

RAINBOW
Mathematics
Encyclopedia

Leslie Foster

This edition produced exclusively for

Contents

Why Bother About Maths?	8
One, Two, Three . . . a Lot	10
Number Stories from the Past	12
Our Wonderful Number System	14
Measuring Length	16
Mass and Weight	18
Marking Time	20
Money Matters	22
Hogsheads and Litres	24
Some Shapes and Sizes	26
Machines that Count	28
Signs and Symbols	30
Two of the Branches . . .	32
The Other Two Branches . . .	34
Guessing and Estimating	36
Fun with Numbers	38
Numbers Magical and Mysterious	41
Little and Large	43
Numbers in a Sieve	46
A Piece of Cake	49
The Most Important Invention?	52
How an Octopus Counts	55
Every Picture Tells a Story	59
Letters Start Algebra	62
Odd and Amazing Numbers	64

$4 = \sqrt{16}$

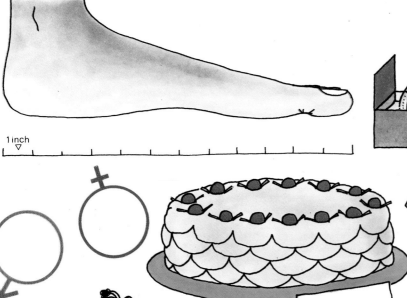

1 inch

Guess the Weight

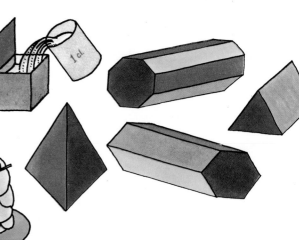

Edited by John Paton

Fun with Number Patterns and
   Shapes   67
A Building Brick   70
Geometry Set   72
Solid Stuff   75
Plane Shapes: Triangles   78
Plane Shapes: Quadrilaterals and
   Others   81
Curves   85
Are You Square?   89
Some Laws of Arithmetic   91
Angles and Rotation   93
Patterns Please   96
Powerful Numbers   98

Home Maths   101
Introducing Sets   103
Maths Around   106
Thales and the Trigon   110
Moebius and his Merry Band   114
Euler and his Networks   116
Bears and Babies   119
Strong and Beautiful Shapes   122
Fun Maths   125
Where do you Live?   126
Calendar Curiosities   129
Toilet Roll Maths   131
Chances   133
Answers   136
Index   138

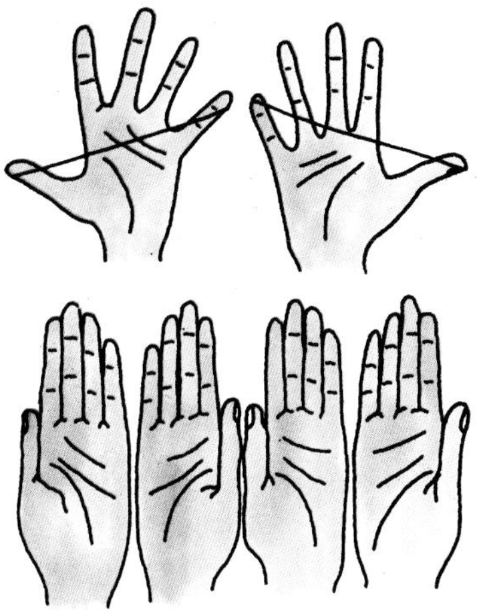

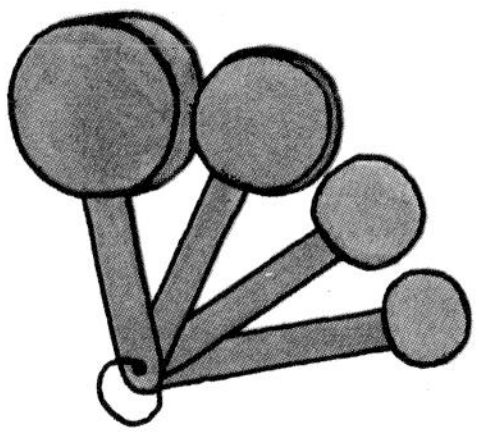

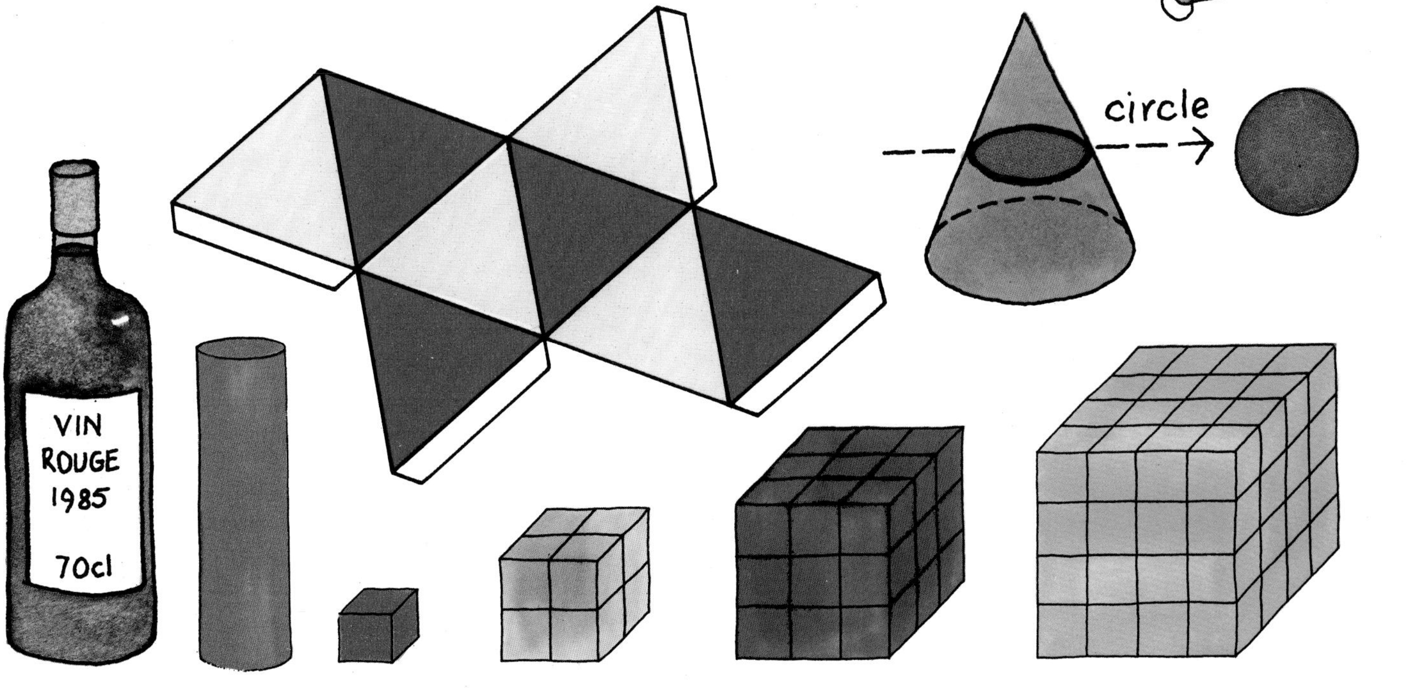

circle

VIN
ROUGE
1985

70cl

Why Bother About Maths?

Have you ever read "A Christmas Carol" by Charles Dickens? The book was written in 1843 and tells of Ebenezer Scrooge, a rich merchant. At the beginning of the story Scrooge was a miserable miser but he was changed into a kind and happy man one Christmas Eve.

Scrooge had a clerk called Bob Crachit who worked in the counting house. At this time Britain was becoming an important trading nation. It was making a great many goods in its factories and sending them all over the world in its ships. This trade meant that a lot of clerks were needed to work out the ships' loads and keep records of all the money involved. Bob Crachit and his fellow-clerks worked long hours doing boring sums and entering columns of figures into thick books.

By 1870 all children had to attend school to learn reading, writing and arithmetic. Britain was an even bigger trading nation by this time and there was still a great need to have lots of clerks. So schoolteachers had to teach children how to do copperplate writing and sums. These were just to help boys find jobs in offices. The mathematics had little to do with the wonderful subject now taught in schools. It is very sad that, for a hundred years after Bob Crachit was doing his boring work, arithmetic books still had "sums" in them which dated from Victorian times.

Bob Crachit at his cold, high stool filled book after dusty book with long columns of figures.

"SUMS" FROM AN ARITHMETIC BOOK OF 1923

Divide 20 tons 15 cwt. 2 qrs. 12 lb . by 27.
Multiply £10 7s. 8½d. by 128.
Reduce 3 miles 6 furlongs 130 yards to feet.
Find the difference between 75 oz. 15 dwt. 21 gr. and 80 oz. 2 dwt. 7 gr.
Find the cost of 2439 articles at 19s. 11½d. each.
If 3 ducks are worth 4 chickens, and a pair of chickens cost 5s. 6d., find the cost of 7 ducks.
Add 5½ cwt. to 3.125 qrs., and reduce the result to the decimal of a ton.

Find the sum:
61244
264496
1675144
1602338
3999762
1733124
1109059
583850
5048027
1261398
78651
1001897

What is Maths?

We now know that maths is not about doing boring sums. Nor is it a subject only for clever people. It is really about patterns and learning how numbers and shapes are related to each other. Just as members of a family are related to one another, so numbers and shapes are linked in interesting and beautiful ways. We find some of these patterns in Nature and some of them in mathematics.

Maths is divided into many topics which link together. New or Modern Maths, which is taught in many schools, helps us to understand how this is done.

What Use is Maths?

Maths is, of course, very useful. It helps us to understand and learn about other subjects like science, geography and history. It is also linked with art, craft, music and movement. Maths is useful in our daily lives for doing things like telling the time and checking that we have the right

Without maths it would be impossible for engineers to build complex road junctions such as this.

change after buying something. It helps us to enjoy our games and hobbies; to cook, build model aircraft or understand the latest athletics results.

Engineers use mathematics to build roads, bridges, reservoirs and power stations. Maths helps people to do their jobs and is needed by mechanics, farmers, plumbers, carpenters and electricians. The High Streets in our towns, with their banks, stores and offices, provide many examples of how maths is used in business. Without maths, and certainly without the computer, the landing on the Moon would not have been possible.

The world is changing all the time and we do not know what things will be like in ten, twenty or thirty years' time. We know that life will be different and we shall be faced with new and fascinating problems. To solve them we shall have to use maths and a special branch of learning known as *logic*. This means that we must think for ourselves and work out new ideas. In the future we shall use computers more and more to help us. But we will also have to tell the computer what to do and how to do it. What an interesting and fascinating task that will be!

Maths is Fun
Maths is so interesting that it is the hobby of many people. It gives hours of amusement with its host of puzzles, tricks, problems and brain-teasers.

There are patterns in shapes and numbers – triangular and square number patterns, above right, and mathematical shapes in the design of the Sydney Opera House.

Even simple activities such as paper-cutting and drawing shapes without taking your pencil off the paper lead to learning interesting mathematical truths. They are also great fun to do.

Maths is Magic
The study of maths leads us into a world of magic and wonder. How did people learn to count and how was our amazing number system built up? How were we able to use numbers to build pyramids and skyscrapers? What wonders will mathematics lead us to in the future? This book tries to answer some of these questions and introduces other topics to interest the Junior Mathematician.

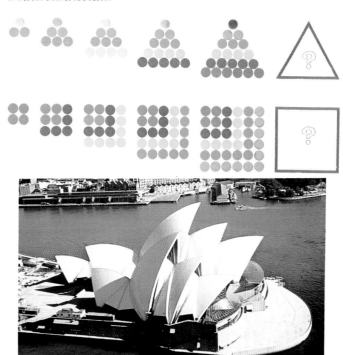

One, Two, Three... a Lot

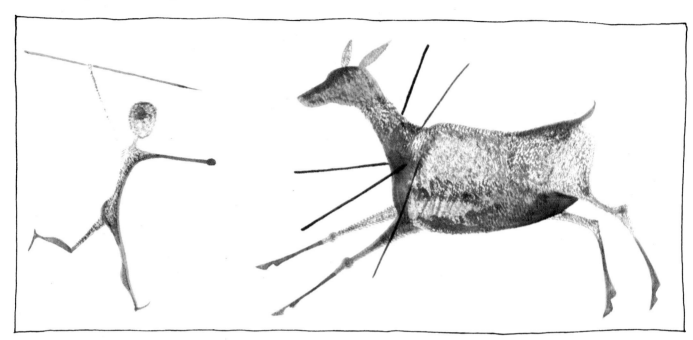

Can you remember when you first started to count? One little girl, whose parents had been helping her, proudly recited her numbers: "One, two, three, five, eight, ten ... Goodness what happened to six?" Before long she could put the numbers in the right order without missing any out. Most of us can count by the time we start school, so it seems strange to think of a time when no-one could count at all.

The Cave-dwellers

Nobody knows how people began to count. In the early days they did not need to count because they did not own many things. In time they began to live in caves and were able to make fire. Men went out to look for food while their wives stayed behind to look after the children and drive away wild beasts. Perhaps the man, returning home, told his family about his hunting. We know from cave paintings that either he, or a member of his family, drew on the wall a picture of what had happened. The artist did not know anything about numbers but he drew a picture to show *how many times* the beast had been hit. Sometimes the cavemen put scratches on the cave wall to represent the number of furs the family had or the animals they had seen. One mark would stand for one thing.

One-for-one Counting

When people began to tame animals and keep them near their homes, they needed to know how many they had. One scratch by a stone on a tree would stand for one animal. A shepherd would put out one stone for each sheep which went out to pasture in the morning. At night the shepherd would remove one stone from the pile for each returning sheep. In this way he would know if any of his flock were missing.

The Inca Indians of South America tied knots in a rope to keep a one-to-one count of things.

During the last war airmen had a picture painted on the side of their aircraft every time they shot down an enemy plane or made a raid over enemy countries.

There are many stories of prisoners making on their cell wall a calendar where a stroke stood for a day.

These are all examples of the one-to-one counting which can be seen when a young child

During World War II, the crews of bomber planes painted a bomb on the fuselage for every raid over enemy territory.

There are stories of prisoners marking off the days of their sentence on the cell walls.

sets a table and puts out a plate for each person saying, "One for me, one for Mummy, one for Daddy . . ."

Fingers and Sounds

We have an idea how counting by using words began because there are some tribes in the world whose lives are like those of the early cave-dwellers.

In the Andaman Islands in the Bay of Bengal in India there is a tribe of people with names only for the numbers ONE and TWO. However, they can count up to ten by tapping their noses with each finger in turn as they make sounds to stand for the ten numbers:

ONE, TWO, AND THIS, AND THIS, AND THIS, AND THIS, AND THIS, AND THIS, AND THIS, AND THIS. By watching which finger taps the nose, and the different sound being used, it is possible to know what number they mean.

Fingers and Toes

At some point in history people began to use parts of their body for counting. Each finger could be matched to objects being counted to stand for one, two, three, four and five. One hand could stand for a set of five things and two handfuls for a set of ten.

In warmer countries, where people went barefoot, fingers and toes were used to stand for a set of 20 things. The Aztecs and Mayans of Central

TALLIES AND SCORES

In olden times, when tribes were fighting each other, the leader would want to know how many fighters the enemy had. He would send out someone to "count" them and perhaps the spy cut a notch on a stick to stand for each of the enemy he saw.

The gunmen in the Wild West used to cut a notch in their six-shooters each time they shot someone.

The proper name for this notch is a *tally* and tally-sticks have been in use until quite recently. When merchants were dealing with each other five or six hundred years ago they kept a record by scoring notches on a tally stick. Sometimes they split the tally-stick down the middle and each merchant would keep a half to prevent cheating. Bank clerks are still called *tellers*. They get their name from the *talliers* who used to match up the two halves of sticks to see if they "tallied".

The British government used to keep tallies that recorded the Treasury's money. In 1834 it was decided to burn all the old tallies in the furnaces which heated the House of Lords. The tallies were so dry, and there were so many of them, they caused a fire which burned down the Houses of Parliament.

A notch on a tally was known as a *score*. From this we get the word we use when playing games.

Tally sticks were used to record sales and loans (left). They were made of willow or hazel. The sticks had notches cut in them according to the amount of money that changed hands. Then they were split down the middle and each party was given one half of the stick. When the debt was settled, the two halves were fastened together to show that the notches "tallied" exactly. The sticks could then be destroyed. Tally sticks were used in the English exchequer in Norman times. They were not abolished by law until the 18th century.

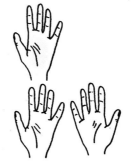

5 → 1 handful

5 10 5 → 2 handfuls

America counted in this set of 20. In Biblical times also this set was used: Moses was "fourscore years old" and Aaron was "fourscore and three".

As time went on, people would count up to five, ten or twenty and put out one stone or pebble to represent this big number. The idea of making one number replace larger numbers was an important step forward in mathematics. It meant that people could begin to count and record their numbers more easily. It also led to our wonderful system of counting in tens and giving names to the numbers.

Number Stories from the Past

If someone were to ask you how old you are, you would give the answer as a *number*. If someone asks you to write down your age you will write a *numeral*.

WE SAY NUMBERS   WE WRITE NUMERALS

Think of a lamb, and another lamb and another lamb. The idea you have in your head is the answer to the question HOW MANY? To write that number you have to make some sort of mark. This mark could be 111 or ≡ or ... or any squiggle you have made up yourself. The important thing is that the mark or squiggle stands for the number you thought of. Of course, if you want people to understand what your mark means, you must use one which everyone knows and uses. The correct word for this mark or symbol or number is NUMERAL.

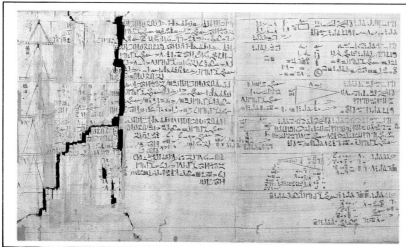

A set of sheep   An idea of the NUMBER   Ways of writing the NUMERAL

A NUMERAL IS THE NAME OR SYMBOL FOR A NUMBER

Numerals are Everywhere

You will see numerals wherever you go. In the kitchen there are numerals on clocks, calendars and dials of cookers and boilers. In the street there are numerals on buses, doors and goods in shop windows. The story of how peoples of long ago began to use numerals, and how we got the ones we use today, is most interesting.

The Chinese

One of the earliest peoples to write numerals and group their numbers in fives and tens were some tribes which lived on the banks of the Yellow River in China. They made their marks on leaves with brushes dipped in black paint. To begin with their marks were like this:

Nowadays the numerals have changed to these:

The Egyptians

One of the first people to work out a number system lived along the banks of the River Nile in Egypt. At first they made marks on walls or pottery, but later they found a way of making a kind of paper from reeds. They wrote on this *papyrus*, as it was called, with brushes filled with black ink. Their number signs looked like pictures of birds and people, but later on they made up another system. These numerals were written from

ANCIENT EGYPTIAN SUMS

The picture on the left shows part of a long roll of papyrus which was found in the ruins of a small bulding at Thebes in Egypt. It is now in the British Museum and is one of the most fascinating documents ever found. The ancient Egyptian scribe who copied it about 1650 B.C. was called A'h-mosè. He was copying from an even older papyrus that was written between 1849 and 1801 B.C. Is is full of mathematical problems for students and they are exactly the sort of problems we do in school today. Things like: "A cylindrical granary is of diameter 9 and height 6. What is the amount of grain that goes into it?" or "A quantity and its $\frac{1}{4}$ added together become 15. What is the quantity?" The ancient Egyptian master who posed the questions shows how to get the answers by using fractions.

right to left, sometimes down the page, but most of the time from left to right.

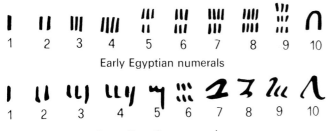

Early Egyptian numerals

Later Egyptian numerals

Babylonian Numerals

Another race of people settled along the valleys between two great rivers in a country we now call Iraq. These Babylonians wrote their numbers from left to right as we do. They grouped their numbers in tens, but they also had a numeral which stood for 60. This number is still used in measurements of time – 60 seconds in a minute, 60 minutes in an hour.

The people of Babylon wrote on clay tablets with a tool which was shaped like a wedge. Many of these tablets have been found, even though they were written on 4000 years ago.

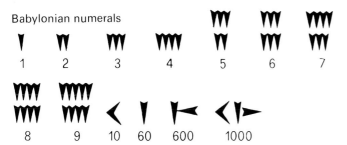

Babylonian numerals

The clay tablet below was written on nearly five thousand years ago. You can see the wedge-shaped marks.

Clock faces still have Roman numerals. These lantern clocks were made in the middle of the 17th century.

The Greeks and Romans

Greece had a number of great scholars and mathematicians. They had several number systems and used their alphabet to represent the numerals.

The Roman way of writing numerals has lasted for hundreds of years and is still used today. It used seven symbols (I, V, X, L, C, D, M) and was based on the idea of grouping in fives. The Romans later used the idea of writing the symbols for 4 and 9 as IV (1 less than 5) and IX (1 less than 10). Roman writers used a board on which wax or dust was spread and made marks with a wooden stylus. The system was a good one, but it had two faults. Sometimes the numeral was very long: 3867 would have to be written MMMDCCCLXVII. Also it was impossible to multiply and divide by using Roman numerals.

I II III IV V VI VII VIII IX X
L C D M

Roman numerals from 1 to 10 and 50, 100, 500 and 1000.

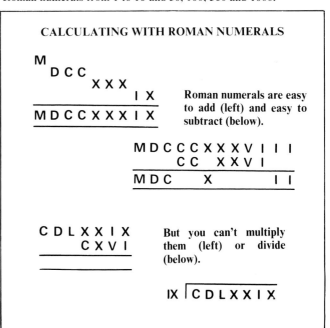

CALCULATING WITH ROMAN NUMERALS

M
D C C
X X X
I X
———————————
M D C C X X X I X

Roman numerals are easy to add (left) and easy to subtract (below).

M D C C C X X X V I I I
C C   X X V I
———————————————
M D C   X   I I

C D L X X I X
C X V I
———————————

But you can't multiply them (left) or divide (below).

IX ⌐C D L X X I X

13

Our Wonderful Number System

The way we reckon with numbers today started in the north of India about 2000 years ago. The Hindus who lived there must have taught these number signs to the Arab traders who travelled through their country. The Arabs became a rich and strong nation. Twelve hundred years ago their armies overran parts of Asia and North Africa. They conquered Spain and their way of numbering spread all over Europe.

We know from Hindu-Arabic scrolls, and later from printed books, how the number signs changed during the last thousand years. Some people think that these symbols were chosen because the number of lines in the numerals was the same as the units they stood for.

The Arabs' number system spread all over Europe.

I	Z	Z	Y	Y	L	7	8	9		1000 years ago
1	Z	3	X	4	ɛ	ʌ	8	9	0	800 years ago
I	2	3	4	5	6	7	8	9	0	600 years ago
1	2	3	4	5	6	7	8	9	10	Today

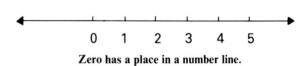

Zero has a place in a number line.

Filling the Empty Space

The Arab merchants began to keep accounts of what they bought and sold. Like the Romans, they were able to write large numbers, but there was one thing they could not do. Although they could record a number like *a hundred and twenty-six*, they could not write down *a hundred and six*. They had no way of writing NO hundreds, NO tens and NO ones. If they wrote a hundred and six it looked like 16, which is a different number altogether. Like the Romans, they often left a space on their dustboards when they did their sums. The merchant at the top of the page has done that.

Then, about 1100 years ago, an Arab had a brilliant idea. He wrote a book about this Hindu way of reckoning. In it he did not show numbers by leaving empty spaces where there were no hundreds and so on. *He put a dot in the empty space.* We call this dot a nought or zero.

```
   2 · 6          2 ⁰ 6
 5 · 3 1        5 ⁰ 3 1
     5 ·            5 ⁰
 ─────────      ─────────
 5 2 8 7        5 2 8 7
```

Zero is Very Useful

This was an important invention because zero has many uses. It is a numeral we use in countdowns –

"four, three, two, one, ZERO!" It is also a number and has a place in the number line. It can give the answer to the question *how many*? How many millions has he got? How many giraffes are there under your bed? How many of your friends speak fifty languages? As you know, the answer is: 0.

0

Zero Holds the Place

The most important use of zero is as a placeholder. It fills the space in a numeral so that no other can come in.

207 means TWO hundreds
NO tens and
SEVEN ones

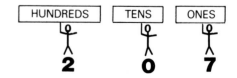

Of course, when we read the number we say "Two hundred and seven". If we had no zero to hold the tens place we would not be able to write the number 207.

How Many is 3?

The Hindu-Arabic system was important for another reason. The answer to the question "How many is 3?" is

IT DEPENDS WHERE IT IS IN THE NUMERAL

In 4583 the 3 is worth 3 ones or 3
In 5637 the 3 is worth 3 tens or 30
In 8368 the 3 is worth 3 hundreds or 300
In 3421 the 3 is worth 3 thousands or 3000

So the value of a numeral depends on its place. This idea means that the same set of numerals can be used to write any number no matter how big. It also means that people are able to calculate by writing numerals in columns.

Words for Numbers

The natives of central Australia count up to four and use *words* to describe their numbers. The Andaman islanders count and use *words* as they tap their fingers on their nose. From earliest times people must have used sounds as they counted. We have words for our numbers, but where did they come from? Many of the number words in Europe come from the Latin language which was spoken by the Romans who lived in Italy. It is easy to see that they are linked in some way if you look at the picture.

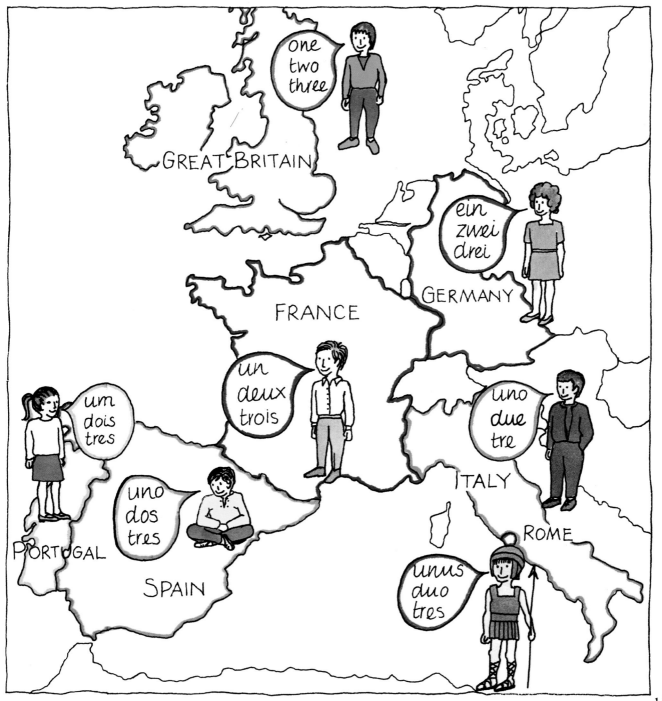

Measuring Length

Many times a day we ask the question "How many?" "How many pieces of chocolate are in that bar?" "How many cakes are on the plate?" Often we have to count before we can give the answer as a *number*.

There is another kind of question we are asked: "How long is that piece of wood?" "How tall are you?" "How far is it from the door to the window?" This time we may have to measure and then give the answer as a *number and a unit of measure*. The units of measure we use may be metres or centimetres.

People did not always have the units of measure we use today. At first they had no need for measures. It was when they began to build and make things that they invented them. They needed to compare the size of the thing they were making with a length they knew. They must have used measures which they could see and which were near to them. These measures were parts of their body.

Body Measures

When the Egyptians built their pyramids and temples they used parts of their arms as units of length. These were the digit or finger, palm, span and cubit. The trouble with these body measures

According to the Bible, Goliath was 6 cubits and 1 span in height.

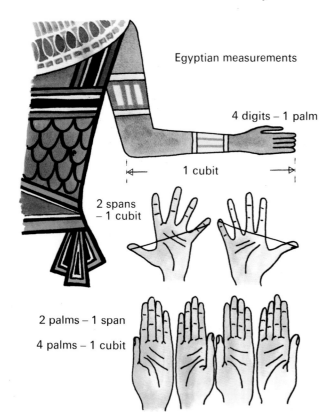

Egyptian measurements

4 digits – 1 palm

1 cubit

2 spans – 1 cubit

2 palms – 1 span

4 palms – 1 cubit

was that everybody's digits, palms, spans and cubits were not all the same length. So the Egyptians decided that the cubit of their king or pharaoh was to be the one unit of measure. Some measuring rods and slabs have been found in Egypt which are 5000 years old. These were the first measuring sticks. We now call them *rules* or *rulers* and use them to compare the length of the stick with the length of the thing we want to measure.

Bible measurements are in cubits and spans. Noah's Ark was 300 cubits long, 50 cubits wide and 30 cubits high. Goliath was a very big man. He was 6 cubits and 1 span in height. How tall do you think that is in our measures?

The English Inch and Foot

The shortest Egyptian unit was the digit, which was equal to the width of one finger. The Romans' shortest length, which they also called the digit, was the width of a thumb. When the English began to take their measures from parts of the body, they called the digit an *inch*. An English king, Edward the First, said that its length was to be that of three corns of barley laid end to end.

People long ago must have used a real foot as a measure, and it was used by the Greeks and Romans many years later. The Romans divided the foot into twelve parts and their word for one of

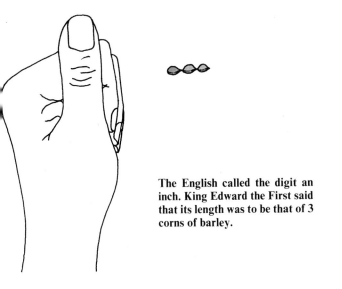

The English called the digit an inch. King Edward the First said that its length was to be that of 3 corns of barley.

these parts gives us our *inch*. The English began to use the foot measure, with its 12 inches, about nine hundred years ago. King Henry the First is said to have based the measure on the length of soldiers' feet. One can only think that their feet must have been quite long in those days.

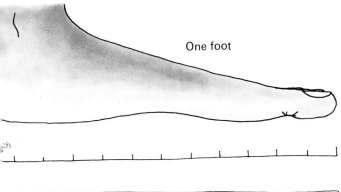

One foot

Was a yard the distance from the nose to the end of an outstretched arm, or the length of an arrow?

The English Yard

We do not know exactly how the *yard* became a measure. One story is that it was the length of King Henry the First's arm. Another story is that it was the distance from the nose to the end of an outstretched arm. A third story is that it was the length of the arrows used by the archers who used long bows (above).

The kings of England seemed quite worried about measures. This was because merchants cheated by giving short measure. Five hundred years ago, King Henry the Seventh decided that there should be a *standard* unit of measure called a yard. So that everyone should know the exact length, some standards were made of brass. These are eight-sided bars with three feet marked on one side, and one of the feet is divided into inches.

Paces and Miles

Often we estimate distances by seeing how many steps or paces it is from one point to another. Two steps are equal to one pace, which is a measure Roman soldiers used. A long distance is called a *mile*. The word comes from the Roman word for 1000, which was *mille*. A thousand paces was a Roman mile.

Roman soldiers paced up and down this road – the Appian Way outside Rome. It was built as a supply line for Roman forces in 312 B.C.

The Metre

Most countries today use the same system of measuring lengths and distances. It is called the *metric* system and was invented in France about 200 years ago. The system takes its name from the unit of length – the *metre*. Scientists all over the world use this system because it can be divided into hundredths of a metre which are called centimetres and thousandths which are called millimetres. A thousand metres are equal to one *kilometre*.

Mass and Weight

It was a long time before people started to weigh things. They had few possessions and had no need of weights and scales. Then some of them began to have more things than they needed. So they exchanged them for something they were short of. Perhaps they exchanged two sheep for three goats or a piece of cloth for some sewing needles. Much later they began weighing things they wanted to sell and exchanged the goods for coins.

Nowadays, most household things are sold by weight. Shops and supermarkets sell cans, bottles and packets which have the weight printed on them. In this way shoppers can tell *how much* they are buying. In factories and engineering works where glass, steel and plastics are made, it is important that things are weighed accurately.

The First Weights

The earliest weights we know of were found in some Egyptian graves. The weights are about 6000 years old and are quite light – about 200 grams. A picture on a papyrus roll shows an Egyptian balance. It was used to weigh grain by balancing it against bronze weights. The balance, with its two pans and upright pointer, is very much like the scales which were used in our shops until quite recently. There are many early weights in museums. Some are made of stone and are in the shape of ducks and rectangular blocks. Some are of bronze in the shape of a lion. Records dating back about 4500 years tell us that stone weights were used to weigh gold. The Babylonians made stone weights in the shape of animals. To buy an ox, an ox weight was balanced against a number of metal rings. This heavy weight was a *talent*, but the

Weighing things today can be done electronically, whether they are heavy objects (above) or a few grams in the kitchen.

An ancient Egyptian using an equal arm balance. This kind of machine has been in use for around 6000 years. Note the bull's head weight.

Babylonians had a lighter weight, a *shekel*, for weighing spices. The Bible mentions talents and shekels. The weight of King David's crown was a talent of gold. Goliath's coat of mail weighed 5000 shekels of brass and the head of his spear had a weight of 600 shekels of iron.

Roman Weights

The Romans traded with the Egyptians and took over some of their measures. One of these was the

18

These Assyrian lion weights were used before the time of Christ.

talent, which they divided into 125 parts. They called each part a *libra*, which was their name for a balance as well as for a pound. This was the weight which was handed on when the Romans invaded Britain. Our way of writing a pound, lb., is the shortened form of libra. The libra was divided into 12 *unciae* from which we got our *ounce* weight as well as our inch. Five hundred years ago the name of the weight changed from *uncia* to *onza*. The abbreviation we use for ounce, oz., is taken from that word. The Saxons decided later that there should be 16, and not 12, ounces to the pound.

The Romans also gave us a new way of measuring weight. This is the *steelyard*, which is a balance with two arms. The short arm holds the thing to be weighed on a pan or a hook. The long arm has marks on it and a weight is moved along it until both sides balance. The weight is seen where the weight stops on the marked rod.

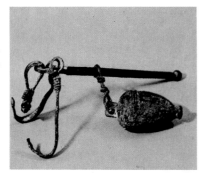

A Roman market trader's steelyard. The authorities in Rome laid down standard weights and measures to be used throughout the empire.

Elizabethan Times

For many years quarrels had broken out in England because of the weighing measures. Merchants cheated when they used the steelyard and the weights on the balances were not the same in different parts of the country. Special courts were set up in the markets to punish people who gave short weight. Special laws were passed so that merchants' weights could be tested against standard ones. If the weights were correct the mark of an ox's head was stamped on them.

For many years people still argued about weights in spite of the special laws and courts. Four hundred and fifty years ago Queen Elizabeth the First asked a group of people to work out a new law. As a result, new weights were made and sets of them were sent to towns and cities so that everybody should know how heavy the correct ones were.

Victorian Times

During the reign of Queen Victoria another body of people decided that yet another set of standard weights should be made. Again one set was kept in a government office and other sets were sent all over Britain and the British Empire to be used to test weights in use. This Imperial System had three kinds of units:

The *Troy* system was to be used to weigh stones like diamonds and rubies, and precious metals. Dealers in gems and gold still use this system.

The *Apothecaries'* system was the one used by chemists. They now use the metric system.

The *Avoirdupois* ("to have weight") system was to be the common one where 16 oz = 1 lb., 14 lb. = 1 st., 2 sts. = 1 qr., 4 qrs. = 1 cwt. and 20 cwt. = 1 ton. This is slowly giving way to the metric system.

Metric Units of Mass

The standard for measuring metric units of mass is a cylinder made of a hard metal called platinum-iridium. It weighs one kilogram (1 kg) and is kept in France. There are copies of it in countries where metric units are used.

A cubic centimetre of water weighs one gram (1 g).

A thousand cubic centimetres of water weigh one kilogram (1 kg).

MASS AND WEIGHT

You will often hear these two words as you learn about weighing. Mass and weight are not the same thing. *Mass* is the amount inside something. What is inside your body is its mass. *Weight* is a force which you notice when you throw a ball into the air and it falls down again. This is because the Earth pulls objects towards its centre. The force on an object because of the pull of Earth's gravity is called weight.

Suppose an astronaut weighs himself before he sets off in his spacecraft. He notices perhaps that the scale reads 75 kg. This mass will stay roughly the same all the time he is in space. However, the farther his body moves from the surface of the Earth, the less it will *weigh*. After a while, if he is not strapped in his machine, he begins to float about. He becomes *weightless*, but the mass of his body is still the same as it was back on Earth.

Mass and weight are related. The units for mass, such as gram and kilogram, are often used as weights.

Marking Time

Not even the cleverest person in the world knows what time is. Yet think what it would be like if we had no clocks or watches to measure time. Buses and trains would go without us. Ships and aircraft would not know where they were. We would have no idea when to switch on the television and schools would have no end to their day. Everyone would be in a terrible mess. But, although time is a mystery, people have been measuring it since they appeared on Earth.

The Dawn of Time
The first people noticed that things around them changed. Plants grew at certain times and then died. Waves of the sea came in and went out. Lights in the sky changed shape and moved about. The Sun came up and woke them. It stayed in the sky and made everything light. Then it sank again and it was time to sleep because it was dark.

Measuring the Day
Astronomers from the ancient countries of Babylon and Egypt were the first to measure the day's length. They noticed that the Sun rose in the east, moved across the sky and disappeared each night. When the Sun returned day after day some people made records by scratching marks on sticks and stones. Stories were told about a god who rose from the sea, drove his chariot across the sky and then sank back into the water.

It was the Egyptians who found out how to record the movement of the Sun during the day. They saw that the Sun cast shadows. They noticed that the shadows were longer in the morning and evening than they were in the middle of the day.

To find the time of day the ancient Egyptians stuck a stick into the ground and marked out the path of its shadow. By checking the position of the shadow, they could measure the Sun's position at any time of day.

The first sundials were made by poking sticks into the ground and making marks where the shadow fell. As different kinds of marks were made for different times of the day, the dial told what hour it was.

Soon, stone pillars were built on a circular base to measure the shadows more exactly. The Babylonians studied the circle and divided it into 360 equal parts. They noticed that the Sun moved half way round the circle during the twelve parts of daylight. The rest of the circle was made up of the twelve parts of darkness. From this they decided that there were 24 hours in a day.

The Babylonians also studied the changing shape of the Moon and tried to work out how long it took from one new moon to the next. They thought it was 30 days and said that there were twelve moons in a year of 360 days. We know that it takes about $29\frac{1}{2}$ days for the Moon to complete its orbit round the Earth. So the Babylonian idea of linking the Moon and the year was not quite right. After some time the year and the four seasons did not fit.

The Calendar
The Egyptians tried to work out the length of the year by studying the Sun and the stars. They decided that it took 365 days for the Sun to make a full journey round the sky during a period of four seasons. The year is 365 days, 5 hours, 48 minutes and 46 seconds long, so the Egyptians were getting closer.

The Romans tried to find the exact length of the year. *Calendar* comes from their word which means the first of the month. At first they had a

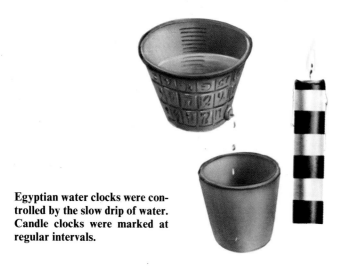

Egyptian water clocks were controlled by the slow drip of water. Candle clocks were marked at regular intervals.

Pocket sundials usually had a compass built into them so that they could be pointed in the right direction.

year of 304 days divided into ten months. This, of course, did not work at all and it was Julius Caesar who made a new calendar. It now was to have 365 days in twelve months, with an extra day in February every four years. This calendar lasted a long time, but it too was not quite right. After some centuries it was ten days out. Pope Gregory tried to put it right 400 years ago.

Weeks and Days

Why are there seven days in a week? Perhaps people tried at one time to divide the phases of the Moon roughly into quarters. This may have led to the Jewish custom of having a rest-day every seventh day. We do not know how the days of the week got their name. Some people think that they were named after the seven "planets" which astrologers said ruled our lives. If this is true, only Sun-day, Moon-day and Saturn's day remain. Tuesday, Wednesday, Thursday and Friday are called after the Norse gods Tiw, Woden, Thor and Fria.

The strange sundial is on a church wall in England. The early sandglass is made from two containers joined in the middle by wax and twine. It timed 15 minutes.

Telling the Time

The Babylonians divided the circle into 360 parts. We call these parts *degrees* and each one is one degree (1°). Astronomers later divided the degree into 60 *minutes*. Much later, when accurate clocks were made, the minute was divided into 60 *seconds*.

The Egyptians had sundials 3500 years ago, and the Romans had public ones 1200 years later. They did not appear in Britain until Saxon times. Even then they were very roughly made and no-one had an accurate way of telling the time.

During the Middle Ages some churches had sundials scratched on their outside walls. Four hundred years ago pocket sundials were very popular. Sundials were used for many years and are still to be seen in gardens and parks.

For many years people tried to make clocks which did not depend on the Sun. The Egyptians, Greeks and Romans used water-clocks. One of these had a float which rose in the vase as water dripped in and turned a finger on a dial. King Alfred used candles as clocks; each candle burned for four hours. Sand-clocks or hour-glasses are at least 500 years old. These are like some modern egg-timers and were used to measure a short period of time like the length of sermons in churches.

Clocks became much more accurate when the *pendulum* began to be used. It was found that a weight on a rope, nearly a metre in length, swings each way every second. Experts were now able to make clocks such as *grandfather clocks* which kept true time.

Very accurate clocks are now made. Those for navigation at sea are called *chronometers*. Electric clocks are excellent when the electricity supply works accurately. Electronic, quartz and atomic clocks and watches keep almost perfect time. Modern timepieces use transistors and silicon chips with tiny batteries. Digital watches sometimes show the time on the 24 hour system, now used for road, rail and air timetables.

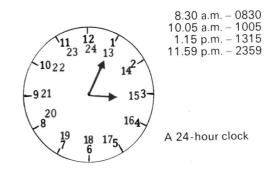

8.30 a.m. – 0830
10.05 a.m. – 1005
1.15 p.m. – 1315
11.59 p.m. – 2359

A 24-hour clock

Money Matters

Can you imagine a world without money? How would we buy ice-cream? Or pay for the cinema? How would we save up for holidays and presents? Money is easy to pass from one person to another in order to buy things. Money is also a measure. When we ask "How much is it?" we compare the thing we want with the money we can afford.

Long ago nobody needed money. People hunted for food and began to grow it. They gave away any food they didn't want. However, when people wanted something they didn't grow or catch, they had to think of a way to get it. At first they exchanged things. One family would take a sheep in exchange for a goat, or a pile of corn in return for some fish. This way of exchange is called *barter*. The trouble arose when a family could not find anyone to take the goods they had to barter. What they needed was something they could accept as barter which everybody would take.

Early Money

The first bartered items were those it was easy to keep such as cattle, skins and salt. People then began to take objects they could carry easily like fishing hooks, shells and precious stones. Metal money in the shape of rings became popular because they did not wear out and could be exchanged by weight. The Chinese used metal money, shaped into small tools and knives, more than 2000 years ago. (They were also the first to use paper money 1300 years later.)

Gold and silver were scarce, so they became suitable to use as money. Sometimes they were made into bars which were exchanged for animals such as oxen. It was only a short step to turn these, and other minerals, into coins which were easy to handle.

Early Coins

The first coins were made in a country called Lydia which is roughly where Turkey is today. These coins were a mixture of gold and silver and were made about 2600 years ago. The coins were brought by merchants to Greece. A hundred years later, coins like them were in use in the countries ruled by the Greeks.

In 500 BC the Persians were the first people to print the head of their king on coins. The Romans

Above: Most currencies have a main unit which is divided into 100 smaller units. The smaller ones are often called cents, centimes, centavos or centimos from *centum*, the Latin for one hundred. Below: An early coin from Phrygia in Anatolia (Asia Minor). It is made of electrum, a mixture of gold and silver.

Below: An ancient Greek stater coin with the head of Apollo. The word *stater* meant standard and was originally the name for a unit of weight.

began to make coins 200 years later and took them to the countries they conquered. They were a rough mixture of copper and tin. Ancient coins were either cast in moulds or were hammered out with a hand-held die. Casting was slow and produced coins with a poor finish. Striking coins by hand gave a cleaner and better result. Sheets of metal were hammered out to the right thickness. Then blank coins were cut out with a punch and trimmed to the right size and weight. The coin design was then stamped on both sides with a hand-held die. Coins were made in this way right up to the middle of the 1500s, when simple machines took over from simple tools. Today, minting machines can stamp out as many as 10,000 coins in a minute.

Above: The Chinese used bronze money in the shape of everyday objects. The small knife above (much enlarged) had the same value as a real knife.
Below: The first British coin to show Britannia was minted by the Romans.

This 16th century painting shows a Flemish banker and his wife weighing gold and silver coins. Many coins at that time were debased with other metals, so bankers had to check their metal content by weighing.

Hogsheads and Litres

A look around will tell you how often we use containers. Our milk arrives in containers. On our food shelves there are containers which hold items like oil, vinegar and drinks. First Aid boxes hold bottles of medicine; bathrooms contain shampoo and other lotions. In outdoor sheds and garages there may be oil, paraffin and liquids to clean the car. All around us there are bottles, cans, packets and boxes of items we use every day.

Containers with liquids in them are sold by *capacity*. This tells us the amount of liquid we are buying. Other things such as refrigerators and water tanks also have a capacity. Car engines are measured by capacity. The great tankers which carry oil and milk, and the massive petrol tanks under a filling station, have a large capacity.

This huge jar was found at Knossos in Crete. Jars like this were used for storing grain, oil and wine.

Skins and Kilderkins

The first containers were probably hollow branches and animal skins. Later people made clay vessels; they stored grain in the large pots and drank out of the smaller ones. When they began to trade they needed containers of a more exact size. They also needed to give a name to their measures.

Until recent times water has not been pure enough to drink, so people drank other liquids. When the Romans invaded other countries they took with them wine which they drank with most meals. They had vessels of different sizes, including the *amphora* which was a large jar with two handles.

The Anglo-Saxons brewed ale, and some of their measures had strange names such as firkins and kilderkins. The drinking vessels they used were beautifully made of horn, silver, wood and even leather.

Measures by Halves

About 500 years ago the French began to trade their wine for English wool. As each country had different measures it became important to have a proper table. So a law passed in 1423 said that wines should be measured in gallons, hogsheads, pipes and tonnels. In the 17th century containers began to be made which doubled in size, starting with the tankard. This is perhaps how the measures grew up which were used almost all over the world. These were the pint, quart and gallon. In 1878 these standard measures were used all over the British Empire and in the United States.

Grain, which can also be poured, has had many ways of being measured. Fruit and vegetables have been sold in pecks, bushels and quarters but also in punnets and baskets. They are now mainly sold by weight.

Metric Measures

The metric unit of capacity is the *litre*. Many items, such as milk, soft drinks and cooking oil, are now sold in litre containers. A bottle of wine may contain less than a litre. Spoons used for cooking or for medicine hold parts of a litre. A garage has dials on its pumps to show how many litres flow into the car's tank. Big tanks which store petrol, and the tankers which fill them, are so huge that they need long dipsticks to measure the thousands of litres they contain.

We do not have to use the whole word when we want to write litre or litres. We can use the letter *l*: 3 *l* stands for 3 litres. The litre measure is linked with the metre. A cube with sides 10 cm (or 1 dm) long holds a litre.

Cooking spoons hold $2\frac{1}{2}$ ml, 5 ml, 10 ml, and 15 ml, equal to $\frac{1}{4}$ teaspoon, $\frac{1}{2}$ teaspoon 1 teaspoon and 1 tablespoon. A medicine spoon holds 5 ml.

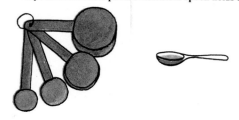

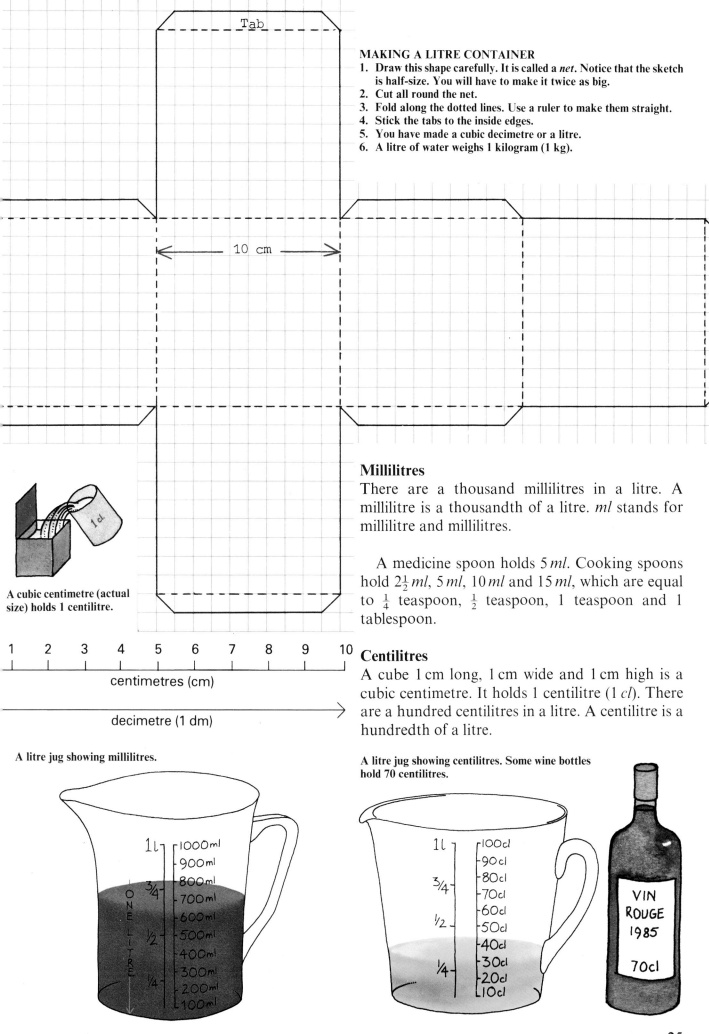

Tab

MAKING A LITRE CONTAINER
1. Draw this shape carefully. It is called a *net*. Notice that the sketch is half-size. You will have to make it twice as big.
2. Cut all round the net.
3. Fold along the dotted lines. Use a ruler to make them straight.
4. Stick the tabs to the inside edges.
5. You have made a cubic decimetre or a litre.
6. A litre of water weighs 1 kilogram (1 kg).

10 cm

A cubic centimetre (actual size) holds 1 centilitre.

1 cl

Tab

| 1 | 2 | 3 | 4 | 5 | 6 | 7 | 8 | 9 | 10 |

centimetres (cm)

decimetre (1 dm)

Millilitres

There are a thousand millilitres in a litre. A millilitre is a thousandth of a litre. *ml* stands for millilitre and millilitres.

A medicine spoon holds 5 *ml*. Cooking spoons hold $2\frac{1}{2}$ *ml*, 5 *ml*, 10 *ml* and 15 *ml*, which are equal to $\frac{1}{4}$ teaspoon, $\frac{1}{2}$ teaspoon, 1 teaspoon and 1 tablespoon.

Centilitres

A cube 1 cm long, 1 cm wide and 1 cm high is a cubic centimetre. It holds 1 centilitre (1 *cl*). There are a hundred centilitres in a litre. A centilitre is a hundredth of a litre.

A litre jug showing millilitres.

1 l

1000 ml
900 ml
800 ml
700 ml
600 ml
500 ml
400 ml
300 ml
200 ml
100 ml

ONE LITRE

3/4
1/2
1/4

A litre jug showing centilitres. Some wine bottles hold 70 centilitres.

1 l

100 cl
90 cl
80 cl
70 cl
60 cl
50 cl
40 cl
30 cl
20 cl
10 cl

3/4
1/2
1/4

VIN ROUGE 1985

70 cl

25

Some Shapes and Sizes

Have you ever stopped to look at the buildings around you? Houses, churches, offices, schools and shops; they are all built in a different way. All over the world there are various styles of building. The Parthenon in Athens is an example of ancient Greek style. Saint Basil's Church in Moscow is highly coloured and decorated. Notre Dame Cathedral in Paris is elaborate.

The style of all these buildings tells us something about the times in which they were built and what they were used for. Although buildings are different, there are some things which they share. They all have shape and size. Their size is reckoned like many other solid things, by how long, wide and tall they are. We call these measures of length, width and height the three dimensions, or 3-D for short.

Modern Buildings

Modern buildings are often used as offices. They are very much like tall boxes and copy the shape of solids. Cubes and cuboids are solids and, like all other solids, they take up space. The amount of space they take up is called *volume*.

The Volume of Solids

Volume is measured in cubic units. The unit of measure for the volume of a solid is the cube. To find the volume of a solid we find out how many cubes will fill the space. If we know the size of one cube we can find the volume of the solid.

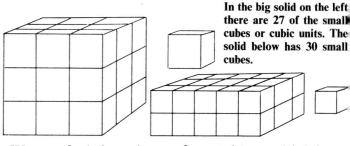

In the big solid on the left there are 27 of the small cubes or cubic units. The solid below has 30 small cubes.

We can find the volume of a solid by multiplying the length (l), width (w) and height (h).

Example: A solid is 5 cm long, 4 cm wide and 3 cm high. Its volume is $5 \times 4 \times 3$ (or 60) cubic centimetres. The way to write this is:

$V = l \times w \times h$
$\quad = 5\,cm \times 4\,cm \times 3\,cm$
$\quad = 60$ cubic centimetres
$\quad\quad (60\,cc$ or $60\,cm^3)$

The Parthenon (right), the UN building (below), St. Basil's (far right, below) and Notre Dame (below right) are all different in style and shape, but they all take up space – they have volume.

A Metre of Sand

Builders buy sand by the metre or yard. This is really a cubic metre or a cubic yard, which is quite a large amount. Try making a cubic metre to see how large it is. You can make it from sticks or canes one metre long and sticky tape or plasticine. If your shape is to be a cube how many sticks will you need?

Capacity and Volume

Have you seen how these are linked? The cubic decimetre and the litre have the same size. The cubic decimetre has a volume of 1000 cubic centimetres ($1000 \, cm^3$). The litre has a capacity of 1000 millilitres. They take up the same amount of space. A cubic decimetre of water and a litre of water both weigh 1 kilogram (1 kg).

Flat Shapes

Some shapes have no thickness. They have length and width but no height. We call these the shapes with two dimensions. These 2-D shapes are seen on the faces of solids.

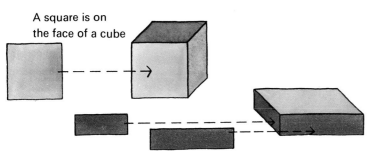

A square is on the face of a cube

Rectangles are on the faces of a cuboid. Other solids have 2-D shapes on their faces (below).

On the faces of a cube there are squares. There are rectangles on the faces of a cuboid. Opposite faces of a cuboid are the same size. Other solids have on their faces 2-D shapes such as circles and triangles.

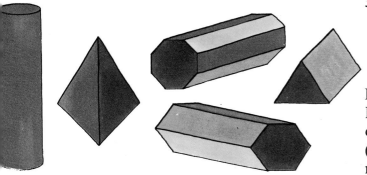

Measuring Flat Shapes

The 2-D shapes have sizes which can be measured. This measure is called *area*. Area is the amount of surface an object or a shape has. It is the amount taken to *cover* the surface. Although surfaces are not all square, the measure is always in square units. Floors, walls, table-tops and books have surfaces. To cover these surfaces we find their area. This can be done in three ways.

1. *By covering with any objects.* The floor can be covered with newspapers. The area of the floor is 29 newspapers. This is not a good measure of area because newspapers are of different sizes. The shopkeeper will be a bit puzzled to be asked for a carpet with an area of 29 newspapers!

2. *By covering with squares.* If squares 1 cm long and 1 cm wide are used to cover a book 8 cm by 6 cm, 48 squares will be needed. The area of the cover is 48 square centimetres ($48 \, cm^2$).

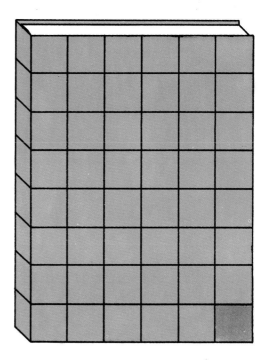

3. *By measuring and doing a sum.* The lid of a box is 12 cm long and 10 cm wide. Its area is $12 \, cm \times 10 \, cm = 120$ square centimetres ($120 \, cm^2$).

Larger Areas

Larger surfaces may be measured in square metres or square yards. The area of a field may be in acres (4840 square yards) or hectares (10000 square metres). A football pitch has an area of about 1 hectare or $2\frac{1}{2}$ acres.

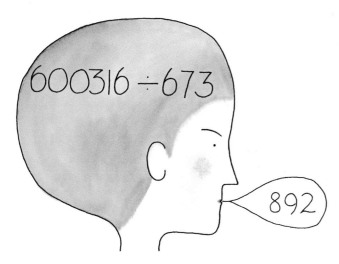

Machines that Count

John Napier, the Scottish mathematician who invented logarithms. In 1617 he explained how small rods or "bones" could be used to multiply and divide.

There are some people who can do long and difficult sums in their heads. Ask them to multiply 468 by 279, or add up a long column of figures, and out come the answers in a few seconds. These people are very rare. Most of us take a long time to work out problems. Some of us need a lot of paper as well as our fingers to help!

Young children use things like beads, sticks and counters in their early learning. They need to handle objects because these help them to understand how numbers behave. All through history, machines and other devices have been invented to make mathematics easier. A lot of people think there is no point in wasting time working out a problem if a machine can do it better and more quickly. But, of course, we must know how the machine works and tell it what to do.

Dust and Pebbles

It is possible that the first sums were marks on the ground made with a finger or a stick. The Romans used to add by moving pebbles on a board sprinkled with sand. The Latin for pebble is *calculus*, which gives us the word "calculate" or work with numbers. Greeks and Romans used to calculate on a square board or counting tablet. It is from this tablet that we get the name of one of the first calculators, the *abacus*.

The Abacus

The abacus helps to show place value in the number system. It is also used to add and subtract and for other calculations. Abacuses are still used in many countries. In China there is the *suan pan*, in Japan the *soroban* and in Russia the *s'choty*. A simple abacus can be made easily from a piece of wood, a few rods and some beads or washers to fit on them.

Napier's Bones

John Napier, who lived from 1550 to 1617, was a mathematician from Scotland. He invented some rods, which were made of bone, to help people to multiply and divide. To make a model of these bones is quite easy. You will need some thin card or squared paper, ruler, pencil, scissors and coloured pens.

1. Copy the square carefully.
2. Cut along the dotted lines so that you have eleven strips.
3. *To multiply 48 by 6*, take the strips which have a green 4 and 8 at the top. Put them at the side of the multiplier strip (in red).

The Chinese abacus below dates from the middle of the 19th century. The beads in the smaller upper half, known as "Heaven", count five when they are down on the central divider. Those on the lower portion, called "Earth", count one when they are up. Can you work out the number shown on the abacus? As the first two positions are not being used, the number is 1 532 786.

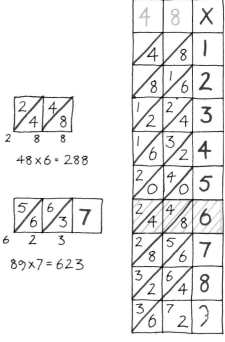

2, 4, 8
2 8 8

48 × 6 = 288

5, 6, 7
6 2 3

89 × 7 = 623

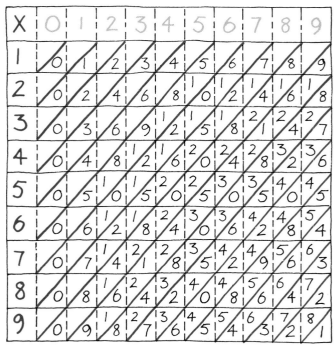

4. Read off the answer by adding diagonally between the red lines as shown in the green box: 2, 4 + 4, 8 = 288.
5. Use your strips to multiply 87 by 7.
6. Multiply 96 by 8.

An Adding Machine

Two rulers make a good adding machine.

1. Put the two rulers side by side with the edges touching.
2. To add 8 and 9 place the zero of ruler B over the 8 of ruler A.
3. Find the 9 on ruler B.
4. Use the 9 to show the answer: 17

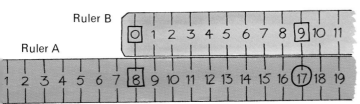

This is a simple example of the use of a *slide-rule*, as it is called. Very difficult calculations can be done with a slide-rule. Slide-rules were used a great deal by people like architects and engineers before calculators and computers were invented. Three people helped to invent the slide-rule. Edmund Gunter started the idea in 1620. William Oughtred invented the slide-rule in 1633. Robert Bissaker in 1654 made the slide-rule which was used widely for 300 years.

Calculating Machines

For many years mathematicians tried to invent a machine which would do calculations for them. A Frenchman called Blaise Pascal was only 19 years old when he invented a machine which could add and subtract.

Twenty-nine years later, Gottfried Leibniz improved on that machine. In 1671 he invented one which would multiply and divide. His ideas were later used by a man called Odhner who made the first desk calculators.

Calculating machines are based on an idea you will have seen inside a car. On the dashboard is an *odometer* which measures the distance of journeys. It has numerals which show through a window. After each mile the numerals change from, say, 134 to 135, or from 6899 to 6900.

This is what a calculating machine does. It adds in ones. Turning the handle of the machine clockwise makes it add (and multiply). Turning the handle anti-clockwise makes it subtract (and divide).

Calculators

There was a time, not very long ago, when electronic calculators were desk-top machines. They were expensive and used mainly in offices. Today, almost every family has a pocket calculator. These machines become smaller and cheaper every year. They are powered by very tiny batteries and even by the Sun.

Computers

The most amazing machines of all are computers. The word *compute* means to work with numbers, but computers do far more than that.

Signs and Symbols

What should we do, and where would we be, without signs? There are signs to tell us where to catch the bus, which door to use and what time the next train or plane departs. Health signs warn us not to take dogs into food shops and ask us to drop our litter in the bins. Signposts explain how far it is to the nearest town or car park. Traffic signals tell us when to stop and go. Road signs tell a story to car drivers as they explain the route:

> Be careful here because some men are carrying out road repairs. Go carefully around the next corner as the road is slippery. There's a roundabout just ahead and, by the way, you mustn't turn in this road. There are some deer in this area and there is also a danger from falling rocks!

The clever thing about these road signs is that they use very few, if any, words. The signs explain everything by using shapes and pictures.

Symbols

These shapes and pictures are known as *symbols*. Symbols are signs which stand for objects or ideas. A horseshoe and a sprig of heather may represent Good Luck. A day-old chicken or a rabbit could represent Spring. A dove stands for Peace and a lion for Courage. The badges on soldiers' uniforms explain what regiment they are in, what their rank is and what jobs they do. In science there are symbols for liquids, chemicals and gases. H_2O stands for water, NaCl for common salt and O_2 for oxygen.

Symbols can explain things or tell us how a job should be done. The symbols on a television set show which knobs to turn or press to change a programme or alter the sound or picture. Symbols on the labels of clothes explain how they should be washed.

Number Symbols

In mathematics, many signs and symbols are used, but very few words. Roman and Arabic numerals stand for numbers. The symbols explain the value of numbers. The Greek letter π (*pi*, pronounced "pie") stands for a number.

16.38   569 $1\frac{3}{4}$ π   XV111

$\frac{1}{2}$ 4^3 MCMLXXXV   0

Letters of the alphabet are symbols which are used in geometry and algebra. Shortened forms of words are also symbols.

A	area	l	length
c	circumference	r	radius
d	diameter	V	volume
h	height	w	width

mm	millimetre	cl	centilitre
dm	decimetre	dl	decilitre
cm	centimetre	l	litre
m	metre	cm²	square centimetre(s)
km	kilometre	m²	square metre(s)
g	gram	h	hectare
kg	kilogram	cm³	cubic centimetre(s)
t	tonne	m³	cubic metre(s)

Operations

Important symbols in mathematics are the four main ones which give orders. These symbols carry out operations. They tell numbers what work they must do.

Symbol	Command	Operation
+	Add!	addition
×	Multiply!	multiplication
—	Subtract!	subtraction
÷	Divide!	division

Plus and Minus

The name of the symbol for the operation of addition is *plus*: $4 + 3$ is read "four plus three". Some people believe that the symbol + was a short way of writing the Latin word *et* which means *and*. This was often written & and changed into + like this to make it different from 4 and 9.

& ᕄ + 4 +

Minus is the name for the symbol for the operation of subtraction. 4 minus 3 is written $4 - 3$. It means *less* in Latin and was at first written as *m*. There is an idea that, through being written quickly, it changed its shape.

ᶆ ᶆ ⌒ ⌒ — —

There is a belief that the plus and minus signs were in use long before they were used for addition and subtraction. Merchants used to mark their goods with a plus sign if they were overweight and a minus sign if they were underweight.

Merchants used signs on their goods if they were over or under weight.

The multiplication sign was first used as a symbol for multiplication by William Oughtred, an English mathematician who lived from 1575 to 1660.

Although the division sign is ÷, many mathematicians used the bar to separate two numbers. $\frac{100}{4}$ means "100 divided by 4" or "How many 4s in 100?"

SYMBOL	MEANING	DESCRIPTION
∠	Angle	Measure of amount of turning
△	Triangle	Three-sided figure
▭	Rectangle	Four-sided figure with parallel sides and right angles
▱	Parallelogram	Four-sided figure with both pairs of opposite sides parallel
⊙	Circle	Line whose points are the same distance from the centre
∥	Parallel lines	Lines which never meet
°	Degree	The measure of angle A right angle has 90°
=	Equals	As in $4 + 3 = 3 + 4$
≠	Is not equal to	As in $4 + 3 ≠ 5 + 4$
<	Is less than	As in $6 < 8$
>	Is greater than	As in $9 > 7$
%	Percentage	A number e.g. 50% of 20 is 10
′	Minute or foot	60′ are 1 hour 3′ are 1 yard
″	Second or inch	60″ are 1′ 12″ are 1′

Two of the branches...

"I only took the regular course."

"What was that?" enquired Alice.

"Reeling and writhing, of course, to begin with," the Mock Turtle replied: "and then the different branches of Arithmetic – Ambition, Distraction, Uglification and Derision."

"I never heard of Uglification," Alice ventured to say. "What is it?"

Through the Looking Glass

Lewis Carroll is here making jokes about his favourite subject, Mathematics, and the part of it called Arithmetic, which has to do with numbers. In his lifetime it became so important that people still call it one of the 3 Rs: Reading, (W)riting and (A)rithmetic.

Arithmetic solves problems which have numbers in them. It helps with buying things and counting money. It is used to tell the time and keep the score in games. Shopkeepers use it to order their goods and sell them. Engineers need numbers to build aeroplanes and roads. Scientists use arithmetic to help them make discoveries. Office and factory workers depend on arithmetic every day.

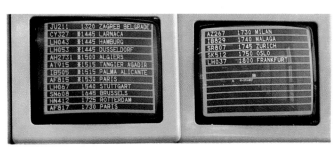

Airports use arithmetic to plan timetables.

Whole Numbers

There are many kinds of numbers. The ones like one, two and three are known as the counting numbers or the *whole numbers*.

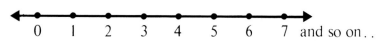

Four main operations are used in arithmetic to solve problems. In spite of what the Mock Turtle said, the different branches of arithmetic are addition, subtraction, multiplication and division.

Addition

This is collecting together to find *how many* there are. Three sets of dots can be counted or added.

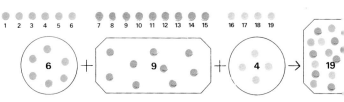

Collected things can be counted or added.

Young children first add by counting. Later it is better to add by remembering *number bonds* to 10 such as $2 + 3$, $4 + 5$ and $1 + 6$. Important number bonds are those of 10. These must be known. It must also be remembered that $1 + 9$, $2 + 8$, $3 + 7$ and so on, give the same total as $9 + 1$, $8 + 2$, $7 + 3$, etc.

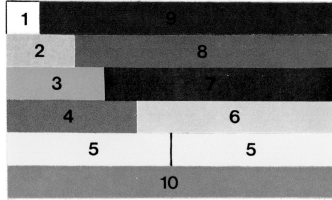

The number bonds which make up 20 must also be known, such as $3 + 9 = 12$, $4 + 7 = 11$ and $6 + 8 = 14$. To add two numbers which have a total more than 10 we have to *regroup*, or make one number up to 10:

$$9 + 7 = 10 + 6$$
$$= 16$$

Adding three numbers:

$$5 + 8 + 9 = 13 + 9$$
$$= 10 + (3 + 9)$$
$$= 10 + (10 + 2)$$
$$= (10 + 10) + 2$$
$$= 22$$

To add larger numbers: $63 + 29 + 36$

$$
\begin{array}{r}
63 \\
+ 29 \\
+ 36 \\
\hline
^{1\,1}128 \\
\end{array}
$$

(1) Add the ones: $6 + 9 + 3 = 18 = 1$ ten and 8 ones.

(2) The 8 goes in the ones answer column.

(3) Carry the 1 ten to join the other tens.

(4) 1 ten + 3 tens + 2 tens + 6 tens = 12 tens = 1 hundred and 2 tens.

(5) Put the 2 tens in the tens answer column.

(6) Carry the 1 hundred to the hundreds answer column.

Still larger numbers are added in exactly the same way. It must be remembered that a numeral in the tens column is ten times the value of the same numeral in the ones column. A numeral in the hundreds column is ten times the value of the same numeral in the tens column and so on. 10 ones = 1 ten, 10 tens = 1 hundred, 10 hundreds = 1 thousand, etc.

Multiplication

This is an easy way to add equal numbers. Suppose a shopkeeper wants to know how many cans are in a box. He could count them, but that takes time He notices that there are four rows of cans with 6 cans in each row. He could add $6 + 6 + 6 + 6$ or $4 + 4 + 4 + 4 + 4 + 4$. But he knows that 4 sixes are 24 and 6 fours are 24, which is much easier than adding. The shopkeeper knows his multiplication facts. There are some ways to make these facts easy to learn, as the shopkeeper found out: 4 sixes and 6 fours are both equal to 24. So if we know that $4 \times 6 = 24$, we shall also know that $6 \times 4 = 24$.

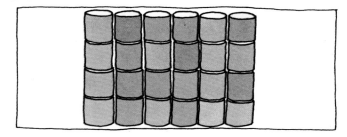

A multiplication square which makes use of this idea can be easily made.

X	1	2	3	4	5	6	7	8	9	10
1										
2		4	6	8	10	12	14	16	18	20
3			9	12	15	18	21	24	27	30
4				16	20	24	28	32	36	40
5					25	30	35	40	45	50
6						36	42	48	54	60
7							49	56	63	70
8								64	72	80
9									81	90
10										100

Some Questions and Answers

Q. Why are there no answers to 1×1, 1×2, 1×3, 1×4 etc?

A. Because $1 \times 1 = 1$, $1 \times 2 = 2$, $1 \times 3 = 3$, $1 \times 4 = 4$ etc.

Q. Why is it easy to learn $5 \times 2, 5 \times 3, 5 \times 4 \ldots$?

A. Because the products (or answers) end in 5 or 0: $10, 15, 20 \ldots$

Q. Why is it still easier to learn $10 \times 2, 10 \times 3, 10 \times 4 \ldots$?

A. Because these products end in 0: $20, 30, 40 \ldots$

Digits

The numbers from 0 to 9 have one digit. The numbers from 10 to 99 have two digits. Numbers like 247 and 596 have three digits.

To multiply by one digit

(i)
$$43 \times 2 = (40 \times 2) + (3 \times 2)$$
$$= 80 \qquad + 6$$
$$= 86$$

(ii)
$$36 \times 8 = (30 \times 8) + (6 \times 8)$$
$$= 240 \qquad + 48$$
$$= 200 + 40 + 40 + 8$$
$$= 288$$

To multiply by two digits

(i)
$$39 \times 36 = (39 \times 30) + (39 \times 6)$$
$$= (39 \times 3 \times 10) + (39 \times 6)$$
$$= (117 \times 10) + (234)$$
$$= 1170 \qquad + 234$$
$$= 1404$$

(ii)
$$214 \times 29 = (214 \times 20) + (214 \times 9)$$
$$= (214 \times 2 \times 10) + (214 \times 9)$$
$$= 428 \times 10 + 1926$$
$$= 4280 + 1926$$
$$= 6206$$

The Other Two Branches...

"What must I add to 13 to make 20?" This sounds like a problem in addition. Young children may solve it by adding, or counting on, from 13 to 20.

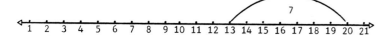

It can also be done by *subtracting*. Subtraction is another way of looking at addition. We say that the two operations are related and that one is the opposite of the other.

Sets and Subsets

Sets help us to think about the link between addition and subtraction. Suppose a set of 9 apples is split up into a subset of 5 apples and another subset of 4 apples. If 4 apples are eaten, 5 are left. If 5 apples are left, 4 were eaten.

This way of comparing two subjects can be shown with coloured rods. Notice that there are four number bonds:

$$4 + 5 = 9 \qquad 9 - 4 = 5$$
$$5 + 4 = 9 \qquad 9 - 5 = 4$$

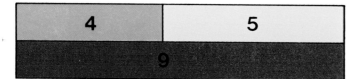

Many Words but One Operation

Many different words are used in the operation of subtraction. Here are some of them:

How many *more*?	How many are *left*?
What is the *difference*?	What *remains*?

Although these are all different questions, they all come from one idea: one set is split into two subsets. The bonds show the link between addition and subtraction.

Example 1: Beth wants to buy a ruler for 35 pence.

She has 27 pence. *How many more* pence does she need?

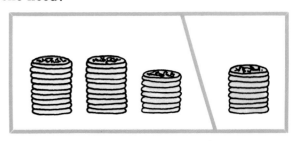

Example 2: What is the difference between 28 and 19?

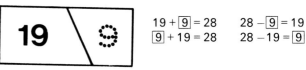

$$19 + \boxed{9} = 28 \qquad 28 - \boxed{9} = 19$$
$$\boxed{9} + 19 = 28 \qquad 28 - 19 = \boxed{9}$$

Example 3: Nine skittles were set up. Mark knocked over 2 of them. *How many remained standing?*

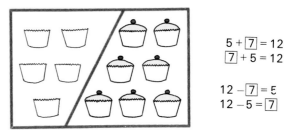

$$2 + \boxed{7} = 9$$
$$\boxed{7} + 2 = 9$$

$$9 - \boxed{7} = 2$$
$$9 - 2 = \boxed{7}$$

Example 4: There were 12 cakes on the plate. Five have gone. *How many are left?*

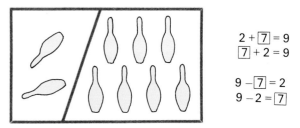

$$5 + \boxed{7} = 12$$
$$\boxed{7} + 5 = 12$$

$$12 - \boxed{7} = 5$$
$$12 - 5 = \boxed{7}$$

Example 5: What must be added to 22 to make 30?
Example 6: How much more than 10 is 15?
Example 7: How much less than 12 is 8?

Taking Away

Numbers are subtracted: "from 16 subtract 7". Real things, like ice-cream and cakes, can be *taken away*. "There are 9 chairs round the table. Please take away 4 of them."

Understanding Subtraction

There are many ways of subtracting numbers. All

the methods use the same ideas of regrouping.

2 − 1, 3 − 2, 4 − 3, 5 − 4 and so on are all equal to 1.

When the same number is added to 2 and 1, 3 and 2, 4 and 3, 5 and 4, etc., the differences remain the same. Look how these numbers have been regrouped:

Example 1
131 − 76
= 135 − 80   Add 4 to 76 *and* to 131
= 55   Subract 80 from 135

$$\begin{array}{rcr} 131 & \text{or} & 135 \\ -\ 76 & & -\ 80 \\ \hline & & 55 \end{array}$$

Example 2
131 − 76
= 61 − 6   Subtract 70 from 76 *and* 131
= 55   Subtract 6 from 61

$$\begin{array}{rcr} 131 & \text{or} & 61 \\ -\ 76 & & -\ 6 \\ \hline & & 55 \end{array}$$

Example 3
131 − 76
= (130 + 11) − (80 + 6). Add 10 to 131 *and* 76
= 50 + 5   (130 − 80) and (11 − 6)
= 55

Division

There are two kinds of division: sharing and grouping.

Sharing When sharing, the size of the set and the number of subsets are known. What is not known is the size of each share. To divide 12 oranges among 3 children we need to separate the set of 12 oranges into 3 equal subsets.

This division can be seen in a diagram.

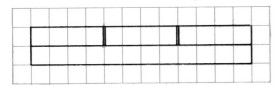

Grouping

With grouping, the size of the set and the size of each subset are known. What is not known is how many subsets there are. Examples of grouping are: How many squares can be made with 20 matches? How many threes are there in 12?

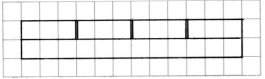

How many threes in 12?

Multiplication and Division Bonds

Division is opposite of multiplication. They are related to each other in the same way as addition and subtraction. Multiplication and division bonds can be learned together after understanding how they work.

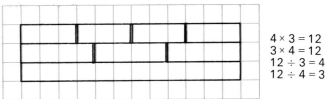

$4 \times 3 = 12$
$3 \times 4 = 12$
$12 \div 3 = 4$
$12 \div 4 = 3$

Ways of Dividing

Grouping and sharing problems are done in the same way. There are several ways of asking the question:

1. Share 36 pears among 2 people.
2. Divide 36 into 2 parts.
3. What is half of 36?
4. How many twos in 36?
5. If I have 36 bananas, to how many people can I give two?
6. If I divide 36 books between 2 children, how many will each have?
7. $\frac{1}{2}$ of 36
8. $\frac{36}{2}$
9. $36 \div 2$
10. $2\overline{)36}$ or $2\underline{)36}$

These last two are ways of setting out the problem.

Short Division

$2\underline{)36}$ (i) How many tens of twos in 30? 1
$\ \ 18$ remainder 10
            (ii) How many twos in 16? 8

Long Division

$$\begin{array}{r} 18 \\ 2\overline{)36} \\ 20 \\ \hline 16 \\ 16 \\ \hline \ \ \ \end{array}$$

(i) How many tens of twos in 30? 1
(ii) $20 \times 1 = 20$
(iii) $36 − 20 = 16$
(iv) How many twos in 16? 8
(v) $8 \times 2 = 16$
(vi) No remainder

$$\begin{array}{r} 42 \\ 23\overline{)982} \\ 920 \\ \hline 62 \\ 46 \\ \hline 16 \\ \hline \end{array}$$

(i) How many hundreds of 23s in 982? None
(ii) How many tens of 23s in 982? 40
(iii) $23 \times 40 = 920$
(iv) $982 − 920 = 62$
(v) How many 23s in 62? 2
(vi) $23 \times 2 = 46$
(vii) $62 − 46 = 16$ remainder

Guessing and Estimating

Are you good at guessing? Can you guess what the height of a building is? Or the number of spectators at a football match? There are many guessing competitions at fêtes. Visitors are invited to guess the weight of a cake. Or how many peas in a jar. Or what time a clock will stop. Or how far a car will travel on a certain amount of petrol. Some people guess wildly and give answers which are not sensible. Those who guess that there are only 20 peas on a jar, or that the car will travel 500 miles on a gallon of petrol are not going to win many prizes. Those people who take their time to *estimate* will be much nearer the correct figure. There is a great difference between guessing and estimating. Guessing is done with very little thought and care. Of course there are some things it is not possible to guess correctly. Nobody can guess at what time a clock will stop because there is no way to calculate it. No-one knows what the weather is going to be ten years from today because it is too far in the future. Someone may like to *foretell* what may happen, but it would be pure guess-work, or luck, if they guessed correctly.

Estimating

Estimating is quite different from guessing and is also useful. In mathematics it helps us to use numbers and measures sensibly. It also stops us from making careless errors. Estimation is used many times in everyday life. Families estimate how long it will take to walk to the railway station or what the distance of a coach journey is. When planning a holiday, the family estimates how much petrol will be needed, how much the hotel will be and how much money will be needed for amusements and presents.

When furnishing a home, people need to estimate how much carpeting will be needed and what the cost of the curtains and furniture is likely to be. Perhaps a builder needs to be called in to give an estimate for repairs which have to be carried out. When new houses are built, architects and surveyors spend time estimating what the costs will be and what materials are needed. At school, teachers make an estimate of the numbers present at parents' meetings. For the school concert, an estimate will need to be made so that enough chairs are put in place.

Can you guess, roughly, how many people are in this picture of St. Peter's Square, Rome?

Careful Estimates

There are times when we have to be accurate. When asked for a date of birth, the answer "Sometime in May" is not accurate enough. Neither is "About eleven" when an exact age is required. Car-drivers have to estimate accurately. They must judge the distance between cars carefully. They have to estimate their speed. They need to know exactly if the width of their car will allow them to pass through a gap or park safely. Children need to estimate accurately when crossing the road. They must estimate the speed of vehicles coming in both directions. They need to estimate how long it will take them to cross the road by the most direct route. Someone once wrote that, to cross the road, we have to make

Although we are unaware of it, we have to make all kinds of calculations when crossing a road.

accurate estimates and use every branch of mathematics. Fortunately, we have a built-in computer inside our head to help us to do all these things!

Rough Estimates

At other times there is no need to be so accurate. Police often give the estimate of a crowd at between 10 and 15 thousand. The population of a country may be given as *about* 50 million. Gardeners are advised to plant a *few* rows of carrots or to sprinkle *some* seeds in a drill. The distance between Paris and Berlin may be given in the road atlas as 667 miles. It is doubtful if the odometer on the car will record that mileage exactly because the car may have made a detour. What is needed is an approximate or near estimate. The distance can be said to be between 660 and 680 miles. In these cases an accurate estimate does not matter.

Round Numbers

People often use *round* numbers when estimating. The population of a town alters daily, so it is impossible to give an exact number. It is much more sensible to round off numbers like 368,359 and 48,493 to 368,000 and 48,500.

It is a good idea to round off temperatures. People are aware, when sitting in a room, that it is cold, or comfortable or hot. The temperature outdoors may be very cold, pleasant or very hot indeed. It is not necessary to know the *exact* temperature but it is interesting to compare how the weather feels with the forecast.

Good and Bad Estimates

Measurement is never exact. Even when the finest instruments are used there will be a small error. Bad estimates arise when they are not sensible or when the wrong kind of measure is used. A good estimate is when the size of the error is small when compared with the thing being estimated.

Hints on Estimating

1. *Take a sample.* Farmers and scientists sometimes want to know how many kinds of weeds are in certain fields. It is impossible to count them, so what do they do? A small area of a square metre is taped off and the weeds are sorted and counted. The numbers are then multiplied by the whole area of the field. In this way the farmer knows what steps to take to get rid of the weeds.

2. *Use the proper tool.* An estimate depends on what is being measured and the tool used to measure it. Using a metre stick to check the size of a small piece of paper is not sensible. A ruler with millimetres on it is needed. On the other hand, the length of the runway at an airport does not need such an exact instrument.

3. *Knowing the facts.* To estimate how far a car will travel on a gallon of petrol, we would need to have more information about the car; how big it is, how old it is, what its engine capacity is and what its make is. Then, after comparing these facts with what we already know about cars, we would be able to make a sensible estimate.

4. *Do a rough calculation.* To estimate the number of peas in a jar we need to think about the size of the pea and that of the jar. How many peas are likely to cover the bottom of the jar? How many layers of peas might there be in the jar? If we multiply the numbers in a layer by the number of layers we shall have a good estimate of the number of peas.

Can you estimate how many sweets are in the bottom part of this jar?

Fun with Numbers

Numbers are not meant to be serious and boring. They were invented to make life easier and better for people, and they have certainly done that. Think for a moment how mathematics has helped us by:

building homes, ships, canals, aircraft and bridges, inventing clever machines and tools, discovering new foods, making clothes, inventing medicines and curing diseases.

Mathematicians started thinking about these things many years ago. They thought about how numbers behaved and the patterns they made. They found that some patterns were rather unusual and did strange things. Mathematicians have found that numbers can also be amusing. Try having fun with these numbers.

A tricky number. The number 142857 has six digits. When it is multiplied by 2 something interesting happens.

$$\begin{array}{r} 142857 \\ \times\ 2 \\ \hline 285714 \end{array}$$

The same digits are in the product and *in the same order*, except that this time the 2 digit leads the rest.

14 2857   becomes   2857 14

Look what happens when the magic 142857 is multiplied by some other numbers:

$$\begin{array}{cccc} 142857 & 142857 & 142857 & 142857 \\ \times\ 3 & \times\ 4 & \times\ 5 & \times\ 6 \\ \hline 428571 & 571428 & 714285 & 857142 \end{array}$$

When 142857 is divided by 2 and 5 the numbers still appear in order. You have to know a little bit about decimals for these:

$$2\underline{|142857} \qquad 5\underline{|142857}$$
$$\ \ \ 71428.5 \qquad \ \ \ \ 28571.4$$

When the number is split in two, and the numerals added, the result is surprising:

The dots on the turtle's back added up to 15 in columns, rows and diagonals.

$$\begin{array}{r} 142 \\ 857 \\ \hline 999 \end{array}$$

The results are even more surprising when 142857 is added, or multiplied, seven times:

$$\begin{array}{rr} 142857 & \\ +\ 142857 & \\ +\ 142857 & \\ +\ 142857 & \\ +\ 142857 & \\ +\ 142857 & 142857 \\ +\ 142857 & \times\ 7 \\ \hline 999,999 & 999,999 \end{array}$$

142857 has been called the roundabout number because its numerals go round and round.

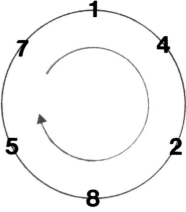

Using all the Numerals

The numerals 0, 1, 2, 3, 4, 5, 6, 7, 8 and 9 can be arranged in a certain way so that they all add up to 100:

$$1 + 2 + 3 + 4 + 5 + 6 + 7 + (8 \times 9) = 100$$

$$\frac{1}{2} + \frac{38}{76} + 49 + 50 = 100$$

and

$(\frac{2}{4}, \frac{3}{6}, \frac{4}{8}, \frac{5}{10}, \frac{16}{32}$, and so on, including $\frac{38}{76}$, are fractions which are all equal to $\frac{1}{2}$.)

How Big is a Million?

$1 \times 10 = 10$	ten
$10 \times 10 = 100$	a hundred
$100 \times 10 = 1000$	a thousand
$1000 \times 10 = 10000$	ten thousand
$10000 \times 10 = 100000$	a hundred thousand
$100000 \times 10 = 1000000$	a million

A million does not look very many, but do you have any idea how big it really is? Suppose a rich uncle left you a million pounds but said that you had to draw £100 of it out of the bank every week. How long do you think you would have to wait until you had drawn out the whole amount? Over 192 years! Of course, if you withdrew £3,846 a week it would only take you 5 years.

Think of a Number

Tell your friends that you can guess a number that they are thinking about. All they have to do is carry out your instructions. You say:

1. Think of a number
2. Add three to the number
3. Now double it
4. Subtract 4
5. Halve it
6. Subtract the number you first thought of
7. The answer is *one*

The answer is always 1 no matter what number your friends thought of.

Magic Squares

Yih King is the name of an old Chinese book written about 3000 years ago. In the book there is a story that a large turtle once came out of the Yellow River. On the turtle's back were marks which puzzled everyone who saw them. The marks were dots which represented numbers. This magic square, or Lo Shu, as it was called, is known as the world's oldest number mystery. It was used to work magic in the East. Seven hundred years ago it was used in Europe to bring good luck and drive away diseases.

The dots in the magic square stand for the numerals 1 to 9. They are entered in the square in such a way that the columns, rows and diagonals give a total of 15.

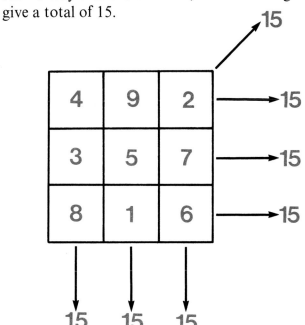

Can you complete these magic squares?

8		6
4		2

6		8
	7	5

2	7	
	3	8

		2
	1	9
	3	

A Magic Circle

A Japanese mathematician called Seki Kowa discovered this magic circle about 300 years ago.

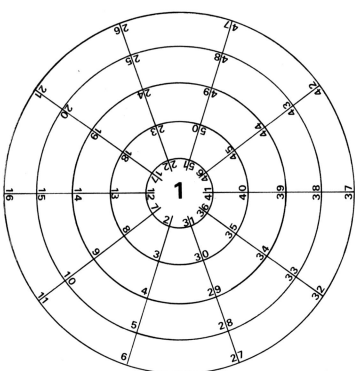

The inner circle has the numbers 2, 31, 36, 41, 46, 51, 22, 17, 12 and 7. If you add these numbers they come to 265. The numbers on the next circumference total 265. Add the numbers on the other circumferences:

$$4 + 29 + 34 + 39 + 44 + 49 + 24 + 19 + 14 + 9 =$$

$$5 + 28 + 33 + 38 + 43 + 48 + 25 + 20 + 15 + 10 =$$

$$6 + 27 + 32 + 37 + 42 + 47 + 26 + 21 + 16 + 11 =$$

What do you notice?
Add the numbers on the diameters but do NOT include the 1.

$$21 + 20 + 19 + 18 + 17 + 36 + 35 + 34 + 33 + 32 =$$

$$16 + 15 + 14 + 13 + 12 + 41 + 40 + 39 + 38 + 37 =$$

$$11 + 10 + 9 + 8 + 7 + 46 + 45 + 44 + 43 + 42 =$$

$$6 + 5 + 4 + 3 + 2 + 51 + 50 + 49 + 48 + 47 =$$

$$27 + 28 + 29 + 30 + 31 + 22 + 23 + 24 + 25 + 26 =$$

What are the totals?
Did you notice that all the numbers from 1 to 51 were used in this magic circle?

Can you make a magic circle with the numbers 1 to 21? Here is a start.

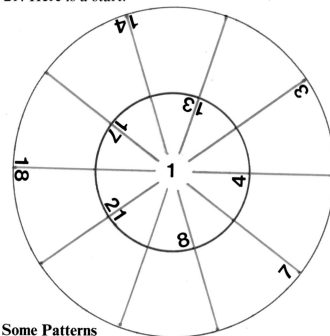

Some Patterns

Sometimes there are problems where numbers and signs are mixed. This is one of them: $1 \times 8 + 1$. In cases like this it is usual to put a part of the expression in brackets:

$$(1 \times 8) + 1 = 8 + 1 = 9$$

Here is an interesting pattern:

$$(1 \times 8) + 1 = 9$$
$$(12 \times 8) + 2 = 98$$
$$(123 \times 8) + 3 = 987$$
$$(1234 \times 8) + 4 = 9876$$
$$(12345 \times 8) + 5 = 98765$$
$$(123456 \times 8) + 6 = 987654$$

Can you finish the pattern? You do not need to work out the multiplication!

Here is another pattern:

$$(1 \times 9) + 2 = 11$$
$$(12 \times 9) + 3 = 111$$
$$(123 \times 9) + 4 = 1111$$
$$(1234 \times 9) + 5 = 11111$$

Can you finish that one?

Here is a neat one:

$$(9 \times 9) + 7 = 88$$
$$(98 \times 9) + 6 = 888$$
$$(987 \times 9) + 5 = 8888$$
$$(9876 \times 9) + 4 = 88888$$

Can you finish it?

Numbers Magical and Mysterious

Some of our newspapers print a special column every day. It is headed YOUR STARS or WHAT YOUR STARS FORETELL. You have to find the name of the star you were born under and you can then see your fortune for the day. People born under the sign Leo the lion (23 July to 23 August) may read something like this:

> Make good plans and keep to them. You are likely to move shortly. Be careful not to become too tired. Try not to lose your temper with a friend. Your lucky number is 4.

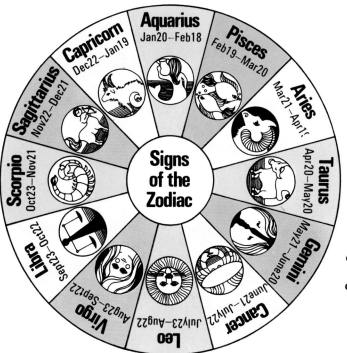

Do you believe in lucky numbers? Many of the old astrologers did and a few people still do. Odd numbers were supposed to be particularly lucky. A saying grew up which Shakespeare copied: "Good luck lies in odd numbers."

The ancient thinkers and mathematicians tried to find special meanings in numbers. Some were thought to be magic and some unlucky. *Golden* numbers took their name from being marked in gold on the Roman and Greek calendars. They are still used to find the date of the new Moon and Easter. The Greeks thought that all the odd numbers were male and the even ones female.

Pythagoras was a Greek thinker and mathematician who was born about 2500 years ago. He was the first to teach that the Sun was round and that the Earth and stars move around in space. Pythagoras taught that number was in all things. He linked numbers with colours and with the way

people behave. It is to him that we owe many of the old beliefs about numbers.

Numbers Around Us

Since the time of Pythagoras numbers have played a big part in people's lives. There are some which are of great importance to some people. Other numbers have become part of our speech and sayings. Here are some of them:

1 One has always been linked with God: the Great One, the Almighty One. It is also applied to oneself. If people say that they are going to look after Number One it means that they are going to take care of themselves. It is a number which has been connected with sadness. At a funeral the bell is rung in *ones*. At a shipping office in London, called Lloyds, the Lutine Bell is struck once when a ship is sunk.

2 Two was looked on by the Greeks and Romans as an unlucky number connected with death. The second month of their calendar was sacred to Pluto who ruled the Lower World.

There are many sayings with *two* in them:
> Two's company. Three's a crowd.
> Two heads are better than one.
> Two wrongs cannot make a right.
> A bird in the hand is better than two in the bush.
> When two Friday's come together ... (meaning NEVER).
> To have two strings to one's bow means to have two ways of reaching one's object.

41

There are lots of names for two: a brace, a couple, a duet, a pair and twins. Words beginning with bi-, such as bicycle and bisect, often have something to do with two.

3 Three was a lucky and a happy number to some people. We still give three cheers to show that we are pleased about something or to congratulate somebody. It was such an important number to some people that they worshipped it. Christians believe in a group of 3 or Trinity: God, Son and Holy Spirit. The Hindu priests or Brahmins represent their god with three heads. Myths and legends have many stories with three gods in them. The world was supposed to be ruled by three gods: Jupiter in heaven, Neptune under the sea and Pluto in the underworld. There were three Fates, three Furies, three Graces and three Harpies. Words starting with tri-, such as trio, trice, triple, triplet and tricycle, usually have a connection with three.

4 Four was fairness and perfection. It is the first real *square* number (2 × 2) and, of course, there are four sides to a square. We talk about a square deal as being honest, and someone who pays a debt is said to square the account. Words like quadrangle and quadrilateral have a connection with four or square. The ancient thinkers imagined that all things were made up of four elements or parts: earth, water, air and fire.

5 The five-pointed star was used by the Greeks as a secret symbol. It is also a Jewish symbol called the Star of David. Five became a symbol for marriage because it is the union of man (2) and woman (3). Five is one of the numbers mentioned in the Bible many times.

Did you know that you have five wits or senses? They are common sense, imagination, fantasy, estimation and memory. The five real senses are better known: taste, sight, hearing, smelling and feeling. Words beginning with quin-, like quintet, mean fivefold. A *pentagon* is a five-sided figure and the first five books of the Bible are called the Pentateuch.

6 Six was looked on as the perfect number because its *factors* (1, 2 and 3) give a total of 6 when added. In many religions God created the world in 6 days. In some worship today people regard 6 as a powerful number and have the six-pointed star as a protecting symbol.

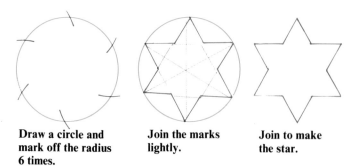

Draw a circle and mark off the radius 6 times.

Join the marks lightly.

Join to make the star.

7 Seven has for long been known as a magical and lucky number. There are many stories which use this number. In the Bible, Peter was told to forgive his brother seventy times seven times. In the Middle Ages the patron saints of the seven European countries of England, Scotland, Wales, Ireland, France, Spain and Italy were known as the Seven Champions of Christendom. In Japanese folklore there were Seven Gods of Luck. There were Seven Heavens, Seven Joys and Seven Names of God. There were also said to be Seven Planets and there were Seven Wonders of the World. Shakespeare wrote about the Seven Ages of Man and we talk of the Seventh Heaven to mean complete happiness. There are seven days of creation and seven days of the week.

8 It is amazing how many events are connected with seven. Eight, on the other hand, is a very dull number. It was looked on at one time as the number which stood for making a fresh start. This was because it was 7 + 1. Words beginning with oct- sometimes have a connection with eight. An octopus has eight legs and eight people play in an octet.

9 Nine was another important number because it was a product of 3 × 3. This made it a perfect and magical number. There were nine Roman gods and nine rivers in the underworld. In folktales you had to wrap nine grains of wheat in a four-leaved clover in order to see the fairies. To cure a sprained ankle you had to tie nine knots in a piece of black wool. It is well known that a cat has nine lives and that a stitch in time saves nine. If you are dressed to the nines you are very smart indeed.

Little and Large

Which is the odd one out of these?

$2, \frac{1}{4}, -6, \sqrt{3}, 0, \triangle, 1\frac{1}{2}, 7^2, \text{VIII}$

Difficult, isn't it? Well, $\triangle$ is the odd one out because it is a symbol which is not a numeral. All the rest belong to a set of numbers.

We must keep remembering that, once upon a time, there were no numbers at all because nobody needed them. However, as people began to need numbers they had to invent them.

Natural Numbers

As we know, the first numbers which were invented were the counting numbers: 1, 2, 3, 4, 5 ... They are also called *natural* numbers because people thought they grew naturally. Suppose you were to start counting today and went on counting all your life. It would be very boring, but do you think you would get to the end of the numbers? It is a silly question because this set of numbers has no end. There is no last or largest number. That is why some dots are put after a number. In that way everyone knows that the sequence goes on indefinitely, or without end:

$$1, 2, 3, 4, 5, \ldots$$

There are many sets of numbers which go on and on. Here are just three of them:

The odd numbers: 1, 3, 5, 7, ...
The even numbers: 2, 4, 6, 8, ...
The multiples of 10: 20, 30, 40, ...

A large part of mathematics is based on the natural numbers.

The Number Line

A useful way, when studying numbers, is to think of them as points on a line. To do this, we have to imagine a line like this:

We have to imagine as well that the line goes on and on in the direction of the arrows. We choose a point on the line and give it the number 1.

We can then mark off numbers in equal spaces to the right to represent 2, 3, 4, 5, ...

"Hush! Daddy's inventing numbers."

In this way every natural number can be represented by one point on the line. The collection of all these points gives us a picture or *graph* of the set of natural numbers.

Zero

Nought, or zero, is a number. It is an important one too because it has more than one use. We know that a symbol like 2 means something different in the number 352 from what it means in 253. It has a different value when it is in a different place. The zero has no value whatever its position is, but it does have importance. Its position in the numbers 320 and 302 makes a difference of 18. Zero is also the number of an empty set. The number of Eskimos living in our house is 0.

Do you know the song *Ten Green Bottles*?

Ten green bottles standing on the wall
Ten green bottles standing on the wall
And if one green bottle should accidentally fall
There'd be nine green bottles standing on
   the wall.

The song goes on until the last verse:

One green bottle standing on the wall
One green bottle standing on the wall
And if that green bottle should accidentally fall
There'd be no green bottles standing on
   the wall.

Ten green bottles standing on the wall, and then continuing to fall until none is left, can be written as $10 - 10 = 0$.

So zero is a number which can be reached by counting back: 10, 9, 8, 7, 6, 5, 4, 3, 2, 1, 0, ... Zero finds its place on the number line and we have a graph of the set of *whole* numbers.

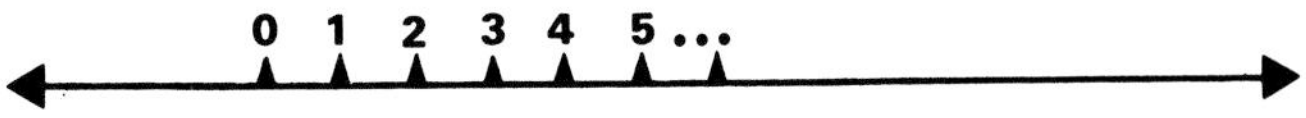

43

Integers

This is a strange word for something quite simple. An integer is a whole number and one which is not divided up like a fraction. Before entering some integers on the number line we must look at some situations in real life. We all know what happens at the *count-down* before a rocket or missile is fired: five, four, three, two, one, zero; we have Lift-off! What is happening is that the commentator is counting in two directions: up to zero and then beyond. A way of counting in two directions is seen in weather charts. If a record is kept during cold weather, the outside temperatures will be seen to rise above and fall below zero.

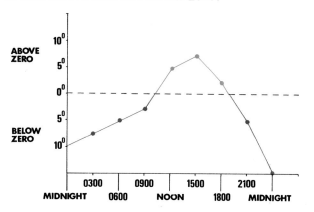

The outside temperatures rise above and fall below zero.

A bank account shows us another way of counting in two directions. If you have a healthy balance in your account everything is fine and the Bank Manager smiles at you. But you may write a cheque for more money than you have in your account. The Manager then writes a letter to say that you are *in the red*. You have less than no money. You owe some.

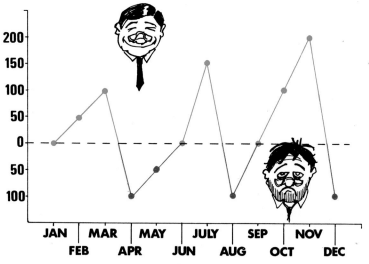

The red lines show when money was owed to the bank.

When the rocket count-down starts at the count of 5 below zero we give it the sign ⁻5. The temperature of 10° below zero is ⁻10°C. Owing £100 to the bank means that the customer is minus £100. These numbers were invented because people did not know of a way to write the answer to 3 − 8 for example. Mathematicians wanted to express a number less than zero. The sign is like a minus sign but, to avoid confusion, it is best to put it above the line. 8 − 3 means 8 subtract (or minus) 3, which is 5, but 3 − 8 = ⁻5 or 5 less than 0. Numbers like ⁻1, ⁻2 and ⁻3 are called *directed* numbers because they show a direction. Positive numbers (those above zero) are written ⁺1, ⁺2, ⁺3, ... and go to the right of zero. *Negative* numbers (those below zero) are written ⁻1, ⁻2, ⁻3, ... and go to the left of zero.

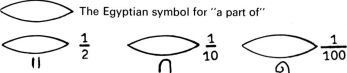

There are many examples of how integers express ideas. Positive numbers can show heights above sea-level and negative numbers show depths below sea-level. Positive numbers show distances north of the equator and negative numbers show distances south of the equator.

Rational Numbers

What did people do when they measured something and found that it was more than 8 cubits long and less than nine? What did they do when they wanted to write down the result of sharing a loaf among 4 neighbours? How do you find the answer to 3 ÷ 2 when you have only whole numbers? A new set of numbers had to be invented. The Egyptians invented a symbol which meant *a part of*. It was their way of writing a fraction or part of a whole number. They used this symbol with a numeral.

The Egyptian symbol for "a part of"

$\frac{1}{2}$ $\frac{1}{10}$ $\frac{1}{100}$

The number system was made bigger to include *rational* numbers. These are numbers which take the form of a *ratio* or fraction. This is a number with two halves: a numerator above the line and a denominator below the line. The denominator must not be zero. This fraction describes three-fourths or three quarters:

3   numerator (whole number)

4   denominator (whole number, not zero)

Irrational Numbers

There are some numbers which cannot be placed on a number line. If 5 is divided by 3 the answer is not exact. It is, in fact, 1.66666··· The three dots mean that the sixes go on and on. We cannot put these *irrational* numbers on the number line because there is no exact point for them. Other numbers which have no special place on the number line are π and $\sqrt{2}$.

Very Small Numbers

The number line shows how, by subdividing, more and more rational number points appear.

The unit ONE can be subdivided into *tenths*.
TENTHS can be subdivided into *hundredths*.
HUNDREDTHS can be subdivided into *thousandths*.
THOUSANDTHS can be subdivided into *ten-thousandths* and so on ...

If this subdivision were continued we would get very small numbers indeed.

Everything in the world is made up of extremely tiny *atoms*: chairs, air, grass, stones and our bodies. Atoms are so small they can be seen only under very powerful electron microscopes. What is amazing is that atoms are made of even smaller particles called *protons, neutrons* and *electrons*. An electron weighs

0.000 000 000 000 000 000 000 000 000 9 grams.

Three drawing pins weigh 1 gram so it is difficult to realize how light an electron is. It is almost weightless. Scientists have to use numbers like that in their calculations. Fortunately they do not have to write lots of zeros when they come across a quantity like the weight of an electron. They have a short way of writing those numbers. This way uses little space but tells scientists the size of a number immediately.

0.000 000 000 000 000 000 000 000 000 9
is written 9.0×10^{-28}.

Very Large Numbers

There are many large numbers. The population of the world must be very large. The number of blades of grass, leaves on the trees and grains of sand on the beaches must be enormously large. Yet these are all definite or *finite* numbers. It is known that there are one million deer in England. It is known that a drop of water contains more than 100 billion billion atoms.

We can represent a million easily as 1 000 000. When the numbers become bigger, mathematicians have a quicker way of writing them. The weight of the Sun is written as 1.9912×10^{30} kg.

Infinite Numbers

There is a difference between very large numbers and *infinite* numbers. Twenty-one hundred years ago there lived a Greek scientist and mathematician called Archimedes. He estimated the number of grains of sand it would take to fill the universe. He did not know the number exactly but he said it was a *finite* number. The set of vowels in the alphabet is finite. The set of numbers from 1 to 10 is finite. The set of natural numbers is *infinite*. There is no end to the set of 1, 2, 3, 4, 5, ...

The sign for infinity is ∞. If you want to have a glimpse of what infinity may be like, look at your face reflected in facing mirrors. The picture below gives us some idea of infinity.

Numbers in a Sieve

For thousands of years people have been interested in certain kinds of numbers. Greek mathematicians liked to discuss how numbers behaved. They thought about the strange things it was possible to do with some of them. One set of numbers which took their attention was the one which could be represented by patterns of objects. For example, they saw that six pebbles, when put into two lines, made a shape. The same shape could be made with 6 pebbles, 8 pebbles and with 10.

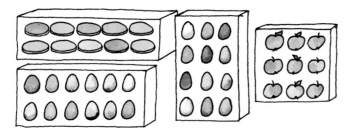

The shape these pebbles make is a *rectangle*. Rectangles are made when, for example, ten biscuits or a dozen eggs are arranged in a certain way. Nine objects can be arranged with three lines of three. Squares are special kinds of rectangles.

The numbers from which these patterns come are rectangle numbers. The rectangle for the number 8 has two lines with four objects in each line:

$$4 \times 2 = 8$$

The rectangle for the number 12 has two lines of six or three lines of four:

$$6 \times 2 = 12$$
$$4 \times 3 = 12$$

A rectangle number is the product of smaller numbers. These smaller numbers are factors. The factors of 8 are 2 and 4. The factors of 12 are 2, 3, 4 and 6.

Prime Numbers

Some numbers of objects cannot be arranged to form a rectangle. Five marbles can be put in 5 lines with one in each line. Or they can be put in 1 line of 5 marbles, which is the same thing. But they cannot be arranged in a rectangle. This also happens with the numbers 7, 11 and 13.

- 5, 7, 11 and 13 are not rectangle numbers.
- 5, 7, 11 and 13 are not the products of smaller numbers. They have no factors.
- 5, 7, 11 and 13 are *prime* numbers.
- 2, 3, 5, 7, 11, 13, 17 and 19 are the first eight prime numbers.

There are many, many more prime numbers. One is not usually included in the set of prime numbers. No even number is prime except 2.

The Sieve of Eratosthenes

How do we know if a number is rectangular or prime? A man called Eratosthenes found out twenty-two centuries ago. He was a Greek mathematician who was the librarian in the University of Alexandria about the year 240 B.C. He found a clever way to measure the size of the Earth and was also an astronomer, athlete and

THE MULTIPLES OF 2 ●

poet. He is famous for discovering a way of telling if a number is rectangular or prime. Imagine a giant kitchen sieve which contains whole numbers. When the sieve is shaken for the first time something magical happens. The first prime number (2) stays in the sieve. The multiples of 2 (4, 6, 8, 10, . . .), or the even numbers, fall through the holes of the sieve (bottom left).

The sieve is shaken again. This time the second prime number (3) also stays inside the sieve. The multiples of 3 which are numbers like 9, 15, 21, 27 and 33, fall through the sieve. All the other ones, such as 6 and 12, have already gone through.

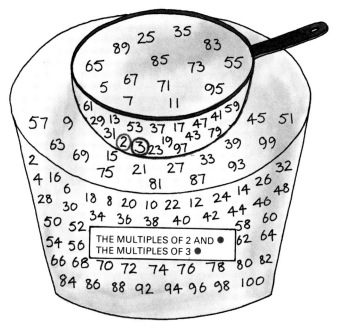

The third prime number is 5. As the sieve is shaken for the third time it holds back 5 and lets through the multiples of 5 which have not already gone. These were the multiples of 2 and 3, like 10, 15, 20 and 30.

Each time the sieve is shaken the next prime number is held back and its multiples fall through the mesh. Each family of prime numbers is dealt with in turn. The numbers finally left in the sieve are the primes:

$$2, 3, 5, 7, 11, 13, 17, 19, \ldots$$

Of course we have only pretended that the numbers up to 100 were in the sieve.

Making a Sieve
You can discover the prime numbers to 100 easily.
1. Draw a square 10 cm long and 10 cm wide.
2. Draw lines 1 cm apart so that you have 100 squares.
3. Inside each square write the numbers from 1 to 100.
4. With a *red* pencil ring the first prime (2). Cross out all the multiples of 2 (4, 6, 8, 10, . . .) because they are not prime numbers.
5. The next prime number is 3. Use a *blue* pencil to ring 3. Cross out all the multiples of 3 by counting in threes: 6, 9, 12, 15, . . . Some of them have already been crossed out. Why?
6. The number 4 has been crossed out already. Why?
7. The next prime number is 5. Use a *green* pencil to ring 5 and cross out its multiples. Why have numbers like 15 and 30 already been crossed out?

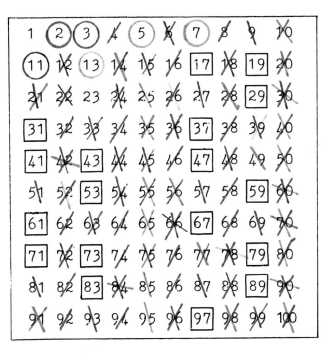

8. Continue to ring primes and cross out their multiples.
In the illustration a circle has been put round all

the numbers whose multiples have been crossed out. The prime numbers left, after all the crossing out has been done, are the ones inside the squares. These are the primes only up to 100. As we shall see, there are many more.

How Many Prime Numbers are There?

This is the question that puzzled the early mathematicians. Over 2000 years ago one of them, called Euclid, found the answer. He proved that there is no end to the set of prime numbers. He showed that no matter how many primes were found by using Eratosthenes' sieve, there are always some larger ones. The set of prime numbers is infinite.

There are still many problems to do with prime numbers which not even modern computers have yet been able to solve. Mathematicians see that there are not so many prime numbers as their size increases. They have also found many which are near to each other. Some of these are: 11 and 13, 41 and 43, 137 and 139, 149 and 151. It is likely that the set of these primes, like the set of prime numbers themselves, is infinite.

What is the *biggest* prime number? Computer experts seem to find larger and larger ones week by week. At the last count the largest prime number would fill the whole of this page with its digits!

Composite Numbers

All the numbers which are not primes are *composite* numbers. Composite means that something is made up of various parts. Composite numbers are made up of factors.

Factor Trees

Check on squared paper, or with apparatus, that you know the factors of 12.

$12 = 2 \times 6$ or 6×2, 4×3 or 3×4
The factors of 12 are 2, 3, 4, 6.

Some of these factors (4 and 6) are not prime numbers. 4 and 6 can be broken down.

$4 = 2 \times 2$ and $6 = 2 \times 3$ or 3×2
The prime factors of 6 are 2 and 3.

A factor tree gives the *prime* factors of a number.

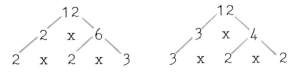
Two trees for 12: the same factors.

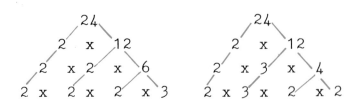

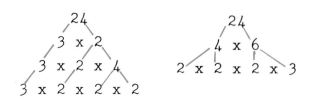
The prime factors of 24: $2 \times 2 \times 2 \times 3$.

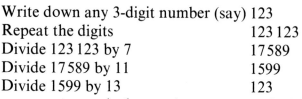

A Trick with Prime Numbers

Write down any 3-digit number (say) 123
Repeat the digits   123 123
Divide 123 123 by 7   17589
Divide 17589 by 11   1599
Divide 1599 by 13   123
                    is the number you started with.

Try this again with another 3-digit number:
$146\,146 \div 7 = 20878$
$20878 \div 11 = 1898$
$1898 \div 13 = 146$
How is it done?
Here is a clue: $7 \times 11 \times 13 = 1001$

Example: $482 \times 1001 = (482 \times 1000) +$
(482×1)
$482 \times 1000 = 482000$
$482 \times 1 \quad = \quad 482$
$482 \times 1001 = 482482$

Divisible Numbers

We say a number is *divisible* by another number when it divides without leaving a remainder.

Example: The number 12 is exactly divisible by 2, by 3, by 4 and by 6.
Like all other numbers it is divisible by itself and 1. The factors of 12 are: 2, 3, 4 and 6 (if we omit 1 and 12).

Here are some tips to see quickly if a number is divisible:

Divisibility by 2
A number is divisible by 2 if it ends in an even number.

Divisibility by 3
A number is divisible by 3 if the sum of its digits is divisible by 3.

A Piece of Cake

There is a kind of number often used in conversations:

> I will meet you in a *quarter* of an hour.
> We were there in *half* the time.
> He left *three-quarters* of his dinner.
> She divided the cake into *eighths*.

These are some of the words which are *fractions*. Fraction comes from the same family of words as fracture. A fractured arm is one that is broken. A fraction is a part broken off, like a piece of cake. Usually it means something small:

> I will return in a *fraction* of a second.
> Just a *fraction* of the sailors were rescued.
> She only had a *fraction* of her money back.

A Need for New Numbers

Until the time when fractions were invented, people had to manage with just *whole* numbers. This was all right for some operations but not for others. There were no numbers to describe what the parts were when a rope was cut into equal lengths. It was not possible to express a length or a weight *in between* two whole numbers. A loaf could be broken into fragments but there was no symbol for the parts which were shared. When something like a bar of chocolate is split up, another set of numbers is needed to describe the parts.

A Need for a New Symbol

The Egyptians used a symbol to describe *a part of* a number. The number was placed under the symbol to express what the part or fraction was (see page 44). About nine hundred years ago a Hindu astrologer, Bhaskara, invented another symbol. In our numerals it looked like this: $\frac{3}{4}$. The Arab traders brought this way of writing a fraction to Europe. By that time a line had crept in between the numerals: $\frac{3}{4}$. Up to 200 years ago several symbols were used:

$$3-4 \quad 3/4 \quad \frac{3}{4}$$

The last one is the one which became widely used.

What Fractions Do

Fractions do three things.

1. A fraction is the result of dividing a *thing* into

equal parts. An apple cut into two equal parts produces two halves. One half of those two equal parts is written: $\frac{1}{2}$.

A bottle of milk can be divided into three equal parts. These are thirds, and one part is one-third or $\frac{1}{3}$.

A block of chocolate can be divided into fourths or quarters. One quarter is written $\frac{1}{4}$.

A melon divided into 5 equal parts produces fifths. One of those parts is $\frac{1}{5}$.

A fraction results from dividing a thing into EQUAL PARTS.

When things are divided we can use words and numbers.

When a thing is divided into	One part is called	and the number is
2 equal parts	a half	$\frac{1}{2}$
3 equal parts	a third	$\frac{1}{3}$
4 equal parts	a fourth or a quarter	$\frac{1}{4}$
5 equal parts	a fifth	$\frac{1}{5}$

Numbers greater than ONE can be divided into equal parts. A platoon of soldiers has 78 in it. A half of that platoon is 39.

$$\frac{1}{2} \times 78 = 39$$

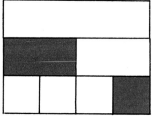

Fractions result from dividing ONE into equal parts.

A half of ONE is a half
$$\frac{1}{2} \times 1 = \frac{1}{2}$$
A quarter of ONE is a quarter
$$\frac{1}{4} \times 1 = \frac{1}{4}$$

$$1$$
$$\frac{1}{2} \times 1 = \frac{1}{2}$$
$$\frac{1}{4} \times 1 = \frac{1}{4}$$

Dividing ONE into equal parts

2. A fraction is a *ratio*. This is comparing two quantities by taking one as a fraction of the other. If David has 9 sweets and Mary has 12, the ratio is 9 to 12, which is written 9:12. This becomes 3:4 or $\frac{3}{4}$.

3. A fraction is a number compared to ONE. $\frac{3}{4}$ means that 1 is divided into 4 equal parts.
Each part is one-quarter ($\frac{1}{4}$) of ONE
Three parts are taken: $3 \times \frac{1}{4} = \frac{3}{4}$

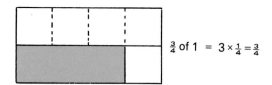

$\frac{3}{4}$ of 1 $= 3 \times \frac{1}{4} = \frac{3}{4}$

A number compared to 1

Fractions of Quantities

We often have to take fractions of the quantities like lengths, weights and other measures. In the *Imperial* system, fractions are used very often.

Examples: $1\frac{1}{2}$ lb. of flour and $\frac{3}{4}$ lb. of sugar.
Pieces of wood $3\frac{1}{4}$ or $7\frac{5}{8}$ inches long.
A third of a pint of milk and $2\frac{1}{2}$ gallons of water.
Half a teaspoonful of baking powder.
A track half a mile long.

Fractions are not used so often with the metric system of weights and measures. It is easy in these cases to use *decimal* fractions (see pages 53 and 54).

Equivalence

Fractions are easy to handle but there is a secret. To operate them they have to be the same kind or from the same family. They have to be *equivalent* or of equal value. Adding a set of 3 apples and a set of 4 apples is easy. The result is a set of 7 apples: $3 + 4 = 7$. Adding one-fifth and two-fifths is just as easy. The result is three fifths: $\frac{1}{5} + \frac{2}{5} = \frac{3}{5}$.

Adding a set of 3 apples and a set of 4 bananas is not possible. Apples and bananas are not the same things. But we can join the two sets if we call them fruit. It is the same with fractions. Adding $\frac{1}{4}$ and $\frac{1}{2}$ is easy because we know that $\frac{1}{2}$ has the same value as $\frac{2}{4}$. $\frac{1}{4}$ and $\frac{2}{4}$ are equivalent.

SOME FRACTION WORDS

Common Fraction An ordinary fraction which has whole numbers above and below the line. $\frac{2}{3}$ is a common fraction. Other names for common fractions are simple fractions, vulgar fractions and rational numbers.

Common means *the same* Two fractions with the same number below the line, like $\frac{2}{5}$ and $\frac{3}{5}$, have a common denominator.

Denominator is the number written below the line. In $\frac{1}{3}$, 3 is the denominator.

Equal or *equivalent fractions* have the same value, like $\frac{1}{2}$ and $\frac{5}{10}$. Some fractions, like $\frac{4}{4}$ and $\frac{10}{10}$ are equal to 1.

Improper fractions, such as $\frac{9}{2}$ and $\frac{8}{5}$, have the numerator bigger than the denominator. Improper fractions are greater than 1.

Line This separates the numerator and denominator.

Mixed numbers have whole numbers and fractions. $3\frac{1}{4}$ is an easy way of writing $3 + \frac{1}{4}$.

Numerator is the number written above the line. In the fraction $\frac{9}{90}$ the numerator is 9.

Proper fractions, like $\frac{2}{9}$, have a numerator smaller than the denominator. Their value is less than 1.

Representative fraction is a way of giving a scale on a map. A representative fraction (R.F.) of $\frac{1}{20000}$ means that the distance on a map represents 20 000 times the distance on earth. This scale can be written 1 to 20 000 or 1:20 000.

Terms are either numerators or denominators. A fraction such as $\frac{1}{2}$ is in its simplest form or *lowest terms* because the numerator and denominator have no common factor except 1. $\frac{4}{8}$ is not in its lowest terms because the numerator and denominator can each be divided by 4 to give $\frac{1}{2}$.

Value is how much the fraction is. $\frac{3}{4}$ and $\frac{6}{8}$ have the same values.

To add $\frac{1}{10}$ and $\frac{1}{5}$ we must find an equivalent fraction for $\frac{1}{5}$. The fractions must have the same *denominator*.

$$\frac{1}{10} + \frac{1}{5} = \frac{1}{10} + \frac{2}{10} = \frac{3}{10}$$
$$\frac{1}{2} + \frac{1}{5} = \frac{5}{10} + \frac{2}{10} = \frac{7}{10}$$
$$\frac{1}{12} + \frac{1}{4} = \frac{1}{12} + \frac{3}{12} = \frac{4}{12} \text{ or } \frac{1}{3}$$
$$\frac{2}{3} + \frac{1}{4} = \frac{8}{12} + \frac{3}{12} = \frac{11}{12}$$

Subtraction is just as easy:

$$\frac{9}{10} - \frac{1}{10} = \frac{8}{10} \text{ or } \frac{4}{5}$$
$$\frac{3}{4} - \frac{1}{2} = \frac{3}{4} - \frac{2}{4} = \frac{1}{4}$$
$$\frac{7}{8} - \frac{1}{4} = \frac{7}{8} - \frac{2}{8} = \frac{5}{8}$$
$$\frac{11}{12} - \frac{1}{2} = \frac{11}{12} - \frac{6}{12} = \frac{5}{12}$$

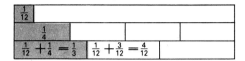

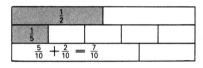

Fractions of Whole Numbers

To find a fraction of a whole number greater than one is a simple operation.

Example: Three motorists decided to share the driving on a journey of 1 737 miles. How far did each of them drive?

To find a third share we divide by three.

A third of 1 737 miles is
$\frac{1}{3}$ of 1 737
$= \frac{1}{3} \times 1\,737$
$= \dfrac{1\,737}{3} = 579$ miles

(Notice that *of* becomes the symbol $\times$)

Example of two ways to find two-thirds of 120:

$$\frac{2}{3} \times 120 \qquad\qquad \frac{2}{3} \times 120$$
$$= \dfrac{240}{3} \rightarrow (2 \times 120)$$
$$\qquad\qquad\qquad = 2 \times 40 \rightarrow (120 \div 3)$$
$$= 80 \qquad\qquad\qquad = 80$$

Fractions of Fractions

Multiplying fractions is really finding a fraction of a fraction. Think about *of* as meaning $\times$.

Examples:

(i) $\frac{1}{4}$ of $\frac{1}{2}$ and   (ii) $\frac{1}{2}$ of $\frac{1}{4}$
$\quad = \frac{1}{4} \times \frac{1}{2}$ $= \frac{1}{2} \times \frac{1}{4}$
$\quad = \frac{1}{8}$ $= \frac{1}{8}$

(iii) $\frac{2}{3}$ of $\frac{1}{2}$ and   (iv) $\frac{1}{2}$ of $\frac{2}{3}$
$\quad = \frac{2}{3} \times \frac{1}{2}$ $= \frac{1}{2} \times \frac{2}{3}$
$\quad = \frac{2}{6}$ $= \frac{2}{6}$
$\quad = \frac{1}{3}$ $= \frac{1}{3}$

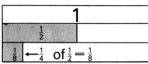

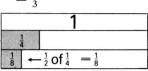

Dividing by a fraction needs care and thought.

How many halves are there in 4?
In 1 there are 2 halves.
In 4 there are 8 halves.
How many halves in 4 is written $4 \div \frac{1}{2}$

So to divide by $\frac{1}{2}$ you have to multiply by 2.

Examples:

(i) How many quarters   (ii) $\frac{1}{4}$ divided by $\frac{1}{2}$
in a half?

$\frac{1}{2} \div \frac{1}{4}$ $\frac{1}{4} \div \frac{1}{2}$
$= \frac{1}{2} \times \frac{4}{1}$ $= \frac{1}{4} \times \frac{2}{1}$
$= \frac{4}{2}$ $= \frac{2}{4}$
$= 2$ $= \frac{1}{2}$

How many quarters in $\frac{1}{2}$?
$\frac{1}{2} \div \frac{1}{4} = 2$

Think of a Fraction

Try this trick on a friend.

	(i)	(ii)
Think of a fraction (say)	$\frac{3}{4}$	$\frac{2}{3}$
Multiply it by 2	$1\frac{1}{2}$	$1\frac{1}{3}$
Add 18	$19\frac{1}{2}$	$19\frac{1}{3}$
Divide by 2	$9\frac{3}{4}$	$9\frac{2}{3}$
Subtract the fraction you started with	9	9

The result is always 9: Why?

Working them out

(i) $\frac{3}{4} \times 2 = \frac{6}{4} = 1\frac{1}{2}$ (ii) $\frac{2}{3} \times 2 = \frac{4}{3} = 1\frac{1}{3}$
$\quad 1\frac{1}{2} + 18 = 19\frac{1}{2}$ $1\frac{1}{3} + 18 = 19\frac{1}{3}$
$\quad 19\frac{1}{2} \div 2 = 9\frac{3}{4}$ $19\frac{1}{3} \div 2 = \frac{58}{3} \div 2 = \frac{29}{3}$
$\quad 9\frac{3}{4} - \frac{3}{4} = 9$ $= 9\frac{2}{3}$
$\quad\quad\quad\quad\quad\quad\quad\quad\quad\quad\quad\quad 9\frac{2}{3} - \frac{2}{3} = 9$

51

The Most Important Invention?

What is the most important thing that was ever invented? Ice-cream? Safety pins? Sliced bread? The wheel? One man said that the most important thing people ever did was to invent the *decimal number system*. It is certainly a most amazing invention. Using only ten symbols it is possible to describe any number there is. We can express mighty numbers and tiny ones. We can describe, not only great distances in outer space, but the weight of the smallest particle of dust.

Ten Numerals

There has been much progress in science, education and trade during the past 400 years. This results from being able to describe numbers and quantities. The simple system of using 0, 1, 2, 3, 4, 5, 6, 7, 8 and 9 is called the *decimal* system. The word means *connected with ten*. The decimal system is based on ten.

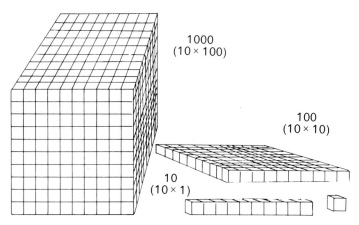

We do not have to say what each numeral stands for because its position tells us. The value of the numeral depends on its place in the number:

The value of 2 in 3*2* is   2 ones   or 2
The value of 2 in *2*9 is   2 tens   or 20
The value of 2 in *2*46 is   2 hundreds   or 200
The value of 2 in *2*876 is 2 thousands or 2000
and so on . . .

The first place on the right is for ONES.
The place to its *left* is for TENS; TEN is ten times greater than ONE.
The third place is for HUNDREDS; HUNDRED is ten times greater than TEN.
The fourth place is for THOUSANDS; THOUSAND is ten times greater than HUNDRED.
This goes on and on. Each place to the *left* is ten times greater.

With our wonderful number system we can describe the size and distance of anything, no matter how large or small. This picture shows the Dumb-bell nebula, a huge group of stars about 1000 light-years away and over 20 million million kilometres across. If we had to write out 1000 light-years in kilometres it would be 9 450 000 000 000 000.

The Great Invention

Suppose a man wanted to invent a way of writing numerals so that they became ten times *smaller* in value. He would know that putting numerals in places to the left made them worth ten times more. Where would he put them to make them worth ten times *less*? The man was Simon Stevin or Stevinus. He was born 400 years ago and became a mathematician and an engineer in the Dutch

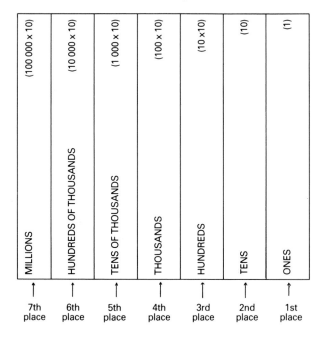

MILLIONS (100 000 × 10)	HUNDREDS OF THOUSANDS (10 000 × 10)	TENS OF THOUSANDS (1 000 × 10)	THOUSANDS (100 × 10)	HUNDREDS (10 × 10)	TENS (10)	ONES (1)
↑ 7th place	↑ 6th place	↑ 5th place	↑ 4th place	↑ 3rd place	↑ 2nd place	↑ 1st place

VALUES ARE TEN TIMES GREATER
EACH PLACE TO THE LEFT

army. He thought that all measurements should be based on ten and wrote a book about this decimal system of measures. He invented a symbol to separate the whole numbers from the fractions.

Whole numbers on this side Fractions on this side

▲
Symbol to separate
the whole numbers
from the fractions

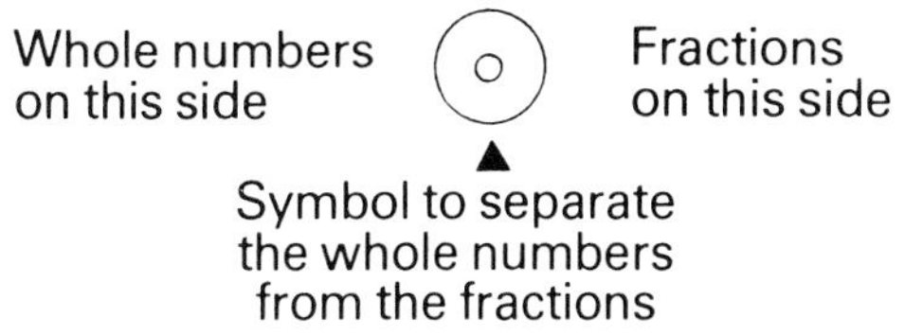

He decided that the numbers to the left of the symbols should be whole numbers. The numbers to the right of the symbols should be fractions. He had invented the system of decimal fractions.

At first the numerals were written like this:

32₀6①5②4③

This stood for 32 whole ones, 6 tenths, 5 hundredths and 4 thousandths.

Other people took up Stevin's ideas. Sometimes they used other symbols like:

32, 6′5″4‴

32 6 5 4

32|654

About 300 years ago everyone used the present way of writing decimal numbers where

$$32 \cdot 654 \text{ means } 32 + \frac{6}{10} + \frac{5}{100} + \frac{4}{1000}$$

So, in the decimal system:

The 6 in 32·654 means 6 tenths   or $\frac{6}{10}$
The 5 in 32·654 means 5 hundredths   or $\frac{5}{100}$
The 4 in 32·654 means 4 thousandths or $\frac{4}{1000}$

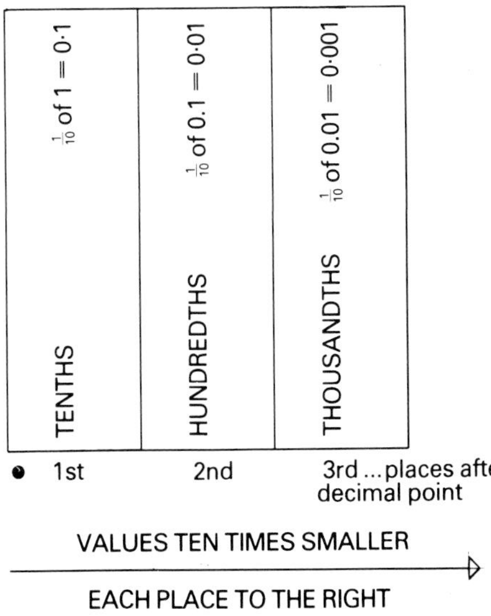

TENTHS $\frac{1}{10}$ of 1 = 0·1	HUNDREDTHS $\frac{1}{10}$ of 0.1 = 0·01	THOUSANDTHS $\frac{1}{10}$ of 0.01 = 0·001
1st	2nd	3rd ...places after decimal point

VALUES TEN TIMES SMALLER

EACH PLACE TO THE RIGHT ⟶

Sometimes there are no whole numbers to the left of a decimal fraction. A zero is then put in to draw attention to the decimal point, as in 0·2, 0·02, 0·002. The point is usually placed *above* the line as in 2·9. Printers of books and newspapers often put it on the line like this: 2.9. On the continent of Europe a comma is used instead of a point, as in 2,9. This is the reason why numbers are now normally written without commas to separate thousands from hundreds, and hundreds of thousands from millions:

21 869 457

An Easy System
Decimal fractions are much easier to use than common fractions. It is a tidy system where columns moving to the right show not only thousands, ten and ones, but tenths, hundredths, and so on.

Decimal fractions do not need a denominator as they are part of the decimal system: $\frac{3}{10} = 0 \cdot 3$.

Any fraction can be expressed as a decimal fraction by dividing the numerator by the denominator.

Examples: (i) $\frac{1}{8} = 0 \cdot 125$ (ii) $\frac{1}{4} = 0 \cdot 25$

There are, however, some which do not divide exactly.

Examples: (i) $\frac{1}{3} = 0 \cdot 33\dot{3}$ (ii) $\frac{1}{6} = 0 \cdot 16\dot{6}$

The dot on the top of the 3 and 6 denotes that those numbers go on to infinity.

Decimals can be arranged in columns for addition and subtraction:

Examples: (i)   Add   (ii)   Subtract

```
      36·45
      82·96               256·82
      17·08               118·87
     ──────              ───────
     136·49               137·95
```

Using Decimal Fractions
Newspapers and television often use this sytem:

2·6 million tonnes of grain are needed this year to prevent famine in Southern Africa.
The painting was sold for £3.2 M.

Lengths can be drawn accurately and their measurements recorded. Because 10 mm are equal to 1 cm, 6 cm 3 mm can be written neatly as 6.3 cm.

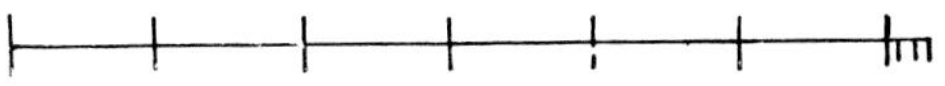

Decimal notation is used at athletic and other sporting events. Times, distances, speeds and other measures are given in decimal terms:

Ni Chin-Chin cleared 2·29 metres in the high jump

Wyomia Tyus ran at 23·78 m.p.h.

The race was run in 19·5 seconds.

3. Try to understand thoroughly the meaning of the first three places of decimals.
4. Use decimals when you are doing practical things. Finding the cost of 8 litres of petrol will be an example of multiplying a decimal by a whole number. When you are sharing the cost of something you will be dividing a decimal by a whole number.

The metric system has a decimal notation. It is, therefore, easy to express weights and measures.

£18 and 99p as £18.99
3 francs and 5 centimes as 3.05 frs.
$109 and 50 cents as $109·50
The field has an area of 36·75 hectares.
The pail holds 7·6 litres.
The potatoes weigh 11·2 kg.

Calculating with Decimals

Here are some things to think about when you are calculating with decimals:

1. You may need sometimes to change common fractions to decimal fractions. You can use a calculator, which will make the operation quick and easy. You may like to calculate some of the common fractions and keep a card which shows the conversions.
2. Use your calculators whenever possible. It will save time and will be accurate. But do estimate beforehand so that you know whether your answer is sensible.

5. Will you need to multiply and divide a decimal by a decimal? Estimate, use a calculator and do not be afraid to *round off* the answer.
6. Line up the decimal points when adding and subtracting decimal fractions.

The Tricky Number

Do you remember the roundabout number 142857? When multiplied by 7 it became 999999, so 999999 ÷ 7 = 142857.

0·142857 is really the number we get when we divide 1 by 7. So 0·142857 × 7 = ONE or nearly one. It is, in fact, 0·999999̇.

There are many decimal fractions which are not exact.

One third is 0·3̇33
One sixth is 0·16̇6
One ninth is 0·0̇9 09 09
One seventh is 0·1̇42857̇   142857142857 ...

Use your calculator to find some of these numbers which repeat numerals. You know that 1 divided by 7 ($\frac{1}{7}$) is 0·142857. What about $\frac{1}{11}$?

How an Octopus Counts

The younger octopupils of Octopus School were showing their teacher how well they count:

One, two, three, four, five, six, seven, one zero; one-one, one-two, one-three, one-four, one-five, one-six, one-seven, two-zero; two-one, two-two, two-three, two-four...

"Very good," said the teacher.

Upstairs the older pupils were adding and subtracting. The ticks in their books showed how well they had learned their lessons.

$$\begin{array}{r} 25 \\ + 47 \\ + 13 \\ \hline 107 \end{array} \qquad \begin{array}{r} 452 \\ - 267 \\ \hline 163 \end{array}$$

Counting in Eights

What were they doing? Octopupils do not count or calculate in the same way that we do. Human beings have five digits on each hand and so our number system grew on a *base* of ten. Octopupils, with eight arms, have a base of eight. We have ten numerals: 0 to 9. They have eight numerals: 0, 1, 2, 3, 4, 5, 6 and 7. Our numerals stop at one less than 10. Their numerals stop at one less than 8. Octopupils count in eights:

1	one	12	one-two
2	two	13	one-three
3	three	14	one-four
4	four	15	one-five
5	five	16	one-six
6	six	17	one-seven
7	seven	20	two-zero
10	one-zero	21	two-one
11	one-one	22	two-two – and so on

Octopupils do not have words like nine, ten, eleven, twelve ... Those words do not mean anything to them. After seven, they count: one-zero, one-one, one-two, and so on. On the right is a list of decimal numerals and the numerals used by octopupils.

Adding and Subtracting in Eights

Octopupils add and subtract in base eight. To show they are using base eight they put a tiny 8 after their numeral:

11_8 means one-one in base eight.

They have a base eight table to help them add and subtract.

+	1	2	3	4	5	6	7	10	11	12	13	14	15	16	17	20 ...
1	2	3	4	5	6	7	10	11	12	13	14	15	16	17	20	21
2	3	4	5	6	7	10	11	12	13	14	15	16	17	20	21	22
3	4	5	6	7	10	11	12	13	14	15	16	17	20	21	22	23
4	5	6	7	10	11	12	13	14	15	16	17	20	21	22	23	24
5	6	7	10	11	12	13	14	15	16	17	20	21	22	23	24	25
6	7	10	11	12	13	14	15	16	17	20	21	22	23	24	25	26
7	10	11	12	13	14	15	16	17	20	21	22	23	24	25	26	27
10	11	12	13	14	15	16	17	20	21	22	23	24	25	26	27	30
11	12	13	14	15	16	17	20	21	22	23	24	25	26	27	30	31
12	13	14	15	16	17	20	21	22	23	24	25	26	27	30	31	32
13	14	15	16	17	20	21	22	23	24	25	26	27	30	31	32	33
14	15	16	17	20	21	22	23	24	25	26	27	30	31	32	33	34
15	16	17	20	21	22	23	24	25	26	27	30	31	32	33	34	35
16	17	20	21	22	23	24	25	26	27	30	31	32	33	34	35	36
17	20	21	22	23	24	25	26	27	30	31	32	33	34	35	36	37
20	21	22	23	24	25	26	27	30	31	32	33	34	35	36	37	40

Example: (i) To add 6 and 7

They find 6 in the red column and 7 in the blue line. Where they meet is 15 (*one-five*, NOT "fifteen").

Decimal numerals	Octo numerals	Decimal numerals	Octo numerals	Decimal numerals	Octo numerals
1	1	17	21	33	41
2	2	18	22	34	42
3	3	19	23	35	43
4	4	20	24	36	44
5	5	21	25	37	45
6	6	22	26	38	46
7	7	23	27	39	47
8	10	24	30	40	50
9	11	25	31	41	51
10	12	26	32	42	52
11	13	27	33	43	53
12	14	28	34	44	54
13	15	29	35	45	55
14	16	30	36	46	56
15	17	31	37	47	57
16	20	32	40	48	60

13 is a group of 8 (+ 5)
So $6_8 + 7_8 = 15_8$

   (ii)   To add 14_8 and 15_8 *base 8*
       Find 14 in the red column   14
       Find 15 along the blue row   + 15
       14 and 15 meet at 31_8 31
       $14_8 + 15_8 = 31_8$

   (iii) Subtract 3 from 12
       Find 3 in the red column   *base 8*
       Go along that row to find 12   12
       Read off the answer in the
         blue row   − 3
       $12_8 - 3_8 = 7_8$ 7

Use the Octopupils' square to make up for yourself some examples of addition and subtraction in base 8.

Other Bases

It is possible to count and calculate in any base. Suppose humans had not had ten digits. Suppose we had had twenty digits, or twelve, or four, or any other number. Our counting set would have been different.

With a counting set of	the numerals are
2	1, and 0
3	1, 2 and 0
4	1, 2, 3 and 0
5	1, 2, 3, 4, and 0
6	1, 2, 3, 4, 5, and 0

The position of the numerals in our base ten gives the value of the number. In 362 the 6 is 6 (tens). The position of the numerals in other bases also gives the value of the number. In 10_2 the 1 is 1 (two).

Base 2
  → eights
  → fours
  → TWOS
  → ones
1 0 1 1

Base 3
  → twenty-sevens
  → nines
  → THREES
  → ones
2 1 0 2

Base 4
  → sixty-fours
  → sixteens
  → FOURS
  → ones
1 3 2 0

Base 5
  → hundred and twenty-fives
  → twenty-fives
  → FIVES
  → ones
3 4 1 2

Notice that, in each case, the column on the right has numerals with a value of ONE. The next column is always the value of the base. As the columns move to the left the *power* of the number increases.

Base 2	Base 3	Base 4	Base 5	Base 10
1	1	1	1	1
10	2	2	2	2
11	10	3	3	3
100	11	10	4	4
101	12	11	10	5
110	20	12	11	6
111	21	13	12	7
1000	22	20	13	8
1001	100	21	14	9
1010	101	22	20	10
1011	102	23	21	11
1100	110	30	22	12
1101	111	31	23	13
1110	112	32	24	14
1111	120	33	30	15
10000	121	100	31	16
10001	122	101	32	17
10010	200	102	33	18
10011	201	103	34	19
10100	202	110	40	20

Base Two

This is an important base. It can be shown by a visit to Mr. Bini's shop. Mr. Bini is a greengrocer and does a lot of weighing. His set of weights are 1 kg, 2 kg, 4 kg, 8 kg, 16 kg and some others out of sight. By combining these weights Mr. Bini can weigh any quantities. He has a chart to help him in case he forgets.

To weigh kg	16 kg	8 kg	4 kg	2kg	1kg
1					1
2				1	
3				1	1
4			1		
5			1		1
6			1	1	
7			1	1	1
8		1			
9		1			1
10		1		1	
11		1		1	1
12		1	1		
13		1	1		1
14		1	1	1	
15		1	1	1	1
16	1				

HE USED

To weigh 9 kg he uses 1 (8 kg) and 1 (1 kg) weights.
To weigh 13 kg he uses 1 (8 kg), 1 (4 kg) and 1 (1 kg) weights.
To weigh 31 kg he uses 1 (16 kg), 1 (8 kg), 1 (4 kg), 1 (2 kg) and 1 (1 kg) weights.

Mr. Bini is well named. His name means *two at a time*. His method of weighing is a model of a number system which groups in twos. It is called the *binary* system. The binary system of counting and calculating is based on 2. It uses only the numerals 1 and 0, and place value. A famous German mathematician, Leibnitz, started calculating in base two about three hundred years ago. Electronic calculators and computers use the binary system. Electrical systems can be switched ON and OFF. Computers can be controlled by a code which represents an ON signal or an OFF signal. The code which is used is the binary code with its two digits 1 (ON) and 0 (OFF). You can make a *binary board* to show these two states of ON and OFF. It will also show the binary system by lighting up bulbs when connections are made. You will need a 3 volt battery, torch bulbs, paper clips and bell wire.

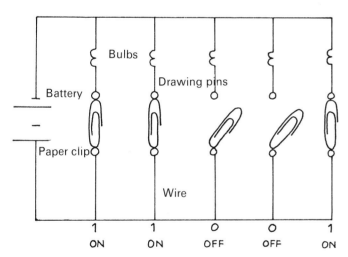

A Binary Code

Binary numerals can represent letters of the alphabet as well as numbers. In this way computers can receive information. You can make a code by letting binary numbers represent letters and symbols as in the table at the bottom.

Rule out a card 16 cm long and 3·5 cm wide into 5 mm squares. Write the letters of the alphabet and other symbols in the left-hand column.

Use a punch to make holes. Punch a hole in the squares where there is a 1 in the binary number. Do nothing where there is a zero in the binary number. Your card will start like this:

	Binary code			Binary code			Binary code			Binary code
A	1	I	1 0 0 1	Q	1 0 0 0 1	Y	1 1 0 0 1
B	1 0	J	1 0 1 0	R	1 0 0 1 0	Z	1 1 0 1 0
C	1 1	K	1 0 1 1	S	1 0 0 1 1	full stop	1 1 0 1 1
D	1 0 0	L	1 1 0 0	T	1 0 1 0 0	comma	1 1 1 0 0
E	1 0 1	M	1 1 0 1	U	1 0 1 0 1	space	1 1 1 0 1
F	1 1 0	N	1 1 1 0	V	1 0 1 1 0	?	1 1 1 1 0
G	1 1 1	O	1 1 1 1	W	1 0 1 1 1	end of word	1 1 1 1 1
H	1 0 0 0	P	1 0 0 0 0	X	1 1 0 0 0		

When you have finished your code card keep it by you. Make another blank card by ruling a piece 16 cm long by 3 cm wide into 5 mm squares. Now make up a sentence on the card in binary code. Send a secret message to a friend using the code. Here is one which uses six letters of the alphabet and some of the first binary numerals.

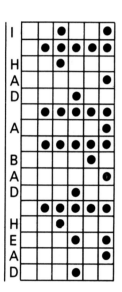

Mr. Murphy's Weights

Mr. Murphy sells potatoes. He has only 4 weights in his shop yet he can weigh any quantity up to 40 kg with them. How does he do it and what are his weights?

Answer. The weights are 27 kg, 9 kg, 3 kg and 1 kg. (What base is connected with these numbers?) To weigh 2 kg of potatoes he puts the 3 kg weight on one side of his scales and 1 kg on the side with the potatoes $(3 - 1 = 2)$. To weigh 4 kg of potatoes he uses the 1 kg and 3 kg weights.

The chart shows how he weighs his potatoes. Can you finish it?

To weigh	He used	To weigh	He used	To weigh	He used
kg	kg	kg	kg	kg	kg
1	1	11	(9+3)-1	21	(27+3)-9
2	3 - 1	12	9+3	22	(27+1+3)-9
3	3	13	9+1+3	23	27-(1+3)
4	3+1	14	27-(1+3+9)	24	27-3
5	9-(1+3)	15	27-(3+9)	25	(27+1)-3
6	9-3	16	(27+1)-(3+9)	26	Can you
7	(9+1)-3	17	27-(1+9)	27	finish
8	9 - 1	18	27-9	28	Mr.
9	9	19	(27+1)-9	29	Murphy's
10	9+1	20	(27+3)-(9+1)	30	table?

Every Picture Tells a Story

For many years people have told stories by drawing and painting pictures. An unknown artist painted an animal on a cave wall in France about 17000 years ago. His picture told the story about his day's hunting.

Other ancient peoples told stories in pictures. The Egyptians painted and carved picture writing on their temples and tombs. They also drew symbols to represent numbers. The Aztecs of South America carved pictures on stone. The North American Indians painted on animal skins. Both peoples used symbols to tell the history of their nation.

People still use pictures to tell stories. Sometimes the pictures depict scenes and objects. Sometimes the pictures stand for ideas. For example, the Egyptian symbol for a million shows a man with his arms outstretched. It is as though he were saying "What an enormous number".

Pictures tell us things in interesting ways and save using a lot of words. There are many sayings about this:

Pictures speak louder than words.
Seeing is believing.
Every picture tells a story.
A picture is worth a thousand words.

Pictures in Mathematics

Pictures are used in mathematics to present information. Newspapers and magazines often give facts and figures by using interesting illustrations. Computer and television screens

Computers can be made to draw shapes and then change them so that you can view them from different angles.

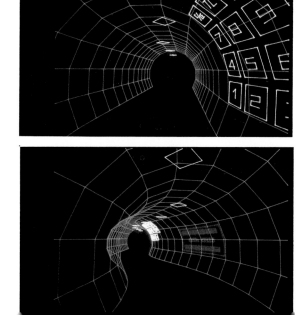

This famous Aztec Sun Stone is over $3\frac{1}{2}$ metres in diameter and weighs about 26 tonnes. It tells the Aztec story of the world's history and the inner circle shows the 20 days of the Aztec month.

show facts with numbers by their use of *graphics*. These visual presentations are able to move and change shape to explain how things work or increase in size.

Graphs

The pictures used in mathematics are called charts or graphs. These are drawings or diagrams which show how numbers are related. There are several kinds of graph. This one tells the story of how high a bean plant grew over a period of seven weeks. The graph is drawn from collected information.

DATE	3 Sep	10 Sep	17 Sep	24 Sep	1 Oct	8 Oct	15 Oct	22 Oct
HEIGHT OF BEAN (cm)	0	2	8	12	16	19	20	21

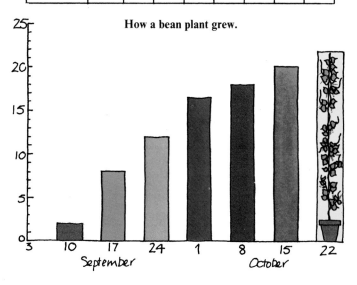

How a bean plant grew.

Bar Graphs or Charts

These show information by bars of the same width. The length of the bars is related to the numbers. This kind of graph is used to compare two or more things. Sometimes the bars are drawn in an upright column. *Column* or *block* graphs show numbers represented by a rectangle. This one explains what the favourite television programmes were of a class of pupils.

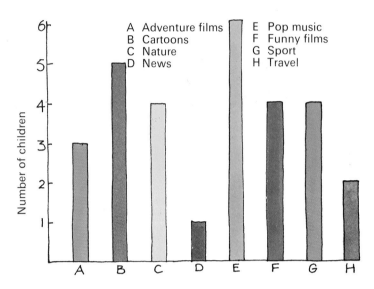

A Adventure films
B Cartoons
C Nature
D News
E Pop music
F Funny films
G Sport
H Travel

Histograms

Histograms are special kinds of block graphs. The width of a histogram's columns are related to the number of times something happened or was measured. This histogram is about the population of a village.

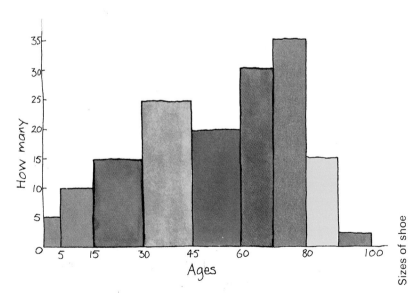

Horizontal Bars

Horizontal bars are sometimes used in a graph. The one on the right shows what size of shoe the children in a certain school take.

Horizontal and Vertical Lines

These can be used instead of bars and blocks. Two graphs give the same information about the number of pets in one class.

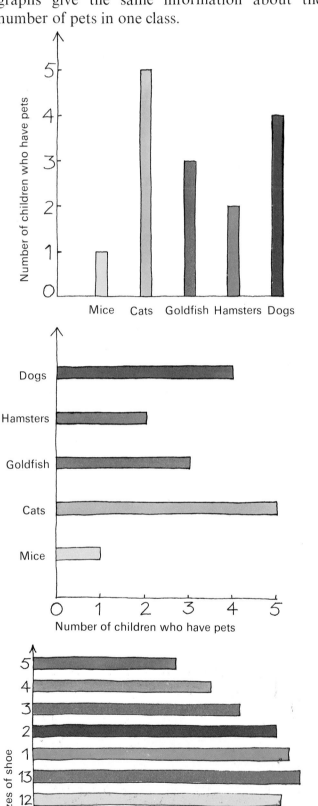

60

Broken Line Graphs

This kind of graph has a set of points joined by lines. It is used to show a trend or what is likely to happen. It can show what may happen if your school decided to raise funds to build a new sports pavilion. Broken line graphs are useful for showing how many goods are made in factories over certain periods. Line can also be used to show the multiples of numbers or be used as conversion tables.

The money for our new pavilion has gone through the roof.

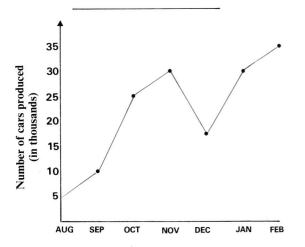

Picture Graphs

These are sometimes called pictographs or pictograms. They use symbols to give information. The ones on the right give two ways of showing the number of vehicles which passed a school between 9 and 10 a.m. one day.

Pie Graphs

Pie graphs are diagrams which use a circle divided into slices or sectors. Each sector shows a fraction of the whole circle.

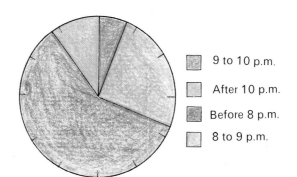

- 9 to 10 p.m.
- After 10 p.m.
- Before 8 p.m.
- 8 to 9 p.m.

Number of children	Bedtime
2	before 8 p.m.
10	8 to 9 p.m.
24	9 to 10 p.m.
4	after 10 p.m.

Bicycles	16
Buses and coaches	58
Cars	90
Lorries and trucks	12
Motor cycles	18
Vans	6

One picture represents 10 vehicles

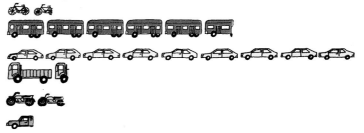

61

Letters Start Algebra

The Ancient Greeks used letters of their alphabet as numbers about 3500 years ago. They had nine letters for the numbers to 9, nine more for the tens and a further nine for the hundreds. They placed a little mark after the letters to show that they were numbers.

Letter	Name	No.	Letter	Name	No.	Letter	Name	No.
α'	alpha	1	ι'	iota	10	ρ'	rho	100
β'	beta	2	κ'	kappa	20	σ'	sigma	200
γ'	gamma	3	λ'	lambda	30	τ'	tau	300
δ'	delta	4	μ'	mu	40	υ'	upsilon	400
ϵ'	epsilon	5	ν'	nu	50	ϕ'	phi	500
ς'	stau	6	ξ'	xi	60	χ'	chi	600
ζ'	zeta	7	o'	omicron	70	ψ'	psi	700
η'	eta	8	π'	pi	80	ω'	omega	800
θ'	theta	9	ϱ'	koppa	90	λ'	sampi	900

Using letters for numbers is a branch of mathematics. It is called *algebra*, a word which comes from the Arabic work *Ilm Al-jebra-W'al Muquabalah* of AD 825. Algebra became more widely used 400 years ago and is now a most important subject.

What is Algebra?
Mathematicians noticed in the past that the same kinds of calculations kept being repeated. For example:

$$5 + 3 = 3 + 5 \quad 8 + 2 = 2 + 8 \quad 6 + 4 = 4 + 6$$

They worked out a rule which was true for *all* statements like those. The rule was that numbers can be added in any order: the total of $5 + 3$ is the same as $3 + 5$. If the letter a stands for the first number, and b stands for the second one, then the rule states:

$$a + b = b + a$$

Mathematicians studied other examples and made a list of laws. They used letters each time to make rules for some kinds of calculations and for working out problems. Algebra uses letters to stand for numbers. A letter can represent one number at one time and an entirely different number at another time. Algebra also uses signs to represent connections between letters.

Example: The area of one rectangle 13 units long and 7 units wide is 13×7 square units.

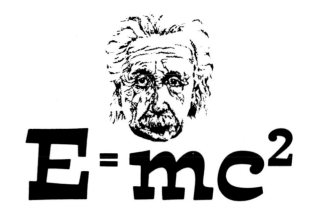

$$E = mc^2$$

If l stands for the length of the rectangle and w stands for its width, the area of *all* the rectangles in the world can be written: $A = lw$ (which means l multiplied by w).

This kind of statement is called a *formula*. The plural of formula is formulae. Notice that there is no multiplication sign between l and w. This is so that the multiplication sign ($\times$) is not mixed up with the letter x.

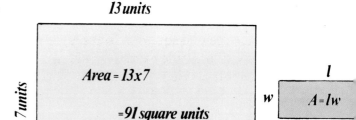

13 units

7 units

Area = 13 x 7

= 91 square units

l

w

$A = lw$

A Famous Formula
A formula is a rule which has an equals sign. It is a rule written as an *equation*. The most famous formula of modern times is $E = mc^2$. It was stated by Albert Einstein. E stands for energy, m for mass and c for the speed of light. (c^2 means c multiplied by itself.) The formula says that great amounts of energy result from a small mass if it is completely changed into energy. This means that a mass of only one gram could produce enough energy to burn a light bulb for 30000 years. Einstein's formula led to the production of atomic energy.

Other Formulae
Example 1: The perimeter of a rectangle is the distance around its sides. To find the perimeter of a rectangle we have to add the lengths of its two sides to the widths of the other two sides.

If P is the perimeter, l is the length of one side and w is the width of one side, then $P = 2l + 2w$

Again notice that there is no multiplication sign between 2 and *l*. 2*l* means $2 \times l$ and 2*w* means $2 \times w$.

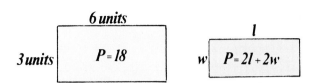

Example 2: A square is a special kind of rectangle whose 4 sides are equal in length. The perimeter of a square is found by adding the lengths of the 4 sides, or by multiplying the length of one side by 4. The perimeter of a square whose sides are 6 units long is $6 + 6 + 6 + 6$ or 6×4. The formula is $P = 4l$.

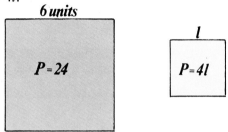

Example 3: The area of a square is found by multiplying the length of one side by itself. This is called *squaring* the side. If a side is *x* units long, its area will be $x \times x$ or x^2.

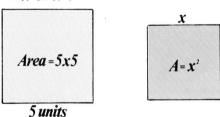

More About Equations

Is this statement true: $x + 4 = 9$?
If *x* stands for 6 it is *not* true because $6 + 4$ is not 9.
If *x* stands for 5 it *is* true because $5 + 4 = 9$.

A true statement is called an *equation*. In an equation both sides of the equals sign balance each other. Solving an equation means finding the number which makes the statement true.

Example 1: An equation is like a balance scale. If 9 kg are put on one pan, and 4 kg + 5 kg on the other pan, the scales will balance.

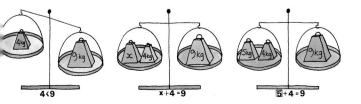

Example 2: Solve the equation $x + 3 = 8$.

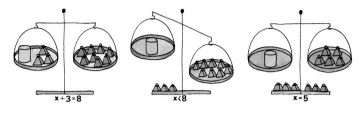

	left-hand side		*right-hand side*
1st scale:	$x + 3$	=	8
2nd scale:	*x* is smaller than		8
3rd scale:	x	=	$8 - 3$
	x	=	5

Example 3: Solve the equation $4x - 3 = 9$

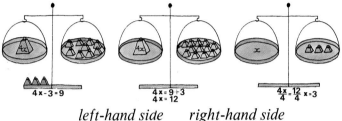

	left-hand side	*right-hand side*
1st scale:	$4x - 3$	$= 9$
2nd scale:	$4x$	$= 9 + 3 = 12$ (add 3 to both sides)
3rd scale:	x	$= 3$ (divide each side by 4)

Example 4: Solve the equation $2x + 4 = 12$

	left-hand side	*right-hand side*
Step 1:	$2x + 4$	$= 12$
Step 2:	$2x$	$= 12 - 4$ (subtract 4 from each side)
Step 3:	$2x$	$= 8$ (subtract 4 from 12)
Step 4:	x	$= \frac{8}{2}$ (divide each side by 2)
Step 5:	x	$= 4$ (divide 8 by 2)

Solve these:

1. $x + 9 = 12$ 2. $8 + x = 14$
3. $x - 2 = 7$ 4. $x - 15 = 25$
5. $3x - 4 = 8$ 6. $5x - 5 = 25$
7. Mary is *x* years old. Her brother John is 5 years younger. How old is John?
8. Their ages added come to 25 years. How old are they?
9. Tom is *y* years old. His sister Jane is twice as old. How old is Jane?
10. Their added ages total 24 years. How old is Jane? (Answers on page 136.)

Odd and Amazing Numbers

We have already met some kinds of numbers. Natural, whole, integers, rational and prime are a few of them. There are many others. Some are ordinary, some are peculiar and others are astonishing. The ancient mathematicians spent much time exploring numbers. They, and the people who lived after them, found curious links between certain numbers.

Pure numbers are the ordinary numbers we use such as "two" or the numeral 2 in the statement $1 + 2 = 3$. These numbers are not linked with any special things or measures. When numbers are related to objects, units or measures they are called *quantities*. Three apples, 5 centimetres or 20 minutes are examples of quantities.

Odd Numbers

Odd numbers are whole numbers which, when divided by 2, have a remainder of 1.

$$9 \div 2 = 4 \text{ rem } 1 \qquad 397 \div 2 = 198 \text{ rem } 1$$

If n is a whole number, $2n + 1$ is odd.

Example (i) $n = 13$
$$2n + 1 = (2 \times 13) + 1$$
$$= 26 + 1$$
$$= 27 \text{ (odd)}$$

(ii) $n = 28$
$$2n + 1 = (2 \times 28) + 1$$
$$= 56 + 1$$
$$= 57 \text{ (odd)}$$

Odd numbers appear in strange places. When odd numbers are arranged in order starting at 1, and added, the sum or total is always a square number.

Adding odd numbers makes squares.

Examples:
(i) $1 + 3 = 4 = 2 \times 2 = 2^2$
(ii) $1 + 3 + 5 = 9 = 3 \times 3 = 3^2$
(iii) $1 + 3 + 5 + 7 = 16 = 4 \times 4 = 4^2$
(iv) $1 + 3 + 5 + 7 + 9 = 25 = 5 \times 5 = 5^2$

Odd numbers are linked with cubes. When increasing sizes of cubes are built from small cubes they look like this:

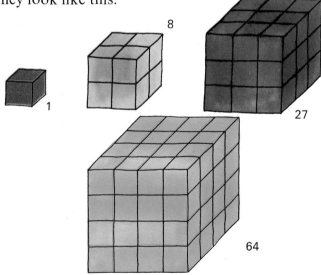

When odd numbers are arranged in this series:

$$1 \qquad 3 + 5 \qquad 7 + 9 + 11 \qquad 13 + 15 + 17 + 19 \ldots$$

the totals are:

1	8	27	64	
(odd)	(even)	(odd)	(even)	...

Even Numbers

Even numbers and odd numbers alternate:

1	3	5	...
(odd)	(odd)	(odd)	
2	4	6 ...	
(even)	(even)	(even)	

64

Even numbers have no remainder when divided by 2, e.g. 2, 4, 6, 8, ...

Even numbers are any form of $2n$:

Examples: (i) When $n = 3$
$$2n = 6 \text{ (even)}$$
      (ii) When $n = 84$
$$2n = 168 \text{ (even)}$$

Cardinal Numbers

Some people think that this word comes from the Latin *cardinis*, a hinge. In other words, the system of numbers turns, or depends on, the cardinal numbers. Other people say that it comes from the Greek *kardia*, a heart. As the heart is the most important part of the body, so cardinal numbers are at the heart of the number system.

Cardinal numbers describe *how many* there are in a set. The cardinal number of set A is 4.

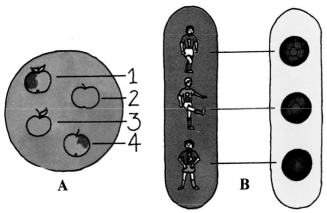

A   B

Each set at B has a cardinal number of 3 because their members (or elements) can be matched one-to-one.

Ordinal Numbers

Ordinal numbers give the order or position of members of a set. Athletes finishing a race come in "first", "second", "third", etc. A child may be "second" in the family. Another may be born on the 8th of March. Ordinal numbers are used to arrange sizes, lengths and measures.

1st   2nd   3rd   4th   5th
first   second   third   fourth   fifth

Perfect Numbers

The numbers 1, 2, 3 and 6 divide exactly into 6. The factors of 6 are 1, 2, 3 and 6. When the factors of 6 (but not 6 itself) are added, the sum is 6. 6 is a *perfect* number because it equals the sum of its factors. The factors of 28 are 1, 2, 4, 7 and 14. $1 + 2 + 4 + 7 + 14 = 28$, a perfect number. The next two perfect numbers are 496 and 8128.

Euclid was born about 2350 years ago. He started a centre of learning in Alexandria, Egypt. His geometry has been taught in schools for 2000 years. Euclid was very interested in perfect numbers. He and his followers found the first four. They thought that they were so rare and interesting that they gave them the name of "perfect".

It was 1400 years before the 5th perfect number was found. It is 33 550 336. The sixth one is 8 589 869 056. The latest perfect number is colossal.

Friendly Numbers

Friendly numbers are also called amiable and amicable. The Arabs gave them this name because they thought that these numbers brought friendship to people.

The factors of 220 (not including itself) are:

1 2 4 5 10 11 20 22 44 55 and 110
$$1 + 2 + 4 + 5 + 10 + 11 + 20 + 22 + 44 + 55 + 110 = 284$$

The factors of 284 (not including itself) are:

1 2 4 71 and 142
$$1 + 2 + 4 + 71 + 142 = 220$$

220 and 284 are called friendly numbers because the factors of the first number add up to give the second number. The factors of the second number add up to give the first number. It is thought that the Greek mathematician Pythagoras discovered that 220 and 284 are linked in this way. A second pair of friendly numbers, 17296 and 18416, was found 320 years ago. The Swiss mathematician Léonard Euler added 59 more pairs about 250 years ago. A sixteen years old boy was the first person to find the friendly numbers 1184 and 1210.

Fibonacci Numbers

Fibonacci is the nickname of the greatest mathematician of the Middle Ages. His real name was Leonardo of Pisa and he was born about 800 years ago. His teachers could do nothing with him, but Fibonacci found mathematics interesting. He used it to solve problems with money and later became a successful merchant. He discovered a list, or sequence, of numbers which is remarkable. It is built up like this:

Start with 0 and 1   : 0, 1 (these are terms)
Add the terms 0 and 1   : $0 + 1 = 1$
Add this 1 to the last term : $1 + 1 = 2$
Add this 2 to the last term : $1 + 2 = 3$
Add this 3 to the last term : $2 + 3 = 5$
Add this 5 to the last term : $3 + 5 = 8 \ldots$

This gives the sequence:

0 1 1 2 3 5 8 13 21 34 55 89 144 ...

Here are some of the amazing things about this sequence:

1. Choose any three numbers that follow each other (say, 2, 3 and 5).
   Square the middle number: 3^2 or $3 \times 3 = 9$
   Multiply the first and third numbers:
   $2 \times 5 = 10$
   Subtract the two numbers: $10 - 9 = 1$
   The result is always 1.
   Choose another three numbers: 5, 8 and 13.
   $(5 \times 13) - 8^2 = 65 - 64 = 1$
   Try three numbers for yourself.

2. Take any four terms which follow each other.
   For example: 3, 5, 8 and 13
   Multiply the outside numbers: $3 \times 13 = 39$
   Multiply the inside numbers: $5 \times 8 = 40$
   Subtract the outside numbers from the inside ones $40 - 39 = 1$
   The result is always 1.
   Take another four numbers: 8, 13, 21 and 34
   $(13 \times 21) - (8 \times 34) = 273 - 272 = 1$
   Choose four numbers yourself.

3. Write the *squares* of each term of the Fibonacci members: 1 4 9 25 64 169 441 1156 3025 ...
   Add each pair, e.g. $1 + 4, 4 + 9$:

   5 13 34 89 233 610 1597 4181 ...

   These are the *odd* terms, (*not* odd numbers) in the sequence.
   Subtract each term from the following term,

e.g. $13 - 5, 34 - 13, \ldots$
You now have the *even* terms (*not* the even numbers) in the sequence: 8 21 55 144 377 ...

4. Take any term from   1 1 2 3 5 8 13 21 34 55 89 144 ...

   For example: 5
   Multiply 5 by $2 = 10$
   Find the term after the 5: 8
   Subtract 8 from $10 = 2$
   That is the 2nd term before 5
   Try it again: $(13 \times 2) - 21 = 5$

5. 1 1 2 3 5 8 13 21 34 55 89 144
   Add the terms in the sequence, e.g.
   $0 + 1 = 1, 1 + 1 = 2, 2 + 2 = 4, \ldots$
   The new sequence is
   1 2 4 7 12 20 33 54 88 143
   Each term is 1 less than the term two steps along in the Fibonacci sequence.

Astonish Your Friends

Write the Fibonacci numbers in a column:

    1
    1
    2
    3
    5
    8
    13
    21
    34
    55
    89
    144
    233

Ask a friend to draw a line anywhere in the column between two numbers. Secretly write down a number on a piece of paper. Fold the paper and ask someone to hold it. Now ask your friend to add all the numbers above the line which has been drawn. Show your friend the number you wrote down.

How did you do it? You subtracted 1 from the second number below the line.

Examples: (i) Suppose the line was drawn above the 21
   The answer is $34 - 1 = 33$
   $1 + 1 + 2 + 3 + 5 + 8 + 13 = 33$
   (ii) The line drawn above 55
   The answer is 88

Fun with Number Patterns and Shapes

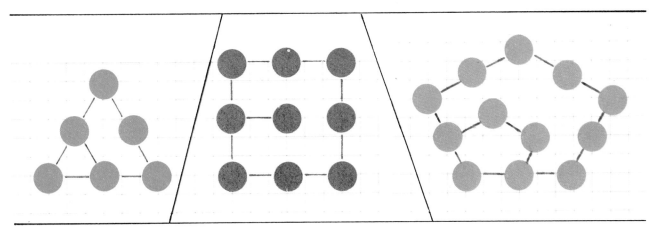

Some of the ancient Greek mathematicians were very rich. They did not have to teach or earn a living as merchants. They were able instead to amuse themselves at times with sets of points which could be made into figures or shapes. *Greek arithmetic* is a name given to the study of these *figurate* numbers. They are numbers which make interesting patterns. Many-sided figures or shapes such as triangles, squares and pentagons are known as *polygons*. This comes from the Greek word meaning *many angles*. The numbers which come from figures and shapes are called polygonal numbers.

Sequences and Series

The study of these patterns led to the discovery of sequences and series. A *sequence* is a list of numbers or *terms* which usually have a link between one term and the next. For example, this sequence has a list of terms which double: 2 4 8 16 32 64 ... The sum, or total, of the terms of a sequence is a series: $2 + 4 + 6 + 8$ is a *finite* series – it has an end. $7 + 9 + 11 + 13 ...$ is an *infinite* series – it goes on and on.

Triangle Numbers

With a handful of counters it is possible to make triangle or triangular numbers.

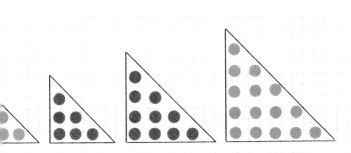

The triangles can be arranged in another way.

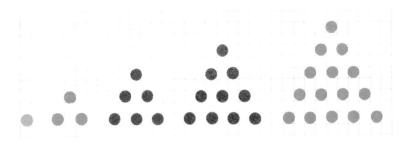

The number of counters gives the sequence for the first five terms:

$$1 \quad 3 \quad 6 \quad 10 \quad 15$$

What will the 6th term be? There are 3 ways to find out.

Method 1: Draw the next triangle number and count.

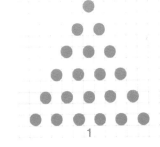

Method 2: Make the triangle into a rectangle and halve the number of counters.

$$7 \times 6 = 42; \quad \frac{42}{2} = 21$$

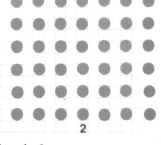

What will the next triangle number be?

Method 3: Form a series.

Triangle numbers	Series	Number of counters
1st	1	1
2nd	1 + 2	3
3rd	1 + 2 + 3	6
4th	1 + 2 + 3 + 4	10
5th	1 + 2 + 3 + 4 + 5	15
6th	1 + 2 + 3 + 4 + 5 + 6	21

What will the 7th and 8th triangle numbers be?

Every whole number is the sum of two or three triangle numbers.

Examples:

(i) $2 = 1 + 1$

(ii) $4 = 1 + 3$

(iii) $7 = 1 + 3 + 3$

(iv) $8 = 1 + 1 + 6$

(v) $9 = 3 + 6$

(vi) $11 = 1 + 10$

(vii) $12 = 3 + 3 + 6$

(viii) $13 = 3 + 10$

(ix) $14 = 1 + 3 + 10$

Which triangle numbers add up to 16, 29 and 48?

Square Numbers

To make the squares, one counter is put on a line. The second square has two lines with 2 counters in each line, giving a total of 4 counters. The two is squared to get 4, which we call "two squared", written 2^2. The next square takes 3 lines with three counters in each line. This gives a total of 9, or 3 squared (3^2).

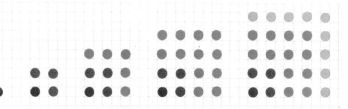

Notice how the squares can be formed from the triangle numbers.

The sequence of the first five square numbers is

$$1 \quad 4 \quad 9 \quad 16 \quad 25$$

The sixth square number can be found in three ways.

Method 1: By drawing or setting out counters.

Method 2: Square the number of counters in the next line. This is 6, and 6^2 is 36.

Method 3: Form the pattern of numbers. The sequence of square numbers is

$$1 \quad 4 \quad 9 \quad 16 \quad 25$$

The difference between these terms is

$$3 \quad 5 \quad 7 \quad 9 \quad (11)$$

This is the set of odd numbers. By adding the next odd number (11) to the 5th square number we find the 6th square number:

$$25 + 11 = 36.$$

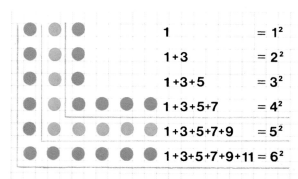

1	$= 1^2$
1+3	$= 2^2$
1+3+5	$= 3^2$
1+3+5+7	$= 4^2$
1+3+5+7+9	$= 5^2$
1+3+5+7+9+11	$= 6^2$

What are the 7th, 8th, and 9th square numbers?
The square numbers are found on the diagonal of a table of products.

X	1	2	3	4	5	6	7	8	9	10
1	1	2	3	4	5	6	7	8	9	10
2	2	4	6	8	10	12	14	16	18	20
3	3	6	9	12	15	18	21	24	27	30
4	4	8	12	16	20	24	28	32	36	40
5	5	10	15	20	25	30	35	40	45	50
6	6	12	18	24	30	36	42	48	54	60
7	7	14	21	28	35	42	49	56	63	70
8	8	16	24	32	40	48	56	64	72	80
9	9	18	27	36	45	54	63	72	81	90
10	10	20	30	40	50	60	70	80	90	100

Pentagonal Numbers

A pentagon has 5 sides. After one dot is drawn for the first number, a pentagonal number can be drawn with five dots.

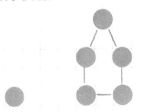

The pentagonal numbers combine the triangular and square numbers.

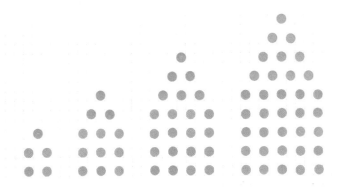

Triangular numbers	1	3	6	10	...
Square numbers	4	9	16	25	...
Pentagonal numbers	5	12	22	35	

Continue the sequence of the pentagonal numbers.

Hexagonal Numbers

A hexagon has 6 sides. Its numbers can form hexagonal patterns.

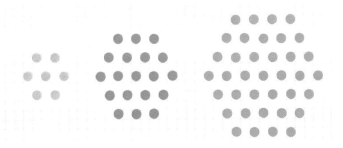

The sequence of dots is 1   7   19   37   ...
The difference is   6   12   18   ...

What will be the next hexagonal number?

Stellate (of Star) Numbers

These are also made up from the shapes of squares and triangles (right).

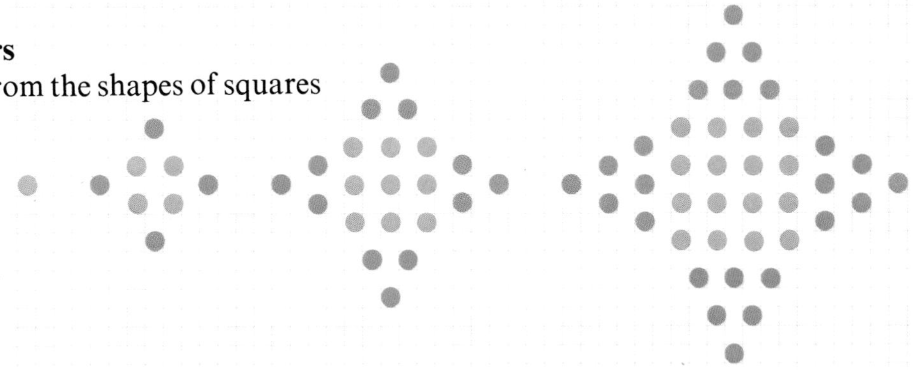

The sequence of dots is   1   8   21   40   ...
The difference is   7   13   19   ...

What is the next stellate number?
What do you notice about 7, 13 and 19?

An Amazing Array

Mathematicians from Persia, India and China were also interested in triangular numbers. They probably were the first to form parts of this array.

```
                    1
                 1     1
              1     2     1
           1     3     3     1
        1     4     6     4     1
     1     5    10    10     5     1
  1     6    15    20    15     6     1
1     7    21    35    35    21     7     1
```

It is called *Pascal's triangle* after the French mathematician (1623–1662). The sequences across all start and finish with 1.

Try to find:

(i)   the natural numbers 1, 2, 3, ...
(ii)   the triangular numbers 1, 3, 6, ...
(iii)   the sum of the triangular numbers 1, 4, 10, ... equal to 1, 1 + 3, 1 + 3 + 6, ...
(iv)   the sum of those numbers in (iii) e.g. 1 = 1; 1 + 4 = 5; 1 + (1 + 3) + (1 + 3 + 6) = 15 ...
or   1 + 4 + 10 = 15, ...
(v)   any other patterns.

Have you noticed that the number 2 in the third row is the sum of 1 + 1 in the second row? That the 3s in the fourth row are the sums of the numbers above, and on either side of, them? Can you check that this kind of addition continues? What happens when you add each row of numbers. e.g. 1, 2, 4, 8, ...?

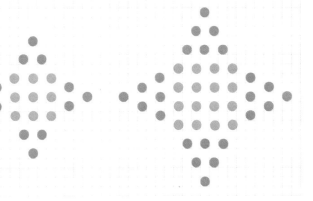

69

A Building Brick

Almost every baby plays with simple building bricks. Very young children try to build these blocks one on top of the other and then enjoy seeing the tower collapse. Children's building blocks are not as easy to build as those in the shape of builders' bricks. Children's bricks are the simplest of all bricks. They are *cubes*.

Making a Cube

A cube is easy to make.

1. Draw a rectangle 8 cm by 2 cm on thin card or stiff paper. Use a ruler, and a protractor or set square for the right angles.

2. Divide the rectangle into 4 squares.

3. Draw squares on either side of the rectangle.

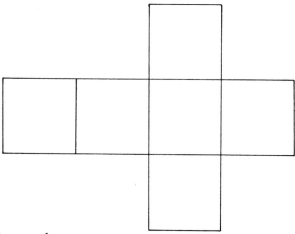

4. Draw tabs.
5. Fold along the red lines.

6. Cut out the net and glue the tabs to make a cube.

Examining the Cube

A cube is a solid shape with 6 square faces. It has a most interesting shape.

1. Like all shapes which have 3 dimensions (length, breadth or width, and height) it is called a solid.

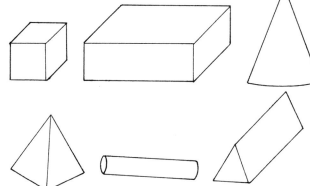

2. Notice that it has 6 *faces* (top, bottom and sides). Another name for cubes is *hexahedra*, which means 6 faces. One cube is a hexahedron. (It belongs to the same family as polyhedra which have "many faces". *One* is called a polyhedron.)

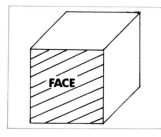

FACE

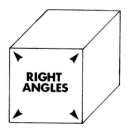

RIGHT ANGLES

. Notice that each face is a *square*. Squares have 4 equal straight lines and 4 right angles.

4. Notice that a cube has 12 edges (top, bottom and sides). The edges are all of equal length. Each edge is perpendicular or at right angles to the edges which join it.

5. Notice that a cube has 8 *vertices* or points. A vertex is a point where lines or edges meet.

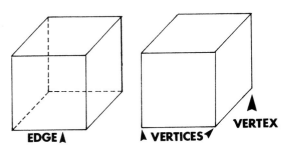

EDGE ▲   ▲ VERTICES ◀   VERTEX

6. Note that all cubes are hexahedra, but not all solids with 6 faces are cubes.

Euler's Formula

A cube has 6 faces, 8 vertices and 12 edges. Léonard Euler, more than 200 years ago, discovered a link among the faces, vertices and edges of the hexahedron and four other polyhedra. Have you discovered what it is? If you add the number of faces to the number of vertices, and subtract the number of edges, the result is 2.

$$(6 + 8) - 12 = 14 - 12 = 2$$

The equation or formula is $F + V - E = 2$. It is thought that Archimedes and the French mathematician René Descartes both knew about this relationship.

Volume of a Cube

The formula for finding the volume (V) of a cube is $V = 1^3$ where 1 is the length of an edge. The volume of a cube of edge 10 units is $10^3 = 10 \times 10 \times 10 = 1000$ cubic units.

Cubic Numbers

These are numbers which can be arranged as cubes grow in unit size.

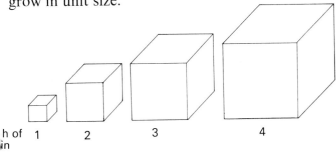

h of   1   2   3   4
in

uct $1 \times 1 \times 1$ $2 \times 2 \times 2$ $3 \times 3 \times 3$ $4 \times 4 \times 4$

The sequence is 1 8 27 64 125
Can you continue the sequence?

Notice that
$$1 = 1^3 = 1$$
$$8 = 2^3 = 3 + 5$$
$$27 = 3^3 = 7 + 9 + 11$$
$$64 = 4^3 = 13 + 15 + 17 + 19$$
$$125 = 5^3 = 21 + 23 + 25 + 27 + 29$$

What are 1, 3, 5, 7, 9, 11, ...?
Can you continue the series?

Powers

In algebra the second power is a number multiplied by itself, for example $2 \times 2 = 2^2$, $8 \times 8 = 8^2$. The third power is a number multiplied by itself and multiplied by itself again.

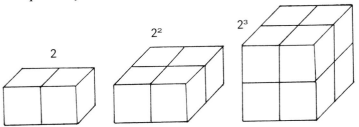

2   2^2 2^3

For example:
$3 \times 3 \times 3 = 3^3$ (three cubed) or 3 raised to the *power* 3.

The cube of a number is the product when a number is used as a factor 3 times.
$5^3 = 5 \times 5 \times 5 = 125$.
What are 4^3, 10^3, 1^3, 6^3 and 8^3?

Archimedes

Archimedes was born about 287 B.C. in Syracuse, Sicily, which was then a colony of Greece. He may have gone to school in Alexandria in Egypt, which was the centre of Greek education. He returned to Syracuse where his father was an astronomer. Archimedes became a great mathematician and scientist. He was very interested in mechanics and studied levers and pulleys. He invented war machines to use against the Roman enemy.

The Romans captured Syracuse when Archimedes was 75 years of age. The Roman commander, Marcellus, told his soldiers that they must not harm the old man. Archimedes was working out a problem when a soldier entered his house. The soldier did not recognize the great scholar and ordered him to go to the Roman commander. Archimedes said that he must finish his problem first and continued to work on it. While Archimedes was drawing the geometric figures in the sand the soldier drew his sword and killed him.

Geometry Set

Geometry is the branch of mathematics that deals with lines, angles, points, shapes and surfaces. These are linked to solids and measurements. The word geometry means earth or land measurement. The Egyptians used geometry to *survey* land and to construct their buildings. The Greeks learned from this and *Euclid* gathered together all that was known about the subject.

Euclid made a list of statements about geometry. They are called *axioms*, which are truths. One of the statements he made is: A line is the shortest distance between two points. In the study of geometry nobody disagreed with statements like that. Euclid's work was taught for 2000 years, but geometry has changed in modern times. It is now a practical subject, as it was when it was used by the Egyptians.

In ancient Egypt there were floods in the valley of the Nile every year. This meant that the boundaries dividing the land were swept away. These had to be restored when the river had subsided. At first, priests used to do the land measuring and had to discover things about geometry to carry out the work. Nowadays the practical side of geometry is very important. It is used by engineers, architects and surveyors. You will enjoy doing practical geometry too.

A Geometry Set

To do geometry you will need a geometry *set*. Set is a good word to use because it is a collection of things which have something in common. This collection is one of geometrical instruments. A geometry set is one of the best presents you can receive, but you can also collect the instruments yourself.

You will need:

a ruler marked in centimetres and inches,
two or three pencils (soft and hard)
a pencil sharpener and an eraser
two set squares: 45° and 60°/30°/90°,
a protractor and a pair of compasses
a tin box or case to hold the instruments

To make the solids on the pages that follow you will also need thin card or cartridge paper.

How to Draw a Line

It may seem very simple to draw a straight line, but

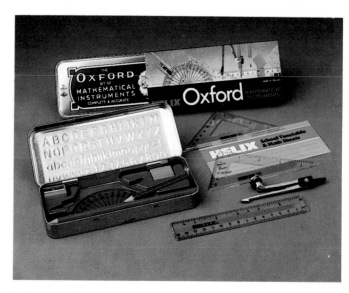

it is very important. Here is the correct way.

1. Mark with dots the *exact* length of the line to be drawn.
2. Put a sharp pencil point on A.
   Draw a line just over half way towards B.
3. Put the pencil point on B.
   Draw the line from B towards A.

How to Draw an Equilateral Triangle

1. Screw a hard pencil tightly into your compasses. (A *compass* gives the direction and is quite different!) Make sure that the points of your pencil and the compasses are level.
2. On a piece of paper draw a line AB 5 cm long.
3. Open your compasses so that the distance from the pencil point to the point of the compasses is 5 cm. This is called the *radius* when a circle is drawn.
4. Put the point of the compasses on A and draw an *arc* near where C is going to be. (An arc is part of the *circumference* of a circle.)
5. Put the point of the compasses on B and draw an arc of the same radius to meet (or cut) the first arc. This is point C.
6. Join lines AC and BC.

You have drawn an equilateral triangle. What do you notice about lines AB, AC and BC? What do you think *equilateral* means?

How to Bisect a Line

To bisect a line (or divide it in two):
1. Draw a line AB 5 cm long. Leave some space above and below the line.
2. Open the compasses to a radius just over half way along AB.
3. Draw arcs from A above and below the line.
4. Draw arcs from B, with the same radius, to cut the first two arcs.
5. Call these two points C and D. Join CD.

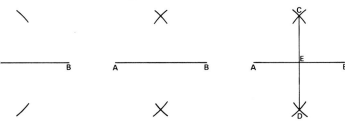

6. You have bisected the line AB. Check by measuring that AE = BE.
7. One angle at E is called angle BEC or ∠ BEC. It is a *right angle*. A right angle has ninety degrees (90°). There are 3 more right angles in the sketch. ∠ AEC is one of them. What are the names of the other two?
8. Line CD is called a *perpendicular bisector*. It bisects AB at right angles.

How to Bisect an Angle

1. Draw any angle BAC.
2. Draw arcs from A to X and Y.
3. From X and Y draw arcs to cut at Z.
4. Join AZ. AZ has bisected ∠ BAC.

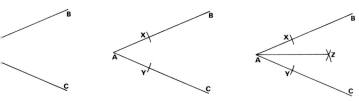

How to Use a Protractor

A protractor is an instrument for measuring and constructing angles. It can be circular, semi-circular or rectangular in shape. The common

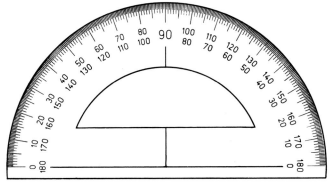

protractor is like half a circle and is transparent.

To draw an angle of 90° from a point

1. Draw a line of any length AB and place a point somewhere along it. Point X.

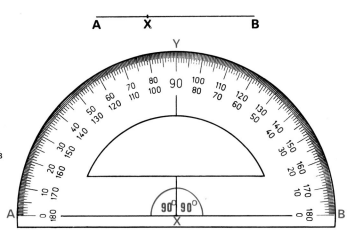

2. To draw a right angle from point X, place the protractor on line AB. Line AB must be positioned to correspond exactly with the horizontal line at the base of the protractor. This line runs from 0° to 180°.
3. Where the vertical line from 90° cuts the base line is the point to be placed over point X.
4. Mark a point at 90° on the circumference of the protractor. Call this point Y. Join XY.
5. The angles AXY and BXY are right angles. Check with a set square that they are right angles.

To draw an angle of 108° from a point A

1. Draw a line AB.
2. Place the protractor on the line so that A is at the point where the 0° to 180° line and its perpendicular bisector meet.
3. On the circumference of the protractor find 108° (or 180 − 108 = 72°). Mark this point X.

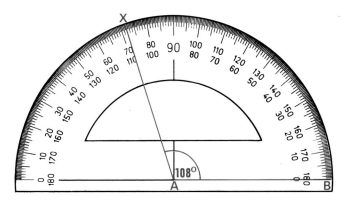

4. Join AX.
5. Angle BAX is 108°.

Using a Set Square

Set squares can be used for:

1. Testing if surfaces are horizontal and vertical.

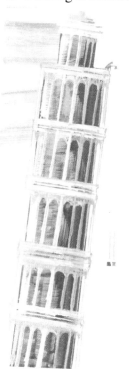

Had the Leaning Tower of Pisa been vertical, Galileo would have found it more difficult to carry out his experiment with the weights.

3. For drawing rectangles, parallel lines and lattices.

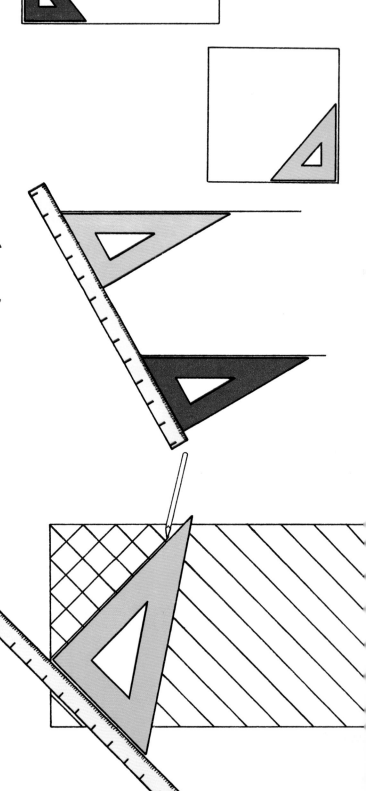

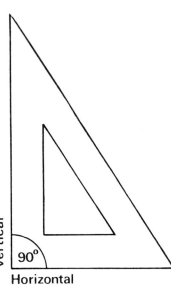

2. For checking and drawing angles of 30°, 45°, 60° and 90°.

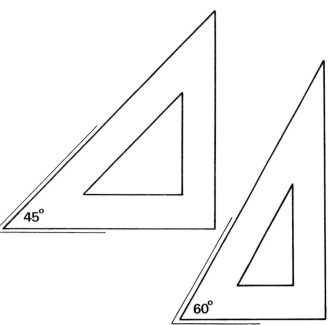

Solid Stuff

The most common objects we see and handle are those with three dimensions. All around us there are trees, walls and vehicles. When children are young they build models of houses and castles. At their first schools they construct toy trains and spaceships. Later on they play with balls, handle money and eat hamburgers. All these things belong to the three-dimensional world.

The objects around us are examples of geometrical shapes called *solids*. Solids take up some space. On their outside there may be a closed surface. Or solids may be skeletons of shapes made with wire, drinking straws or pipe-cleaners. Whether they have closed surfaces or are formed just with edges, they are still called solids. A shape which encloses space is a solid. Solids are sometimes called solid shapes or space figures or geometrical figures. They are all names for shapes which occupy space.

A set of solids can be divided into three chief subsets. Some solids have *curved* surfaces. Some have surfaces which are curved and flat (or planar). The third subset has solids which just have a plane surface.

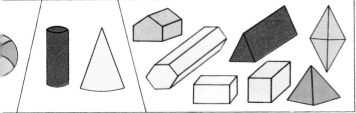

Solids with curved surfaces are balls, spheres and globes. Solids with curved and plane surfaces are cylinders and cones. A *cylinder* is like a tube or a can of beans. If a cylinder were to be cut through, it would have a circular cross-section. A *right* cylinder has ends which are perpendicular to the curved surface. A *cone* has a conical surface and a circular base. A *right* circular cone has a perpendicular from the vertex to the centre of the base.

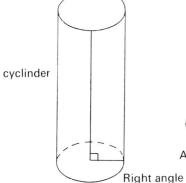

cyclinder

Right angle

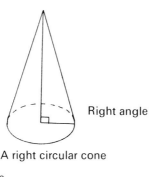

Right angle

A right circular cone

75

Solids With Plane Surfaces

Solids with plane surfaces are of different kinds: prisms and polyhedra. *Prisms* are solids with two faces which are parallel to each other. This means that they are the same distance apart. The other faces of prisms are parallelograms. *Polyhedra* are solids which have "many faces". These faces are called polygons, which are shapes with "many angles".

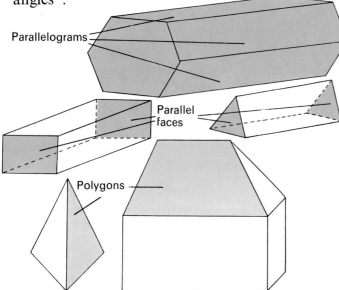

Parallelograms

Parallel faces

Polygons

Regular Solids

Regular solids are most interesting and have a long history. The Greek mathematician Pythagoras studied in Egypt and Babylon before settling in the south of Italy. He may have brought back with him some knowledge about three of these solids – the ones with four, six and eight faces. The other two, with twelve and twenty faces, may have been studied in his own school. Pythagoras formed a secret brotherhood. In this society the solids represented fire, earth, air, the universe and water.

About 2400 years ago these regular polyhedra were studied in the school of another Greek called Plato. It is because of this that these solids are called the five regular *Platonic* polyhedra.

These five polyhedra are regular. Each of them has faces which have the same shape and size. In each polyhedron the edges have the same length. The faces of each have equal angles at the vertices. The faces of each join one another at the same angle.

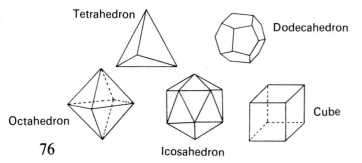

Tetrahedron

Dodecahedron

Octahedron

Icosahedron

Cube

76

Making the Polyhedra

The polyhedra are fairly easy to make, and you will enjoy the practical geometry you will use. Instructions for making the cube (hexahedron) have already been given (page 70). Here are directions for making the other four. You will need thin card or thick paper, a ruler and pencils, compasses and scissors.

The Tetrahedron

This has four faces.
1. Draw the net. The four small triangles are the equilateral ones you have already drawn. AC is 10 cm long and the radius needed is 5 cm.
2. Cut out the net and tabs
3. Fold the edges AF, BC, ED of the tabs.
4. Fold the edges of the net BF, BD and DF upwards.
5. Try to fit the folds together to make the tetrahedron.
6. Use a good adhesive to stick the tabs to the *inside* of the faces.

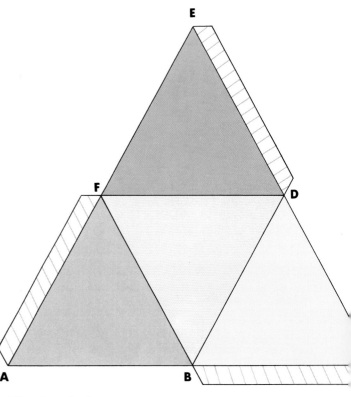

The Octahedron

This has eight faces.
1. Draw the net. The radius of the compasses is 3 cm.
2. Cut out the net.
3. Fold the edges upwards.
4. Try to fit the folds together to make the octahedron.
5. Glue the tabs to the inside of the faces.

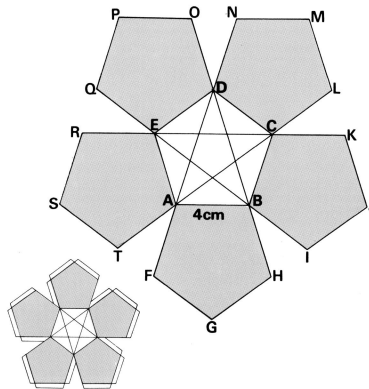

The Dodecahedron

This has twelve faces and is the most difficult polyhedron to make. You may need some help. It is a good idea to make it in two halves which can be stuck together later. You will need two pieces of card or paper.

1. Draw a pentagon with sides 4 cm long in the middle of your paper. Do you remember how to do this?
   1.1 Draw a line AB 4 cm long.
   1.2 With a protractor draw angles of 108° at ABC and BAE.
   1.3 Draw the lines AE and BC 4 cm long.
   1.4 With the point of the compasses at E and C draw arcs of radius 4 cm to cut at D.
   1.5 Join CD and DE to make the pentagon ABCDE.

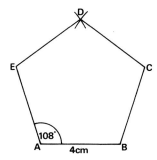

2. To draw the five pentagons round ABCDE
   2.1 Extend the lines AC, AD, BD, BE and CE in both directions.
   2.2 With the point of the compasses at A cut off arcs of radius 4 cm at F and T.
   2.3 Do the same from B to H and I, from C to K and L, from D to N and O, and from E to Q and R.
   2.4 With the same radius draw arcs from F and H to cut at G.
   2.5 Do the same from I and K to cut at J, from L and N to cut at M, from O and Q to cut at P, and from R and T to cut at S.

2.6 Join AFGHB, BIJKC, CLMND, DOPQE and ERSTA to complete the outside pentagons.
3. Draw the other net in the same way.
4. Draw the tabs on the two nets.
5. Fold along the lines, making the folds straight.
6. Cut around the nets and tabs.
7. Try to fit the folds together to make sure they fit.
8. Stick each tab to its next door edge.
9. Glue the rest of the tabs and join the two nets, sticking them to the insides of the edges.

The Icosahedron

This has twenty faces.
1. Draw this net of equilateral triangles. The starting line is 20 cm long and the radius of the compasses is 4 cm.
2. Draw the tabs.
3. Fold along the lines.
4. Try to fit the model together.
5. Stick the tab marked with a cross to the point Y.
6. Glue the other tabs to meet their next door inside edges.

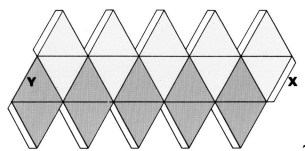

77

Plane Shapes: Triangles

Do you know that a few people still believe that the Earth is *flat*? Thinking people have known for hundreds of years that the world is round. When Christopher Columbus sailed he wasn't trying to *prove* that the world was round. He already knew that as he tried to find a short sea route to the Indies. There is a story that the crew of his ships were afraid of falling off the edge of the Earth, but that is not true either. What they were afraid of was that the strong east wind would blow them back.

But what do you imagine it would be like if the Earth *were* flat? Can you think of a world where people were flat like the gardeners and cards in *Alice in Wonderland*? There are many expressions about flatness in the English language:

Flat as a pancake means quite flat because a pancake is a thin, flat cake, fried in fat.

Flat as a flounder means as thin as a flatfish. The shapes on these pages are flatter than pancakes and flatfish. They are flatter than the gardeners and soldiers belonging to the Queen of Hearts. These shapes have *no thickness at all*.

2-D Shapes

Shapes with no thickness have just length and breadth. They are known as two-dimensional, or 2-D shapes. They are also called plane figures because they have a flat surface.

2-D shapes come from the faces of 3-D solids.

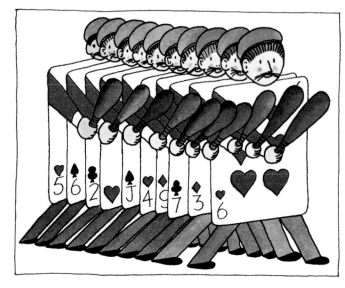

"First came ten soldiers carrying clubs; these were all shaped like the three gardeners, oblong and flat, with their hands and feet at the corners."

Alice in Wonderland

Gummed Paper Shapes

Have you seen the boxes of coloured gummed paper shapes that stationers sell? They are all shapes and sizes.

How could they be sorted? Is this a good way to sort them or classify them?

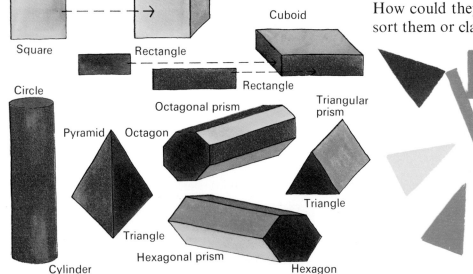

Shapes With Straight Edges

Shapes with straight edges are the polygons, the 2-D shapes with "many angles" (and sides).

Name of Shape	Number of Sides and Angles
Triangle	3
Quadrilateral	4
Pentagon	5
Hexagon	6
Heptagon	7
Octagon	8
Nonagon	9
Decagon	10

Triangles

Triangle means *three angles*.

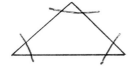

There are different kinds of triangles but they all, of course, have 3 sides and 3 angles. You already know how to draw an *equilateral* triangle. Here are examples of how to construct other triangles.

Example 1: To draw a triangle ABC so that AB = 6 cm, BC = 4 cm and AC = 3 cm.

1. Draw AB with a ruler.
2. Set the compasses at 4 cm. From B draw an arc.
3. Set the compasses at 3 cm. From A draw an arc to cut the first arc at C.
4. Join AC and BC.
5. This is a SCALENE triangle. Scalene triangles have unequal sides. Scalene means uneven.

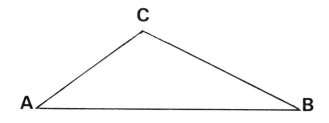

Construct triangles with line (i) 7 cm, 2 cm and 6 cm long, (ii) AB = 3 cm, BC = 2 cm and AC = 4 cm. Why is it not possible to construct a triangle whose sides are 6 cm, 3 cm and 2 cm long?

Example 2: To draw a triangle with 2 sides equal: AB = 5 cm, BC = 4 cm, AC = 4 cm.

1. Draw the base AB with a ruler.
2. Set your compasses at 4 cm. Draw arcs from A and B to cut at C.
3. Join AC and BC.
4. This is an ISOSCELES triangle. Isosceles triangles have two and only two sides equal. *Isosceles* means "equal legs".

Is an equilateral triangle also an isoceles triangle? What do you notice about angles ABC and BAC?

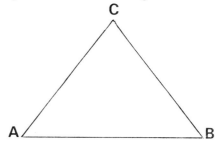

Construct isosceles triangles so that (i) AB = 7 cm, BC and AC = 5 cm, (ii) BC and AC = 7 cm, AB = 3 cm.

Example 3: To draw a triangle which has one of its angles a right angle and sides AB = 4 cm and AC = 3 cm.

1. With a ruler draw the line AB 4 cm long.
2. You know how to construct a right angle from the point A with either compasses or a protractor.
3. With the compasses at a radius of 3 cm cut off an arc along AC.
4. Join this point to B.
5. Measure BC.
6. You have drawn a right-angled triangle.

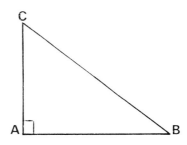

There is more about this kind of triangle on pages 93 and 94. Draw a triangle with AB = 8 cm, AC = 6 cm and angle BAC a right angle.

Some Other Triangles

An *acute* angle is less than a right angle (90°). An

acute-angled triangle (or an *acute triangle*) has all three angles acute.

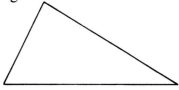

An *obtuse* angle is greater than 90° and less than 180°. An *obtuse-angled triangle* has one angle greater than 90° and less than 180°.

Why cannot a triangle have *two* obtuse angles? Why cannot a triangle have an angle greater than 180°?

Geo-boards

Geo-boards or nail boards can be easily made. You will need a piece of soft board about 20 cm square and some nails 2 cm long. Make a pattern of holes on the board of 1 cm squares before knocking in the nails. Geo-boards are useful for showing shapes of triangles and their areas and perimeters. Elastic bands around the nails make the shapes.

Perimeter

The perimeter of a triangle is the length of the three sides added together. If the lengths of the sides of a

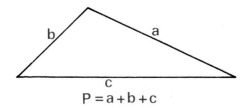

$$P = a + b + c$$

triangle are a, b and c, the formula is:

$$P = a + b + c$$

If the sides of a triangle are 8 cm, 3 cm and 7 cm the perimeter is 18 cm.

Area of a Triangle

The area of a *rectangle* is found by multiplying its length by its width (or base × height). A triangle is *half* a rectangle. So the area of a triangle is a half of the base multiplied by the height.

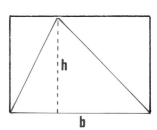
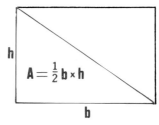

Example: Find the area of a triangle whose base is 6 cm and whose height is 7 cm.

$$A = \tfrac{1}{2}b \times h \text{ or } \frac{b \times h}{2}$$
$$= \frac{6 \times 7}{2}$$
$$= \frac{42}{2}$$
$$= 21 \text{ square centimetres } (21 \text{ cm}^2)$$

Find the area of these triangles:

(i)   base = 10 cm, height = 8 cm
(ii) b = 5 cm, h = 4 cm
(iii) h = 3 cm, b = 9 cm

How many triangles are there in these diagrams? Count them carefully and try not to miss any. Answers on page 136.

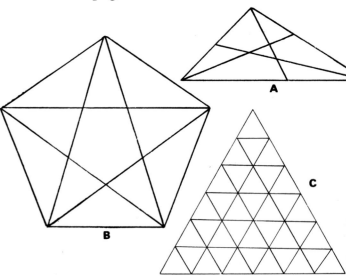

Plane Shapes: Quadrilaterals and Others

Many schools have a *quadrangle*. This is a four-sided court with buildings around it. A *quadrireme* is an ancient galley-ship rowed by four banks of oars. A *quadrille* is a dance for four couples. A *quadruped* is a four-footed animal. *Quadrisyllabic* means that a word has four syllables. When you quadruple a number it makes it four times bigger. *Quadruplets* or *quads* are four children born at the same birth.

Quadrilateral comes from two words. The last part means *side*. What does the whole word mean? Quadrilaterals are flat or *plane* figures with four sides. Some are simple quadrilaterals. The others are called non-simple or complete quadrilaterals.

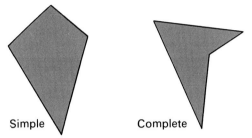

Simple   Complete

There are many kinds of four-sided figures, including rectangles, oblongs, squares, parallelograms, kites, trapezia and rhombuses.

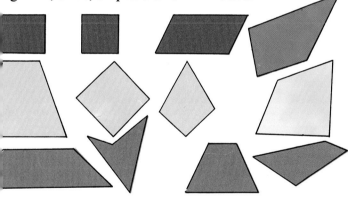

Rectangles

Rectangles have four right angles and their opposite sides are equal. The angles ABC, BCD, CDA and DAB are all 90° angles. AB = DC and AD = BC. The marks on the lines show which lines are equal. The squares in the angles show they are right angles.

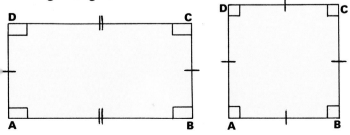

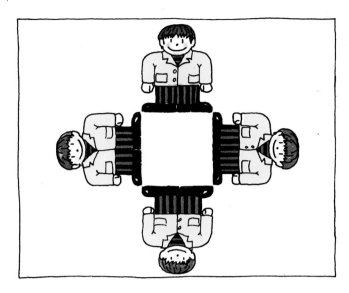

Squares

Squares are rectangles because they also have four right angles and their opposite sides are equal Of course, *all* the sides of a square are equal. The angles ABC, BCD, CDA, DAB all have 90° and AB = BC = CD = AD.

Adjacent Sides

These are sides which are next to each other. In the rectangle ABCD, side AB is adjacent to BC. AB and BC meet at the same vertex, B.

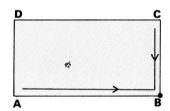

Rectangles and Oblongs

Rectangles are often called oblongs. Oblongs are rectangles with adjacent sides which are *not equal*. A square is a rectangle but it is not an oblong. A square has *equal* adjacent sides. It is a good idea to use the word *rectangle* for a figure with four right angles, whose opposite sides are equal.

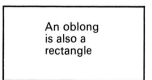

An oblong is also a rectangle

A square is a rectangle but is not an oblong

Parallelograms

Parallelograms are quadrilaterals which have both pairs of opposite sides equal. In the parallelogram ABCD, AB and DC are parallel and AD and BC are parallel. The arrows show which sides are parallel to each other. As you see, AB = DC and AD = BC.

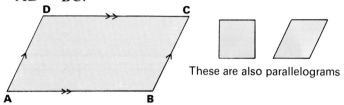

Do you notice that a square is a parallelogram as well? Do you notice that a rectangle is *also* a parallelogram?

Rhombuses

A rhombus is also a parallelogram which has two adjacent sides equal. A rhombus is rather like a square which has been sat on. All four sides of a rhombus are equal. In the rhombus ABCD, AB = BC = CD = AD. AB is parallel to DC and BC is parallel to AD. Do you notice that a square is also a rhombus?

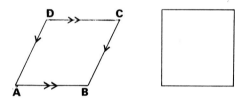

Kites

A kite is a quadrilateral with two pairs of equal adjacent sides. In the kite ABCD, AB = AD and BC = CD. Notice that a kite can be formed by two isosceles triangles which have the same base. Triangles BCD and ABD both have the same base BD.

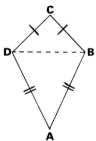

Trapezia

Trapezia are quadrilaterals with one pair of sides parallel but the other two sides *not* parallel. In the trapezium ABCD, the lines AB and CD are parallel. An isosceles trapezium has two sides

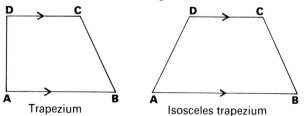

which are not parallel but which are equal to each other. In the isosceles trapezium, AB is parallel to CD and AD = BC.

A *trapezoid* is a quadrilateral with no two sides parallel. In the trapezoid ABCD there are no parallel sides.

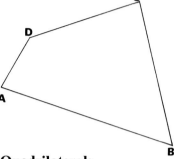

Perimeters of Quadrilaterals

In every case the perimeter of a quadrilateral can be found by adding the lengths of the four sides.

$$P = a + b + c + d$$

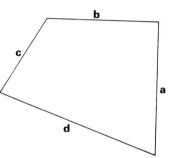

For some there is also a shorter way of finding the perimeter. For parallelograms the perimeter is twice the base and side added. Remember that a rectangle is also a parallelogram.

$$P = 2(b + s)$$

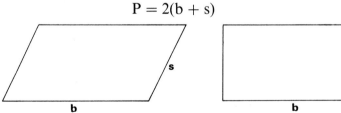

For rhombuses and squares (which are also rhombuses) the perimeter is 4 times the length of one side:

$$P = 4l$$

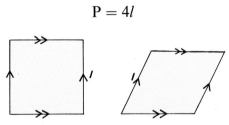

Area of Quadrilaterals

We have already seen that the areas of rectangles (including squares) are found by multiplying the length by the width. There are interesting ways of finding the area of some other quadrilaterals.

The area of a *parallelogram* is found by multiplying the base by the height.

$$A = bh$$

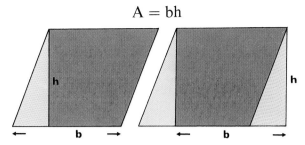

If the base of a parallelogram is 6 cm and the height is 4 cm it will have the same area as a rectangle 6 cm × 4 cm.

$$A = 6 \times 4 = 24 \text{ sq. cm or } 24 \text{ cm}^2$$

The area of a *rhombus* is found by multiplying the diagonals and dividing by 2:

$$A = \frac{\text{diagonal} \times \text{diagonal}}{2}$$

In the rhombus ABCD, AC and BD are diagonals.

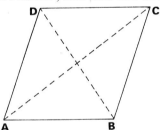

To prove this:

1. Draw the rhombus and number it 1. Call the triangles 2, 3, 4 and 5.

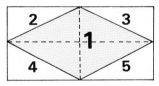

2. Cut out the rhombus and triangles.
3. Compare the area of the rhombus and the area of the triangles which form the rectangle. Do they have the same area?
4. Now calculate the area of the rectangle and that of the rhombus. Are they equal?

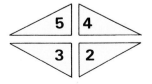

The area of a *trapezium* is found by multiplying its two bases by its height and dividing by two.

$$A = \frac{(b + b)h}{2}$$

(The parallel sides are called *bases*: the shorter one is the lesser base and the longer one is the greater base.) To prove this, halve a trapezium as in the diagram. Turn figure 2 upside down and put it alongside figure 1.

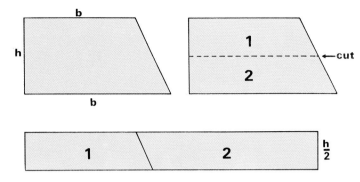

Example: Find the area of a trapezium whose height is 6 cm, whose lesser base is 8 cm and greater base is 10 cm long.

$$A = \frac{(b + b)h}{2}$$
$$= \frac{(8 + 10)6}{2}$$
$$= \frac{18 \times 6}{2} \text{ or } 18 \times 3$$
$$= 54 \text{ sq cm or } 54 \text{ cm}^2$$

Find the area of trapezia whose:

(i) height is 5 cm and bases are 3 cm and 6 cm
(ii) H = 3 cm and b + b = 4 + 7 cm.

About Polygons

Polygons are "many sided" plane figures. Some people look on polygons as having more than four straight lines. Other people include triangles and quadrilaterals in the set of polygons. They all come from the faces of 3-D solids. Polygons can be irregular or regular figures. Irregular polygons do not have all their angles and sides equal to each other. Regular polygons have equal sides and angles.

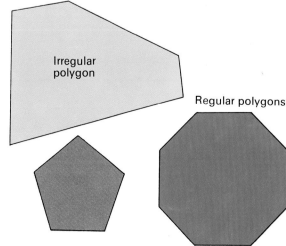

Some Games with Polygons

1. How many rectangles are there in diagram A?
   2. How many rectangles in B? There are more than you think!
   3. How many quadrilaterals in pentagon C?
   4. How many hexagons (regular and irregular) are there in D?
   5. How many quadrilaterals in E?
   6. How many quadrilaterals in F?

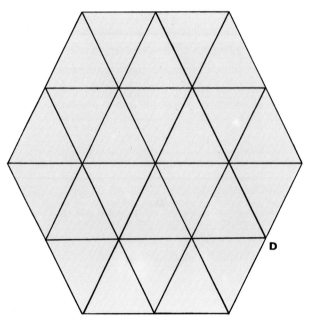

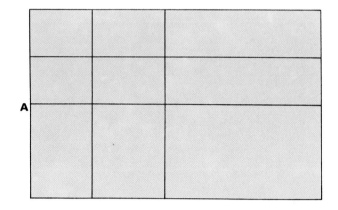

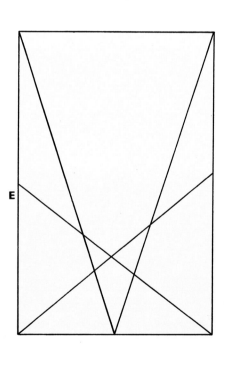

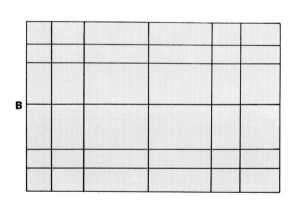

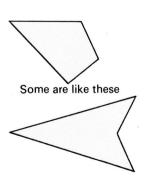

Some are like these

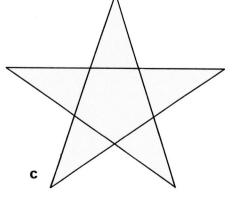

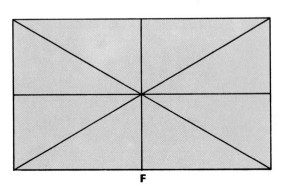

Answers: A = 36 rectangles. B = 441 rectangles. C = 5 simple and 5 complete quadrilaterals. D = 8 regular and 36 irregular hexagons. E = 20 simple and 7 complete quadrilaterals. F = 78 simple quadrilaterals.

Curves

Curves are lines which have no straight parts. Curves can be open or closed. Open curves have end points which closed ones do not have. Simple curves do not cross themselves but non simple ones do.

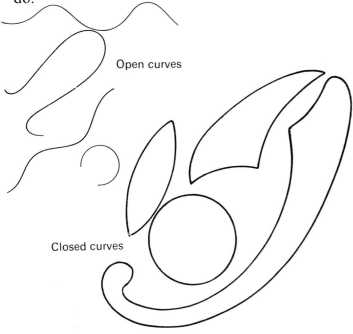

Open curves

Closed curves

The Circle

The circle is an example of a closed curve and can be seen on the end faces of cylinders and on the base of cones.

Many people believe that the circle is the most important thing ever invented. There is no such thing as a perfect circle in nature, so it must have been discovered by a human being. The world today would be completely different if this curve had not been invented. There would be no wheels and therefore no vehicles. There would be no machines of any kind. Without the circle the human race would have made little progress.

To Draw a Circle
1. Stick a drawing pin into a piece of soft wood or cardboard on which a sheet of paper has been placed.
2. Tie a piece of thread around the pin.
3. Attach the thread at the other end to a pencil.
4. Hold the thread tightly as the pencil traces a path which meets itself.

The five intertwined circles on the Olympic flag represent the five continents.

5. The line drawn is a set of points which are the same distance from the centre pin.

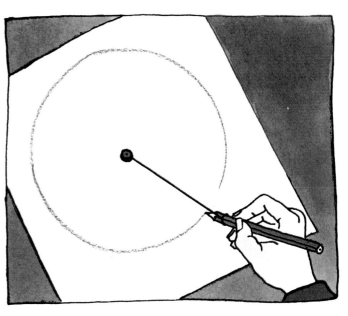

SOME CIRCLE WORDS

Arc: Part of the circumference of a circle.
Centre: The mid-point of the circle.
Chord: A line which joins two points on the circumference. A diameter is a special kind of chord.
Circumference (c): The set of points the same distance from the centre of the circle. The word also describes the *distance* round a circle.
Diameter (d): Any straight line which goes through the centre of a circle and has its end points on the circumference.
Radius (r): The distance from the centre of a circle to the circumference. The plural is *radii*.
Sector: A cut or slice inside two radii and the arc which joins them.
Semicircle: An arc which is half a circle.
Tangent: A straight line which touches a curve at only one point.

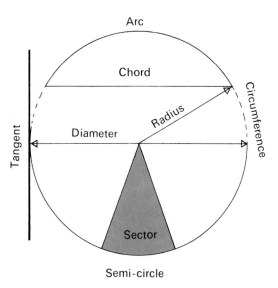

Arc

Chord

Tangent

Diameter

Radius

Circumference

Sector

Semi-circle

When the circumference of a circle its divided by its diameter the result is about 3·14 or roughly $3\frac{1}{7}$. This ratio is called *pi*, which is the Greek letter π. Archimedes used a regular polygon of 96 sides, which is almost a circle, to prove that π was between $3\frac{10}{71}$ and $3\frac{1}{7}$. Just over 100 years ago it was found that π could not be calculated exactly. Computers have worked it out to hundreds of thousands of decimal places. There is no pattern in the digits. Here is π correct to 20 decimal places:

3·141 592 653 589 793 238 46

Finding the Circumference of a Circle

The formula is written $\frac{c}{d} = \pi$ or $c = \pi d$, or $c = 2\pi r$

Example: What is the circumference of a hoop which has a radius of 35 cm?

$c = 2\pi r$

$= 2 \times 3\frac{1}{7} \times 35$

$= 2 \times \frac{22}{7} \times 35$

$= 2 \times 22 \times 5 \ (35 \div 7 = 5)$

$= 22 \times 10$

$= 220 \text{ cm or } 2 \cdot 2 \text{ m}$

Try these:

1. Find the circumference of a wheel which has a diameter of 60 cm. (π = 3.14)
2. How far will a person travel who cycles 14 times round a fountain which has a radius of 14 m? (π = $3\frac{1}{7}$)

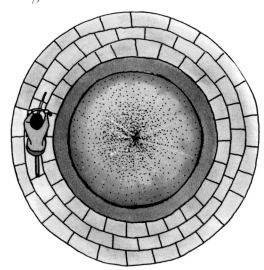

c, d and pi

The diameter and circumference of a circle are linked in a most interesting way. To discover this link you will need: a tin, a piece of string, a pair of scissors, two books or blocks of wood and a ruler.

1. Find the *circumference* of the tin by wrapping a piece of string around it and cutting it at the exact measurement.
2. Find the *diameter* of the tin by placing it between the books or pieces of wood. Measure the distance.

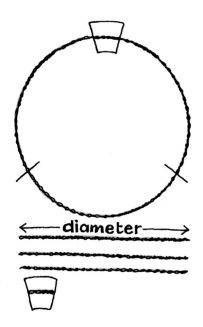

3. How many times does the diameter divide into the circumference? It should be 3 and a bit times.

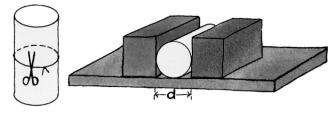

diameter

3. How far does the point at the end of a minute hand of a clock, which is 7 cm long, move between 6 and 7 a.m.?

Answers on page 136.

The Area of a Circle

To find the *approximate* area of a circle:
1. Draw a circle of radius 4 cm.
2. Divide it into 12 sectors. How will you do this?
3. Halve one of the sectors.

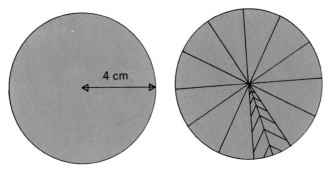

4. Cut out the sectors and re-arrange them as in the diagram. If there were more sectors the figure would more nearly resemble a rectangle.

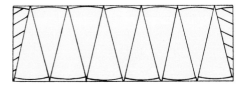

5. The area of the circle has been arranged to form a rectangle whose length is half the circumference of the circle. Its width is the radius. Area of circle = $\frac{1}{2}$ circumference × radius.
6. Circumference of a circle = πd or 2πr
   $\frac{1}{2}$ circumference $\qquad = \frac{1}{2}\pi$d or πr
7. The circle and rectangle are shown again at A.

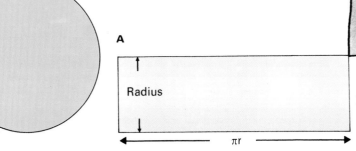

8. The area of the circle $= \pi \times r \times r$ or πr^2 (diagram B).

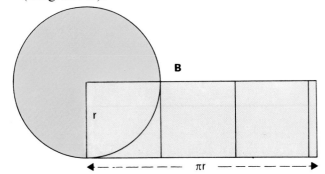

Finding the Area of a Circle

Example: A circular garden has a radius of 7 m. What is its area?

$A = \pi r^2$

$\quad = \dfrac{22}{7} \times 7 \times 7$

$\quad = 22 \times 7 \ (7 \div 7 = 1)$

$\quad = 154$ square metres or 154 m²

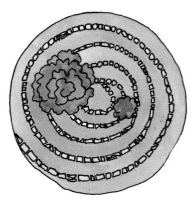

Try these:
1. Find the area of the base of a gas holder which has a radius of 14 m.

2. What is the area of a circle with a radius of 3·5 cm?

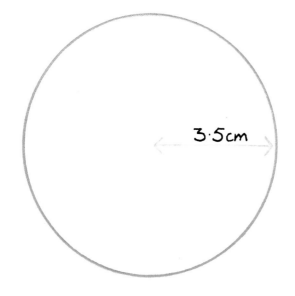

87

3. A circus ring has a radius of 21 m. What is its area?

Answers on page 136.

radius 21 m

Curves in a Cone

Cutting through a plasticine cone can give some interesting curves. When a cone is cut across, at right angles to the base, a *circle* is seen. An *ellipse* is seen when the cone is cut across at any other angle.

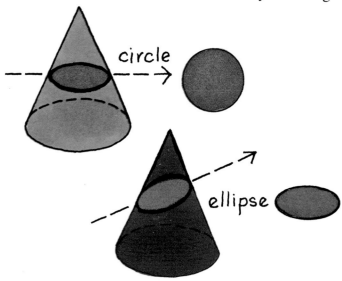

circle

ellipse

To draw an ellipse

1. Fasten the ends of a thread by pins at two points on a piece of paper. The thread must be longer than the distance between the two points.
2. Put a pencil upright against the thread so that it is tight.
3. Draw half the curve.

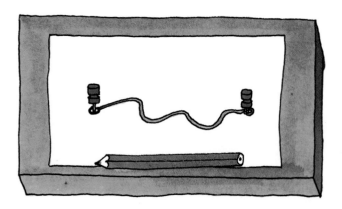

4. Lift the pencil and draw the second half of the curve on the other side of the pins.

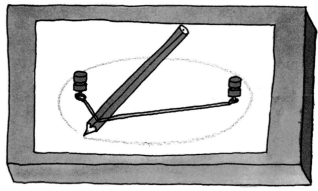

When planets and space satellites are in orbit they make an elliptical curve. The orbit of the Moon is an ellipse.

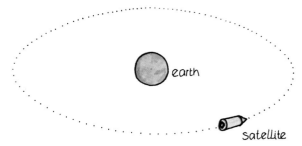

earth

satellite

A *parabola* is another curve formed by cutting a cone. This is the path of a ball thrown up at a slant into the air. It is also the path made by jets of water. A cable which holds up a suspension bridge is also a parabola.

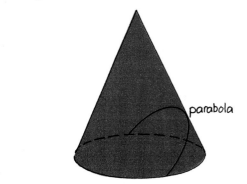

parabola

Are You Square?

What is the most wonderful thing in the world? Is it the decimal numbering system? The circle? The pyramids? Disneyland? The great poet and playwright, William Shakespeare, thought it was *the human body*. In the play *Hamlet* he wrote:

What a piece of work is a man! In form,
in moving, how express and admirable.
In action, how like an angel!

No doubt Shakespeare used the word *man* to include all human beings.

A Family Project

You and your family are invited on these pages to take part in a project which includes measuring activities. The project is called Body Measures. To do it you will need some paper, a tape measure, a ruler, a dictionary and a Bible. There are five aims to this project:

1. To examine the shape and size of the human body.
2. To find out some relationships of body measurements.
3. To trace the history of body measures.
4. To carry out some measuring activities.
5. To draw some conclusions from the activities.

First of all we need to repeat briefly something from earlier pages in the book.

Background Information

In the days of the cave people no measures were needed as there was nothing important to measure When people began to make and build things, they needed units of measure to make the task easier.

The measures which were handy were parts of the body. The Greeks and Romans used hands and feet as units. The early Egyptians used parts of their body as units to build their temples and pyramids. The *cubit* was the distance from the elbow to the finger tip. The *span* was the distance between the tips of a little finger and the thumb of an outstretched hand. They also used a small measure equal to the width of a forefinger.

The Romans also used a small measure which was equal to the width of a thumb. The *foot* measure was divided into *uncia* or twelfths. The *inch* is derived from this word. King Edward I of England decided that an inch was the length of three barley-corns placed end to end. Before Edward's time Anglo-Saxon sailors used to find

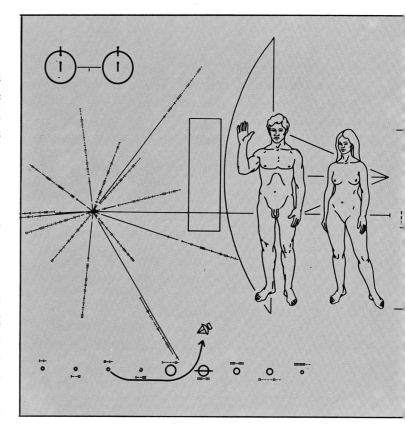

If we manage to make contact with beings on another faraway planet, the first thing they will want to know about us is what we look like. This plaque is being carried by Pioneer 10, the first American space probe to journey beyond our solar system. It shows a man and a woman against a plan of the spacecraft, which indicates their size. At the bottom are the planets and the path of Pioneer 10 from Earth. The symbol at the top represents the molecular structure of hydrogen – the most common element in the universe. The star-like pattern shows the 14 pulsars of the Milky Way galaxy.

the depth of the sea by dropping a stone tied to a rope in the water. When the stone hit the bottom the sailors pulled in the rope. They stretched their arms wide to *reach*, which is the name of an arm-length. The word in their language for out-stretched arms was *fathom*. Fathom later came to mean the length of 6 feet.

The units based on body measures could not be exact because their length varies from person to person. Often there were varying measures in different parts of the country. During the last 1000 years attempts were made to have standard units. About 100 years ago the *Imperial units* became law. The metric system of measures is used in most countries today.

Measuring Activities

When you and your family are measuring, measure with the units you commonly use. If you use metric units remember that m (for metre) and cm (for centimetre) do *not* have capital letters, or an s at the end of the plural, or a full stop at the end.

1. *Personal Statistics*
   1.1 My height is . . . . .
   1.2 The length of my foot is . . . . .
   1.3 My cubit is . . . . .
   1.4 My chest measurement is. . . . .
   1.5 My hip measurement is . . . . .
   1.6 My arm-spread is . . . . .
   1.7 My span is . . . . .
   1.8 My neck is . . . . .
   1.9 My waist is . . . . .
   1.10 My wrist is . . . . .

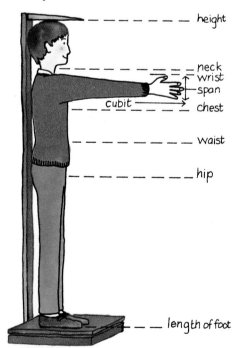

2. The height of the average adult woman is 1.61 m (5 ft. 3 ins.)
   The height of the average adult man is 1·71 m (5 ft. 7 ins.)
   2.1 How do you all compare with these heights?

3. 3.1 Compare your height with your reach (arm-spread).
   3.2 What do you notice?
   3.3 Are your height and reach the same?
   3.4 Are you square?

Your reach and height should be about the same.

4. 4.1 Divide the length of your cubit by the length of your span. Use a calculator to do this if you like and give the answer to one decimal place.
   4.2 The answer is called the *ratio of elegance*.
   4.3 Use your dictionary to find out what these words mean.
   4.4 If your answer is *about 2* it means that you are elegant!
   4.5 Are you elegant?

5. Find out other ratios between some other body measurements, e.g. wrist and neck, cubit and height.

6. From verse 4, chapter 17 of the First Book of Samuel in the Bible find out how tall Goliath was. Give the answer in metric or imperial units.
   6.1 How does your height compare with Goliath's?
   6.2 Draw and cut out figures to represent you and Goliath.

7. Measure the height and reach of a man.
   7.1 Would you have made a good Anglo-Saxon Sailor?

8. Measure the height and cubit of a woman.
   8.1 Find the ratio between them by dividing the height by the cubit.

9. Measure round your forehead at the widest part of your cranium.
   9.1 Find your height/head ratio to one decimal place.

10. Keep a record of your *vital statistics* during the next year.
    10.1 Draw a series of graphs to show the increases.

90

Some Laws of Arithmetic

People have to obey the laws of the country they live in. If some motorists drove on the left side of the road and others on the right, the result would be most unpleasant. Some children may not like the law which says they must go to school, but it has to obeyed.

Arithmetic also has laws which have to be obeyed. You have probably been obeying them for some time without knowing what the laws are. Learning and understanding these laws makes mathematics interesting and enjoyable. The *names* of the laws are a bit difficult but do not worry about them. It is better to understand them than to remember what they are called. There are eleven of these laws altogether. We are going to look at only four of them.

Commutative Law for Addition

Commuters are people who travel to work. Most of them set off to do their job in the morning. When they have finished they *change direction* and go home. In this law, two numbers commute or *change round*.

Imagine three sheep in a pen and four sheep following them. The result is the same if four sheep are in a pen and three sheep follow them.

In other words, 4 + 3 is the same as 3 + 4.

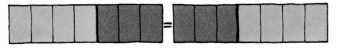

If we give 4 the letter *a* and 3 the letter *b*:

$a + b$ is the same as $b + a$

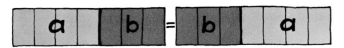

The commutative law for addition says that the order in which numbers are *added* does not affect their sum. For all numbers *a* and *b*, $a + b = b + a$

Notice that this law is *not* true for subtraction:

Traffic can only move if all motorists drive on the right or all motorists drive on the left.

$4 - 3$ is *not* the same as $3 - 4$

$4 - 3 \neq 3 - 4$

Commutative Law for Multiplication

In the same way, the order in which numbers are *multiplied* does not affect their product. Four sets of 3 pencils is the same quantity as 3 sets of 4 pencils.

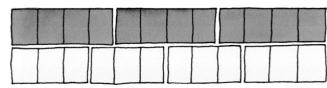

3×4 gives the same product as 4×3

For all numbers *a* and *b*, $ab = ba$

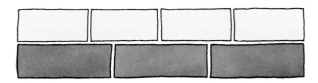

Notice that this law is *not* true for division:

$4 \div 3$ is *not* the same as $3 \div 4$

$$\frac{4}{3} \neq \frac{3}{4}$$

Associative Law for Addition

An association is a society or club. People with the same interests often form a group. Numbers can

be grouped and added *in any order* without changing their sum.

Imagine a man and two children sitting in a restaurant as three women enter. The total number of people is the same as though a man were sitting in the restaurant as two children and three women entered (picture above).

$$(1 + 2) + 3 = 6 \text{ and } 1 + (2 + 3) = 6$$
$$(1 + 2) + 3 \qquad = 1 + (2 + 3)$$

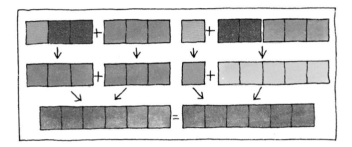

For all numbers *a*, *b* and *c*, $(a + b) + c = a + (b + c)$

This law helps to add numbers quickly:

$$17 + 15 + 23 = (17 + 23) + 15 = 40 + 15 = 55$$

Note that subtraction is *not* associative. Think about $6 - 3 - 2$:

$$(6 - 3) - 2 = 3 - 2 = 1 \text{ but}$$
$$6 - (3 - 2) = 6 - 1 = 5$$

Associative Law for Multiplication

When three numbers are to be multiplied the factors may be grouped in any way without changing the product. Four shelves of cups made up of 2 sets of 3 on each shelf are the same as 2 shelves of cups made up of 4 sets of 3 (right).

$$(2 \times 3) \times 4 = 2 (3 \times 4)$$

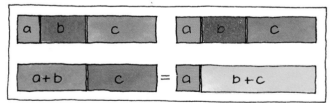

For all numbers *a*, *b* and *c*, $(ab)c = a(bc)$
This law helps to multiply numbers quickly:

Example:
(i) $15 \times 9 \times 4 = (15 \times 4) \times 9 = 60 \times 9 = 540$
(ii) $16 \times 2 \times 5 = 16 \times (5 \times 2) = 16 \times 10 = 160$
(iii) $45 \times 16 = 9 \times 5 \times 2 \times 8 = 9 \times 10 \times 8 = 90 \times 8 = 720$

This law does *not* work for division. Think about $8 \div 4 \div 2$:

$$(8 \div 4) \div 2 = 2 \div 2 = 1 \text{ but}$$
$$8 \div (4 \div 2) = 8 \div 2 = 4$$

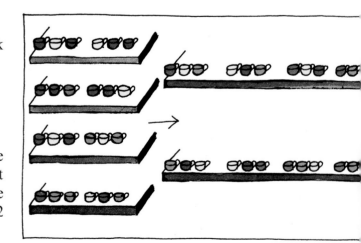

Angles and Rotation

An important part of geometry is about things which turn or *rotate*. The wheels of a vehicle, the turntable on a record-player and the hands of a clock are three of the many things which rotate.

Angles

The amount of rotation is called an *angle*. An angle is also the figure formed by two lines which are joined at a point or vertex. These lines, or rays, are called the sides or arms of the angle.

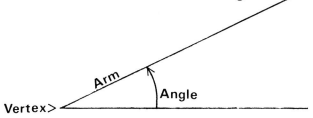

Right Angles

Wherever we look we see square corners or angles. (*Angulus* is the Latin word for corner.) They are seen on windows, picture frames and furniture. They are seen on buildings, walls and books. These *right angles*, as they are called, are the angles which are used most often.

There are hundreds of right angles in this picture of one skyscraper mirrored in the wall of another.

A right angle is a quarter of a complete turn.

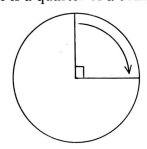

Big Ben's minute hand is just reaching 270°.

In ancient Egypt, surveyors needed right angles for their building. They also needed right angles to survey the land of people whose marks had been washed away by the Nile's annual floods. They made a right angle by *rope-stretching*. They took a long piece of rope and marked off twelve equal divisions by knots. One surveyor held the two ends of the rope together at the point where the right angle was needed. Another rope-stretcher held the knot three divisions from one end. The third held the rope four divisions from the other end. A right angle was made when they stretched the rope tight.

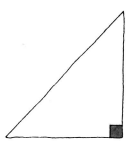

There are other ways of making right angles. An easy way is to fold a piece of paper and then fold it a second time along the crease.

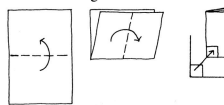

93

Builders and bricklayers make right angles by using spirit-levels and plumb-lines. They put the spirit-level along the top of a brick course and hang the plumb-line vertically from it.

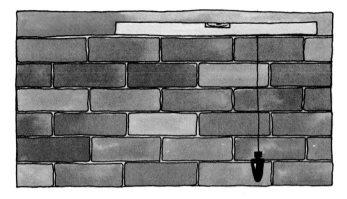

Pythagoras

Pythagoras is probably best known for a rule about right angles which he discovered about 2500 years ago. The rule, or theorem, says that in a right-angled triangle the square on the longest side (the one opposite the right angle) is equal to the sum of the squares on the other two sides.

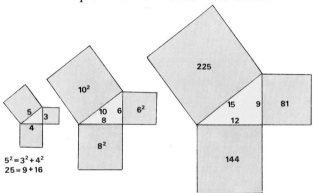

Are these triangles right-angled?
  (i)   12, 16 and 20
  (ii) 5, 12 and 13
  (iii) 8, 15 and 17

Rotation of Angles

Angles are measured according to their amount of turn. This rotation can be seen using geo-strips. The ones which make less than a quarter turn, or a right angle, are *acute* angles.

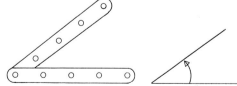

Those making more than a quarter turn and less than a half turn are *obtuse* angles.

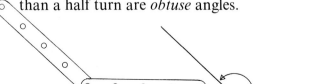

A *straight* angle is half a complete turn, or two right angles.

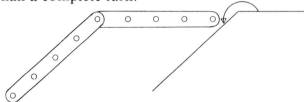

A *reflex* angle is more than a straight angle and less than a complete turn.

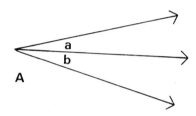

A complete turn is one *revolution*.

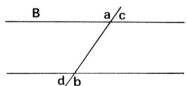

Some other Angles

In geometry you will meet some other kinds of angles.

Adjacent angles are next to each other. They have the same vertex and share one of their sides. In diagram A, angles a and b are adjacent.

Alternate angles are seen when a straight line cuts two other straight lines. When these two other straight lines are parallel, the alternate angles are equal. In diagram B, a = b and c = d.

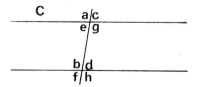

Corresponding angles can also be seen when a straight line cuts two parallel lines. In diagram C, these corresponding angles are equal: a and b, c and d, e and f, and g and h.

Supplementary angles are two angles which make a straight angle or two right angles. In diagram D, angles a and b are supplementary.

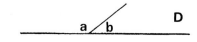

Vertical (or *vertically opposite*) angles are equal. They are formed when two lines cut each other. In diagram E, angles a and c, and b and d are vertically opposite.

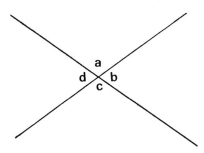

From 12 back to 12 it has gone through a complete revolution, or 360°.

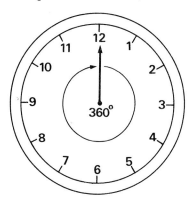

Measuring Angles

Angles have to be measured. The units used for measuring angles are called *degrees*. A degree (1°) is one-ninetieth of a right angle. An arc of 1° is one three-hundred-and-sixtieth of a circle.

When the minute hand of a clock has moved from 12 to 3 it has gone through a quarter turn, or 90°.

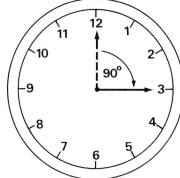

From 12 to 6 it has gone through half a turn, or 180°.

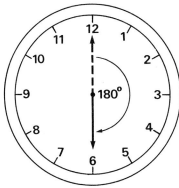

From 12 to 9 it has gone through three-quarters of a turn, or 270°.

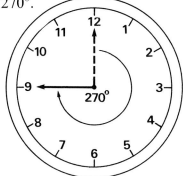

The amount of rotation from 12 to 1 can be found by dividing 360° by 12, which is 30°.

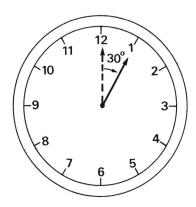

How many degrees are there from 12 o'clock to
(a) 2   (b) 5   (c) 8   (d) 11 o'clock?
Use your protractor to draw the number of degrees from 12 to
(a) 4   (b) 7   (c) 10 o'clock.

The diagram shows the angle between 12 and 5.

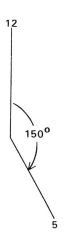

Patterns Please

Patterns abound throughout the whole of mathematics. We have examined some interesting *number* patterns and now we look at some pleasing patterns of *shapes*. They are patterns which may be seen on walls and pavements, on parquet floors and on patchwork quilts. These patterns have one thing in common. They consist of shapes which can be fitted together to cover surfaces completely.

Many years ago the Romans laid down pavements and covered the floors of their houses with *mosaics*. Many of the mosaics were in the form of pictures but some of them were made of repeating patterns. To make these patterns the Romans used small cubes of stone which were set in cement. One of these cubes was called a *tessella*. It is from this word that we have the name of a tiling pattern.

Tessellation once meant tiling by using equal squares. It now means using any shapes which can be repeated in a way that leaves no gaps. *Squares* tessellate easily and square tiles are often seen on bathroom walls. Here are some square repeating patterns, but you can draw some tessellations using squares yourself.

This Roman mosaic is a complicated tessilation. It dates from the early A.D. 200s and can be seen in the Baths of Caracalla in Rome.

Tessellations can also be made by using two squares of different sizes.

Repeating patterns of rectangles are seen on parquet floors and in the bonds which bricklayers use when building walls.

Parquet floors (above left) are usually made up of rectangular pieces of wood. Bricks laid lengthways (above right) are in a stretcher bond pattern.

With the *stretcher* bond the bricks are laid lengthways. The *English* bond has alternate rows of stretchers and *headers*, where the bricks are laid head-on. The *Flemish* bond has a pattern of alternate headers and stretchers in the same row.

In bricklaying, the English bond has alternate rows of lengthways and end-on bricks (left). In Flemish bond, the bricks are laid alternately lengthways and end-on in the same row (right).

Equilateral triangles fit together to form a regular hexagon. This is the shape of the bees' cells. The honeycomb is the best shape for honey because it is strong and gives a lot of storage space.

The bees' honeycomb is made by the workers and is a wonderfully built structure of wax. Each cell is six-sided to give strength and a lot of storage space. You can see in the picture above how the cells fit together perfectly. The queen bee is in the centre being attended by worker bees who clean and feed her. The queen lays one egg in each wax cell.

Six equilateral triangles fit together to make a regular hexagon. This is the shape of the bees' cells.

Squares, equilateral triangles and regular hexagons are the only *regular* polygons which can be used alone for tessellations. There are reasons for this. In order for a tessellation to be possible, the space around a *vertex* must be filled. The vertex is the point where the lines and edges meet.

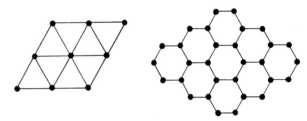

To fill this space the angles of the shapes which surround the vertices must be a complete revolution, or 360°. There need to be at least three polygons at each vertex. The only combinations are 3 regular hexagons, 4 squares and 6 equilateral triangles.

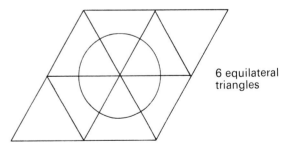

6 equilateral triangles

Shapes Which do not Tessellate
Curved shapes, such as circles and elipses, cannot tessellate either, for the same reason.

No regular polygon with more than six sides can be used *alone* to make a tessellation. This is because the angles in a polygon increase in size as the number of sides increases. Three regular hexagons meet at a vertex to give an angle of 360° (120° × 3), so any polygon with more sides than a hexagon gives an angle greater than 360°. A tessellation of octagons overlaps. The regular pentagon will not tessellate because there is a gap among the vertices. Try it.

Powerful Numbers

Long ago there lived in Persia a Shah who loved playing chess. He liked the game so much that he decided to reward the inventor of the game. The Shah ordered the inventor to ask for anything his heart desired. The clever inventor thought for a moment, then he asked for a grain of wheat for the first square of the chessboard on Monday, two grains for the second square on Tuesday, four for the third square on Wednesday, eight for the fourth square on the following day and so on until the 64th square.

The Shah was very disappointed that the man had asked for so little and the inventor left. A few weeks later, however, the Persian Minister for Wheat appeared before the Shah with a very worried look on his face. He told the astonished Shah that there was not enough wheat in the whole of Persia to give the inventor that day's reward.

There was not enough wheat in all Persia.

The chessboard shows that, by the 16th day, the number of grains of wheat would be near 33 000.

By the 22nd day it would be over four thousand million. On the 64th day it would be the number 184 followed by 17 zeros!

If a grain of wheat is 3 mm long and the grains were placed end to end, how far do you think the chain of wheat would stretch on the 64th day? It would, in fact, stretch from Persia to the nearest star outside the Solar System, Alpha Centauri, and a good deal further! (Alpha Centauri is 4·3 light-years away from us and a light year is 9·45 million million kilometres.)

Our bodies are made up of millions of tiny cells that can only be seen under a microscope. There are about a million million in the body of an adult. This gives some idea of what such a large number of grains of wheat is

18 400 000 000 000 000 000.

Most cells divide and become two cells. These two cells become four cells which become eight cells and so on. The smallest living thing is the *amoeba*. Amoebas have young by splitting in two. These two become four, which become eight, which become sixteen, and so. Can you think of any other things which double?

The Power of a Number
This continual doubling gives the *power* of two. Each power of two gives twice its previous power. 2^2 is the second power of 2: $2 \times 2 = 4$.

$1 = 2^0$ (2 with no power) $= 1$
$2 = 2^1$ (2 to the power 1) $= 2 \times 1$

$4 = 2^2$ (2 to the power 2,
   or 2 squared) $= 2 \times 2$
$8 = 2^3$ (2 to the power 3,
   or 2 cubed) $= 2 \times 2 \times 2$
$16 = 2^4$ (2 to the power 4) $= 2 \times 2 \times 2 \times 2$
$32 = 2^5$ (2 to the power 5) $= 2 \times 2 \times 2 \times 2 \times 2$
and so on.

These powers of 2 can be shown using Colour-Factor blocks.

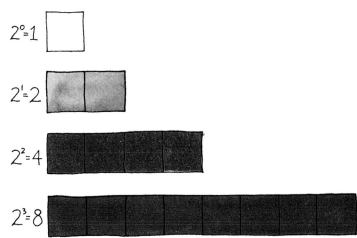

It will be seen that the block 1 is white to represent no power. As the number increases in power, so the block shows a deeper red. Blocks to represent 16, 32, 64, etc. would become darker and darker red.

This increase in power can be shown in the building of blocks.

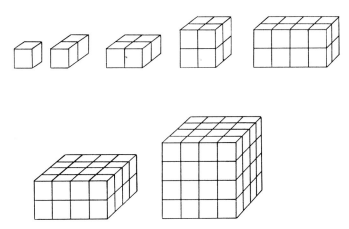

It can also be shown in a graph (right). Notice how the graph of the powers of 2 shows how rapidly the powers grow.

It would be very difficult to show the growth in the powers of 10 because the numbers increase so rapidly: 1, 10, 100, 1000, ...

Indices and Exponents

The number which shows or *indicates* the power is the *index*. (The plural of index is *indices*.) In $4^3 = 4 \times 4 \times 4 = 64$, the little 3 is the index. In $5^2 = 5 \times 5 = 25$, the 2 is the index. Where there is no index written it is taken to be 1. For example, $2 = 2^1$.

Another word for index is *exponent*. When 64 is written as 2^6, the 6 is the index or exponent. It shows that 2 has been raised to the power of 6. Indices are short ways of writing numbers.

Example: 2^6 has a *base* of 2 and an index of 6.

2^6 indicates that 6 twos have been multiplied.

$2^6 = 2 \times 2 \times 2 \times 2 \times 2 \times 2$

2 has been used a factor 6 times.

Indices show how many times a number is multiplied.

Indices are used in square and cubic measure.

Example

(i) A cube is 2 cm long and 2 cm wide.

   Its area $= 2\,\text{cm} \times 2\,\text{cm}$
             $= 4\,\text{cm}^2$

$4\,\text{cm}^2$ means 4 square centimetres.

It does *not* mean 4 centimetres squared.

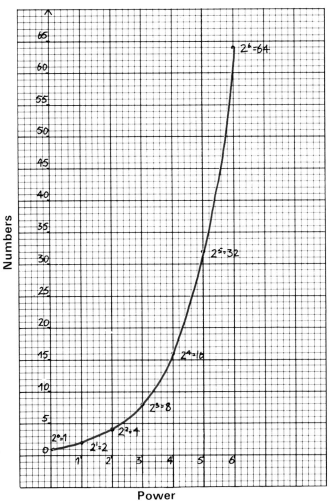

99

Logarithms

$10 \times 10 \times 10 = 1000 = 10^3$: the logarithm of 1000 on base ten is 3.

$10 \times 10 = 100 = 10^2$: the logarithm of 100 on base ten is 2.

$10 \times 1 = 10 = 10^1$: the logarithm of 10 on base ten is 1.

$1 \times 1 = 1 = 10^0$: the logarithm of 1 on base ten is 0.

The table shows the links among numbers, bases, indices and logarithms.

Example 1: Multiply 1000 by 100.

Number	Log
1000	3
× 100	+ 2

$$10^3 + 10^2 = 5 = 100\,000$$

Example 2: Divide 1 000 000 by 100

Number	Log
1 000 000	6
÷ 100	− 2

$$10^6 - 10^2 = 4 = 10\,000$$

Product	Number	Number of zeros in number	Base and Index	Logarithm
1	1	0	10^0	0
1×10	10	1	10^1	1
10×10	100	2	10^2	2
$10 \times 10 \times 10$	1 000	3	10^3	3
$10 \times 10 \times 10 \times 10$	10 000	4	10^4	4
$10 \times 10 \times 10 \times 10 \times 10$	1000 000	5	10^5	5
$10 \times 10 \times 10 \times 10 \times 10 \times 10$	1 000 000	6	10^6	6

Do you remember Napier's Bones? Logarithms were invented by John Napier in 1594. His book on logarithms was published twenty years later. This helped people to carry out long multiplications of numbers by adding their logarithms, and divisions of numbers by subtracting their logarithms. Tables give the logarithms of *all* numbers but here are very simple examples of how they work.

Slide rules multiply numbers by adding their logarithms. It will be seen that the numbers on a slide rule are not spaced evenly.

Try this puzzle. An amazing Persian lily doubled its size every day. On the 30th day it filled the whole area of the lily pond. On which day did it cover *half* the pond?
Answer on page 136.

Before the electronic calculator, engineers, architects and business-men used the slide rule to make quick calculations. The numbers on the slide rule are not spaced evenly – they are arranged logarithmically.

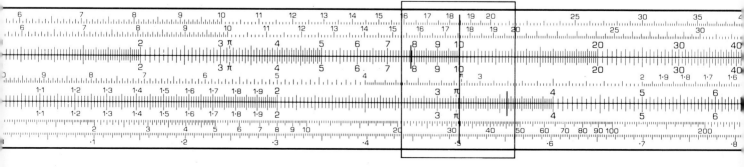

Home Maths

Some people study something called *pure mathematics*. This subject does not set out to solve problems in science or in the world of work. It is studied for its own sake and was of great interest to some early Greek scholars. Pure mathematics helps to give ideas to its sister, *applied mathematics*. This subject is put to practical use in engineering, mechanics, physics and surveying. It is involved with energy, force, mass, space and time. In the past forty years it has been concerned with nuclear physics, electronics and computers. Applied mathematics links science and mathematics. Many examples of this are seen in the building and running of our homes.

Building Houses

Many people take part in building houses. An *architect* designs the house and draws it to scale. On his plan 2 cm may represent a metre, so the scale will be 1 to 50 (1:50). He may make detailed drawings of the building to help the workmen later on.

A *surveyor* works with the architect. He measures the land and marks out the points where the house is to be built. The surveyor uses a *theodolite*, which is a small telescope on a tripod for measuring angles. He also has an instrument for measuring levels as well as a spirit-level, plumbline and a steel tape for setting out distances.

Surveyors use the theodolite (left) to measure angles. The plane table (right) is used to map details of the land.

The *contractor* uses the architect's plans to erect the building, and brings in workmen as they are required. The foundations have to be dug to careful measurements because these, and the walls, have to support the weight of the house and its

Building work looks haphazard, but everything that happens has to be planned in advance.

contents. *Bricklayers* finish the walls, and *carpenters* put in the wooden beams to support the roof. They also put in the staircase, doors and windows.

Electricians put in the wiring, and *plasterers* finish off the wall surfaces. *Engineers* put in the gas supply, and *plumbers* install the water and waste pipes as well as the bathroom and kitchen fixtures. *Painters* decorate the ceilings, walls and woodwork. Perhaps a *gardener* is called in to lay a lawn or set out flower borders.

All these people use machines and tools. Cranes pick up heavy loads. Dumpers level the ground and move earth. Bricklayers use fork-lift trucks. There are wheelbarrows and many other kinds of tools. All these machines and tools are mechanisms that illustrate force.

Force

The most important force is *gravity* which causes a ball to fall to earth after being thrown into the air. Force pushes and pulls. It starts, stops or changes motion. Pulleys, wheels and springs all use force, and mathematics helps to measure it. The force needed to move heavy loads decreases when *wheels* are used. A wheelbarrow is easier to pull up a plane

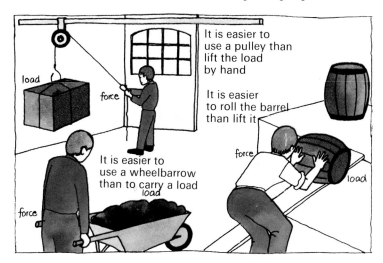

load

force

It is easier to use a pulley than lift the load by hand

It is easier to roll the barrel than lift it

It is easier to use a wheelbarrow than to carry a load

load

force

force

load

which slopes. The mathematicians who built the Pyramids and Stonehenge used the inclined plane to lift heavy stones. A builder uses a single pulley to haul a heavy bucket from the ground to the roof. The huge cranes used on building sites use a system of pulleys, levers and balances to lift steel girders. Mathematics is applied to make work easier.

Decorating and Furnishing

When the house is finished the householders may decorate it. They will want to know how much wallpaper they need and how much paint to buy.

WALLS Height from skirting		Measurement round walls, including doors and windows						
metres	feet	m 9.1 ft. 30	11.6 38	14.0 46	16.5 54	18.9 62	21.3 70	23.9 78
2.15-2.30	7-7½	4	5	6	7	8	9	10
2.30-2.45	7½-8	5	6	7	8	9	10	11
2.45-2.60	8-8½	5	6	7	9	10	11	12
2.60-2.75	8½-9	5	6	7	9	10	11	12
2.75-2.90	9-9½	6	7	8	9	10	12	13
2.90-3.05	9½-10	6	7	8	10	11	12	14
3.05-3.20	10-10½	6	8	9	10	12	13	15
CEILINGS		2	2	3	4	5	6	7

They will have to measure the floors before covering them with carpet or other materials. They will measure the windows to see how long and wide the curtains will have to be. Some people spend time, when they are furnishing the house, on choosing the correct colours, patterns and shapes. This is mathematics in action. If fitted bookcases are required, they will need more measuring.

Machines

Have you ever counted the number of domestic machines in your home? Some, like bottle-openers, whisks and can-openers, are operated by hand, but many of the machines are powered by electricity. These may be the cooker, refrigerator, freezer, dishwasher, washing machine, central heating boiler, food mixer, coffee grinder, radio, television and percolator. The central heating, music centre and washing machine may be operated by electronics. The computer, if you have one, will most certainly be electronically con-

trolled. Many clocks are battery-operated but some have clockwork and a pendulum. All these domestic machines owe their existence to the application of science and maths.

Meters and Measurers

At home, as well as the machines, there are *meters* and *dials* which register what is happening. The *thermostat* regulates the heat in the house. The *thermometer* registers the temperature. The *barometer* records the pressure of the atmosphere and gives an idea as to what the day's weather is to

The table above shows how many rolls of wallpaper are needed for various-sized rooms. Each roll is 10 m (11 yd.) long and 530 mm (21 in.) wide.

be. The dials on the cooker regulate the heat of the oven and the rings, while gas, electricity and water meters record how many units have been used.

The *scales* in the kitchen weigh out the amounts for cooking and baking. Can you think of any more measurers and meters?

There are lots of meters and measurers on electronic equipment such as the hi-fi unit left and the music centre below.

Introducing Sets

One of the ideas in Modern Maths is about *sets*. The study of sets began about a hundred years ago and has been widely used during this century.

George Boole (1815–64) wrote *The Laws of Thought* in 1854. The first ideas on sets came from his work, and his algebra has been used in computer design.

Georg Cantor (1854–1918) was a German who discovered the mathematics of sets at the end of the last century. He tried to answer some questions which had been puzzling mathematicians for centuries. *How many whole numbers are there?* was one of the problems. Cantor used sets to solve them, but his ideas were ignored at first. About 50 years ago mathematicians accepted his work, which is now used to solve problems and to program computers.

Rev. John Venn (1834–1923) was a mathematics scholar at Cambridge. Later he became interested in logic. To represent his ideas he used drawings which gave their name to Venn diagrams, although the great Swiss mathematician Leonhard Euler had used the same drawings years before.

Why Sets are Important

If we study a subject we should know something about the ideas on which it is built. Ideas about sets help the understanding of how arithmetic, algebra and geometry are linked. There can be sets of numbers, shapes and ideas.

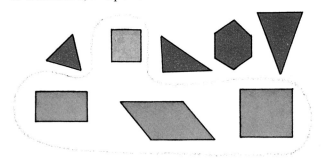

Studying sets shows new ways of sorting and leads to the understanding of how things are related. Studying sets helps in clear thinking about mathematics. It also provides a language so that ideas can be shared with others. The study helps to solve problems and puzzles. It helps in describing geometrical figures and in drawing graphs. Best of all, it provides great pleasure to anyone exploring this mathematical idea.

The idea of sets of things is not new. Sets were first thought of a hundred years ago by the Irish mathematician George Boole (above).

What is a Set?

A set is a *collection* of things. Children play with train *sets* and collect *sets* of stamps. Sometimes we use special words to describe sets: we talk about a *fleet* of ships, a *swarm* of bees or a *pride* of lions. They are all sets. A set is a collection of things which are alike in some way:

> Sparrows, robins and hawks belong to the set of birds.
> A hammer, chisel and pliers belong to the set of tools.
> Knives, forks and spoons belong to the set of cutlery.

(a) What six things are likely to belong to a set of furniture?

The Members (Elements) of a Set

All the things which belong to a set are known as the *members* (or *elements*) of that set. Shoes, slippers, boots are elements of the set of footwear. a, e, i, o, u are elements of the set of vowels. Farm animals make up a set.

(b) Name the sets of which *you* are an element.

Set Notation: Braces

Special symbols are used to save time when elements of a set are put in a list. Curly brackets or braces like this { } are used. *The set of encyclopedias is* written {encyclopedias}. *The set of consonants* is written {consonants}. {Outdoor games} means *the set of outdoor games.* One of two things go inside the braces: *either* a description of the set *or* the elements of the set.

Example: {The trees in our park}
or {Oak, beech, birch, sycamore}

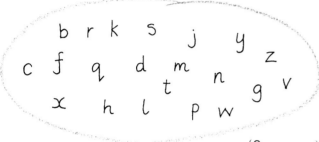

{Consonants}

(c) Use the notation to describe the set of domestic animals.

Set Notation: Element

The symbol for *is an element of* is ε. The symbol for *is not an element of* is ∉. The symbol ε is the Greek letter e called *epsilon.*

Examples: Dog ε {animals} and cup ε {crockery}
Cat ∉ {crockery} and plate ∉ {animals}

Cup ε {crockery}

Soup ∉ {breakfast cereals}

(d) Write, in set notation, a statement about elements which belong to {square numbers}.

Describing a Set

Sometimes it is easier to describe a set than to list its elements, for example, it is shorter to write {months} than {January February, March, April, May, June, July, August, September, October, November, December}.

Sometimes it is easier to list the elements than to describe the set, for example, {2, 4, 6, 8, 10} is shorter than {the even numbers between 1 and 11}.

A capital letter can be used to represent a set. If

Q = {animals}, every time we wanted to refer to the set of animals we could write Q. As tiger ε {animals} we can write tiger εQ. Often the capital letter is connected with the set it represents. For example:

(i) O may be used to represent {odd numbers}, so

O = {odd numbers} and 3 ε O

(ii) S = {square numbers} and 9 ε S

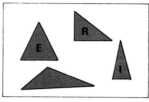

T = Triangles   IεT

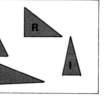

E = Even numbers   5∉E

(e) Write this in set notation: Five is an element of the set of natural numbers (represented by N).

The Size of Sets

Some sets have an infinite number of elements. Some have many elements, some have one element and some have no elements at all.

A set with no elements is a *null* or *empty* set. There are no elements in the set (T) of boys who are 4 metres tall or the set (L) of girls with two left legs. T = {} and L = {} or T = ∅ and L = ∅. The empty set is like zero in the number system and is often shown as a zero with a line through it. This symbol ∅ is the Greek letter *phi.*

There is no end to the number of elements in an *infinite* set. For example, W = {whole numbers} and W = {0, 1, 2, 3, 4, ...}. The elements go on to infinity, so only a few elements have been written in the braces followed by three dots.

Finite sets have a definite number of elements. The set of natural numbers greater than 5 and less than 11 can be represented by A and reads A = {6, 7, 8, 9, 10}. It would be very boring to have to list all the elements in a big set. If the elements follow a pattern, dots may be used to show that some have been omitted. The set of natural numbers less than 500 can be shown as:

N = {1, 2, 3, 4, 5, ... 499}

The number of elements in a set is called the number of the set. The number of this set is 6:

A = {1, 3, 5, 7, 9, 11}

(f) Is this set empty, finite or infinite:
{Whole odd numbers divisible by 2} ?

Universal Set and Subsets

In the world there are many books which make up

the main set of books. Included in this *universal* set are spelling books, reading books, maths books, among others. The universal set is represented by the symbol ∪. Sets which belong to the universal set are subsets. Square numbers and triangular numbers are *subsets* of the universal set of numbers.

The symbol for *is a subset of* (belongs to) is ⊂. If the universal set is the set of whole numbers less than 10, and the subset A has the elements 1, 2, 3 and 4, then A is a subset of ∪:

∪ = {whole numbers less than 10}
A = {1, 2, 3, 4}
A ⊂ ∪

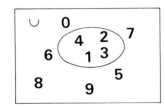

(g) What are the subsets of these universal sets:
   (i) quadrilaterals
   (ii) polygons
   (iii) regular polyhedra?

Venn Diagrams

The links between sets and subsets can be shown in diagrams.

Example 1: ∪ = {children}
       G = {girls}
       B = {boys}

The rectangle contains a circle to represent the girls and a separate circle to represent the boys. A girl cannot be in the same subset as a boy.

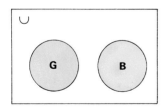

Example 2: ∪ = {children}
       H = {children over 1½ metres tall}
       W = {children who weigh more than 40 kilograms}

(h) This time the circles overlap or *intersect*. What do you know about the children in this intersection?

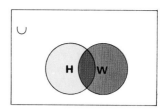

Example 3: ∪ = {animals}
       D = {dogs}
       A = {Alsation dogs}

(i) Can you write this in set notation?

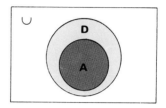

Example 4: ∪ = {children in the school}
       E = {eleven-year-olds in the school}
       M = {children who play a musical instrument}.
       G = {children who like games}

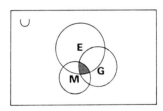

(j) Describe the children represented by the shaded area.

Draw Venn diagrams to solve these problems.
(k) Which numbers below 10 are multiples of both 2 and 3?
(l) Are parallelograms subsets of quadrilaterals?
(m) In a class of 28, 15 passed in Biology, 8 passed in French and 6 passed in both. How many (i) failed in both subjects (ii) passed in Biology *only?* (iii) passed *only* in French?

This is only an *introduction* to sets and there is much more to the subject. Why not find out more about this important and fascinating topic for yourself?
Answers on page 136.

Maths Around

The threads of mathematics run through the world around us. There are sets of things and people to be counted and measured. To do this, numbers and units of measurement are used. There are shapes and sizes everywhere, and patterns which link the branches of mathematics. Mathematics has been called the Queen of Knowledge. She is to be seen in Nature and Art, in Music and Science. Mathematics makes possible the ideas of place in Geography and of time in History. She points the way along the road of learning.

From the world around we take many of our mathematical ideas. There are sets of buildings, animals, vehicles and many other things. These sets lead on to countings and operations with the numbers. Numbers too are all around. They are on cars, road signs and houses. Shops open up a world of money and measurement. Packets of food illustrate volume, shapes and sizes. The fruit and vegetables in greengrocers' windows is arranged in pleasing numerical patterns.

There are shapes in abundance; solid shapes and plane shapes which derive from them. Buildings give us shapes of roofs, windows, doors and bricks. Pavements and shopping precincts show examples of tessellations. Telephone boxes, post boxes and clocks have interesting shapes.

Mathematics and Art

Artists use mathematical ideas in the way they *compose* their pictures. Many artists arrange their figures in geometrical shapes to direct attention to the main point in their work. On the other hand, Piet Mondrian's *Composition with Grey, Red,*

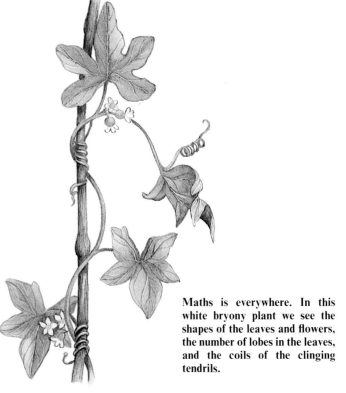

Maths is everywhere. In this white bryony plant we see the shapes of the leaves and flowers, the number of lobes in the leaves, and the coils of the clinging tendrils.

Yellow and Blue (right) is a mathematical composition to be enjoyed for its own sake.

Although artists paint on a flat surface they have to make their pictures look as if they have depth and distance. The Egyptian painters of 5000 years ago were unable to do this. Their wall paintings show stiff figures with heads and feet facing sideways, while their bodies face the front. Important people were painted larger than the others no matter where they were in the picture.

In the ancient Egyptian painting below, a man is making food offerings. The food is drawn without perspective so that each item can be seen clearly. The man himself is in the conventional pose – chest full-face, head, arms and legs profile.

106

Left: Piet Mondrian's *Composition with Grey, Red, Yellow and Blue* was painted in 1920. The colours are set in a grid of black lines. Fra Angelico's *Annunciation* (below) is an early Italian use of perspective. This famous painting is in the Monastery of S. Marco, Florence.

This idea of drawing objects as they appear to the eye from a distance is called *perspective*. It is based on mathematical rules first used by Italian artists 600 years ago.

Perspective uses two ideas. One is that objects appear to get smaller the farther they are away. The other is that parallel lines meet at a vanishing point on the horizon or at eye level.

Perspective makes distant objects look smaller, and parallel lines meet at a vanishing point.

The study of perspective led to a new branch of mathematics founded by a Frenchman called Desargues nearly 300 years ago. It is called *projective geometry* and is about figures that are changed by transforming their points from one shape to another.

The figure $A_1 F_1 D_1 C_1$ is the same shape as AFDC, but larger.

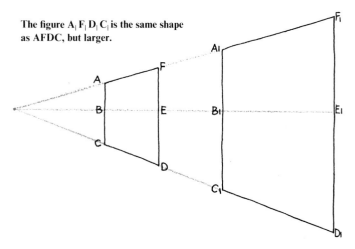

This is a kind of enlargement which is common to mathematics and art. It is a transformation which makes a geometrical figure larger or smaller. This can also be done by using squared paper or by a pantograph (below right).

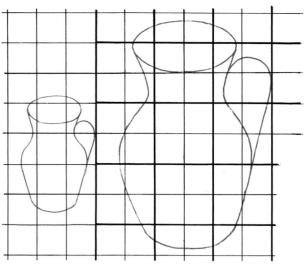

Mathematics and Nature

Mathematicians study the wonderful shapes found in nature. Some crystals take the 4-sided form of tetrahedra, salt crystals are cubes and diamond crystals have 8 faces. Skeletons of tiny animals which lived in the sea millions of years ago are almost perfect 12- and 20-sided polyhedra.

No two snow crystals are exactly alike, but they are all six-sided figures.

The hexagon is a popular shape in nature. The snowflake is a hexagonal crystal of water. A bee's honeycomb is made up of hexagons which tessellate to make roomy and strong cells.

Nature gives us many examples of shapes and curves. The Sun, Moon and stars are almost *spheres*, and the planets move in graceful elliptical curves. Sea creatures have shells that are cone-shaped and perfect spirals. *Composite* flowers like the daisy and dandelion have groups of flowers growing together in a head. One of the members of this family, the sunflower, has on its head a pattern made up of circles and spirals.

Another spiral occurs in new leaves growing from the stem of a plant. As it climbs, the spiral turns a fraction of a complete rotation. This fraction is one made from the Fibonacci series: $\frac{1}{2}$, $\frac{2}{3}$, $\frac{3}{5}$, $\frac{5}{8}$, $\frac{8}{13}$ ...

The sunflower head is made up of a wonderful pattern of circles and spirals.

Mathematics and Music

Sounds in music have *high* and *low* pitch. Musical sounds, or tones, are made by vibrations. *Slow* vibrations produce low tones and *rapid* ones produce high tones. This *number* of vibrations per second is known as the *frequency*.

Some tones are *long* and others are *short*. This is known as the *duration* of the tones. *Intensity* is the name given to the tones' loudness or softness.

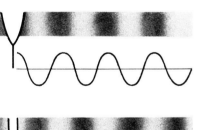

If a tuning fork is struck, it vibrates in the air, making sound.

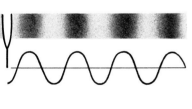

If it is struck gently, the sound is soft.

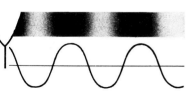

If it is struck harder, the sound is louder.

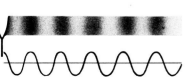

If a smaller tuning fork is struck, the prongs vibrate more rapidly, making a higher sound.

A *scale* is a number of tones put together in a certain way. On a piano keyboard the *distance* between keys, black or white, is always a *half* step. These are called sharps or flats, depending on whether the half steps are above or below the white keys. An *octave*, which means eight, is the interval between two tones of the same name.

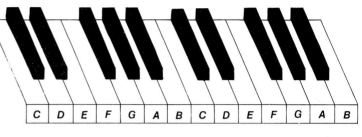

Part of a piano keyboard. Doubling the frequency (number of hertz) of a note increases its pitch by the musical "distance" called an octave.

You will have noticed the number of mathematical words used in music. Pythagoras and his followers made many discoveries in music. They saw music's partnership with mathematics. Pythagoras found out that when a vibrating string is halved in length it sounds an octave higher.

Mathematics Around Us

Mathematics is a tool which most people use every day. Families use it to shop, compare prices and work out what are the best buys. They use it to run the home, to pay bills and to weigh and measure.

Commerce deals with what we buy and sell. Computers play a big part in trading and selling. Electronic eyes in supermarkets list and add the items. At the same time information is passed on to the store's central computer which keeps records of what has been sold and what must be re-ordered.

In *industry*, mathematics helps engineers design new machines and methods of work. Skilled craftsmen use their ideas to measure and calculate as they use the machines. The transport industry is vast. Airlines span the globe and need mathematics to direct aircraft and passengers. Road and rail travel depend on precise calculations to arrange timetables and traffic systems.

Scientists experiment to find out facts in their work. Their equations and discoveries lead to new ideas and inventions. Research in astronomy, medicine, physics, chemistry and engineering widen the field of knowledge to improve life for ordinary people.

Thales and the Trigon

Here is a quiz. Which of these statements is correct about the above title?

(A) It is a story about Outer Space.

(B) It is an account of a fight with a wild beast.

(C) It tells you how the height of the Great Pyramid was measured.

Clue: A poly*gon* is a figure with many angles and *tri* is connected with three. If you chose (C) you were right. *Trigon* is a figure with 3 angles – a triangle. It is the first half of the word *trigonometry* which means the measurement of triangles. Trigonometry deals with the sides and angles of triangles and how they are related. This branch of mathematics is used to measure things which are out of reach like distances to the stars, heights of cliffs and tall buildings, mountains and rocky coasts. *Triangles* can be of different shapes and sizes but some things are true of *all* triangles. They all have 3 sides and their angles all add up to 180°. This can be proved in two ways:

1. Cut out a triangle from a piece of paper. Tear off the three angles and rearrange them so that the sides, angles and corners are together. They make a straight angle of 180°.

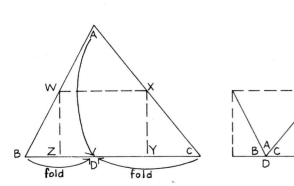

2. Cut out a triangle ABC. Inside it draw the rectangle WXYZ. Fold the angles A, B and C to meet at D. They make a straight angle of 180°.

This fact allows people to find the size of the third angle of a triangle when the other two are known. In the diagram, angle A $= 180° - (30° + 70°) = 180° - 100° = 80°$. Surveyors standing

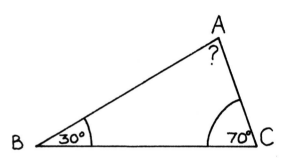

apart at the foot of a mountain can form a triangle with its peak. They can measure the angles to the summit and so calculate the third angle and the distance to the peak.

110

Astronomers use this method to find the distance from Earth to the planets.

Pythagoras showed that, if the lengths of two sides of a right-angled triangle are known, the length of the third side can be calculated.

In the triangle ABC:

$AC^2 = 3^2 + 4^2 = 9 + 16 = 25$, so $AC = 5\,cm$
$AB^2 = 25 - 16 = 9$, so $AB = 3\,cm$
$BC^2 = 25 - 9 = 16$, so $BC = 4\,cm$

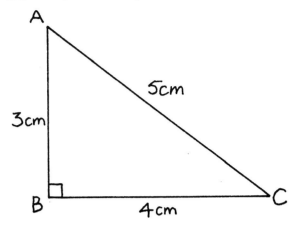

We calculate AC, AB and BC by finding the square root ($\sqrt{\ }$) of 25, 9, and 16.

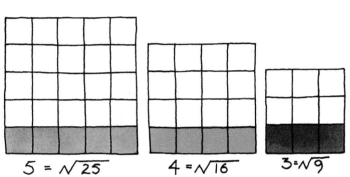

$5 = \sqrt{25}$ $4 = \sqrt{16}$ $3 = \sqrt{9}$

Theodolites

To measure angles, astronomers used an astrolabe, which is like a surveyor's *theodolite*. You can make an astrolabe so that you can measure angles yourself (right).

(a) Draw circles 18 cm and 12 cm in diameter on card.
(b) Divide the larger circle into 360 degrees. (How will you do this?)
(c) Cut out a strip of card 20 cm long and 2 cm wide. Fold the pointed ends and stick the strip to the smaller circle.
(d) Use a pronged paper fastener to fix the larger circle under the smaller one.
(e) To find the angle, line up the pointer on the two positions and read it off the scale.

Triangulation

Surveyors use triangles to draw plans and also to find the area of irregular shapes. A triangle ABC is pegged out. A fourth point (D) is chosen so that a second triangle ACD can be surveyed. All measurements can be calculated when a line and 2 angles of a triangle are known.

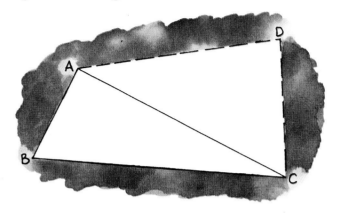

Scale Drawings

Scale drawings can be made to find heights and distances which are out of reach. AC represents the foothills of a mountain being surveyed so that a railway can be built (page 112).

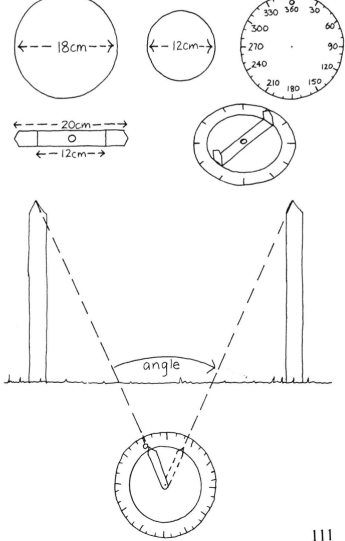

From B to A is 600 m and from B to C is 1 km. The surveyor uses his theodolite to calculate angle ABC (120°). From his scale drawing he finds that AC is 12 cm long which represents 1.2 km.

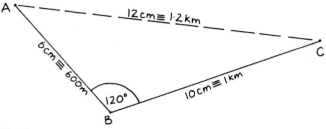

Ratio

In mathematics two things can be compared by division. A plot of land is 50 m long by 100 m – the width is half of the length. Two bags contain 3 apples and 12 apples – the first has $\frac{1}{4}$ of the second. When two things are compared by division, it is called *ratio*. The ratio of the length and width of the land is $\frac{50}{100}$ or $\frac{1}{2}$. The ratio of the apples is $\frac{3}{12}$ or $\frac{1}{4}$.

The ratios are written $\frac{1}{2}$ or 1 to 2 or 1:2; $\frac{1}{4}$ is 1 to 4 or 1:4. The ratio of lines measuring 9 cm and 3 cm is 3 to 1 or 3:1.

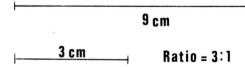

Ratios are used to compare sides of triangles.

Similar Triangles

These pictures are of the same dog, but the second has been *enlarged*. The pictures are different in size but similar in *shape*.

Squares and circles vary in *size* but are similar in *shape*. Changing their size makes no difference to their shape.

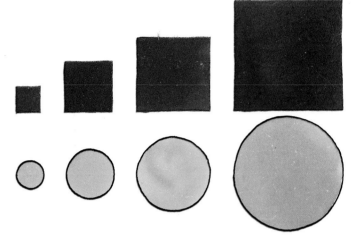

Other shapes are similar, but triangles are not *always* similar. Some are isosceles, some equilateral and some have angles of different sizes. Those which have the same shape are called *similar triangles*. These have angles which are equal to each other. The *ratio* of their *corresponding* sides is also the same. In the diagram the angles are equal – A = D, B = E, and C = F. The corresponding sides are AB and DE, BC and EF, AC and DF. These corresponding sides have equal ratios:

$$\frac{AB}{DE} = \frac{2}{4} = \frac{1}{2}; \ \frac{BC}{EF} = \frac{3}{6} = \frac{1}{2}; \ \frac{AC}{DF} = \frac{4}{8} = \frac{1}{2}$$

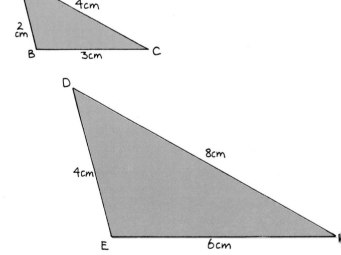

Shadow Reckoning

Shadow reckoning is a way of measuring heights by using the shadow made by the Sun. To estimate the height of the chimney:

1. A stick (AB) of height 2 m is placed upright.
2. The stick's shadow (BC) is 6 m and the length of the chimney's shadow (FG) is 48 m.
3. The height (EF) of the chimney is calculated by similar triangles. Triangles ABC and DEF are similar in shape.

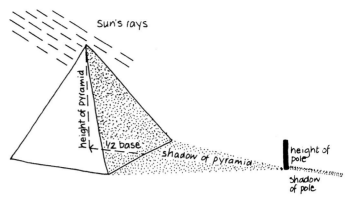

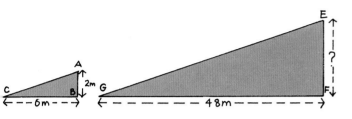

$$\frac{EF}{FG} = \frac{AB}{BC} \quad \frac{EF}{48} = \frac{2}{6} \quad EF = \frac{2 \times 48}{6} \quad EF = 16\,m$$

The chimney is 16 metres high.

Thales

Thales (pronounced THAY-LEEZ) was a Greek born in 640 B.C. in Miletus, one of the largest cities of ancient Greece. He travelled in Egypt where he became interested in geometry. He later founded the first school of mathematics and was the teacher of Pythagoras. He is known as the Father of Geometry and used his skill to foretell an eclipse of the Sun. Thales calculated the height of the Great Pyramid at Cheops.

To do this he used his knowedge of *similar triangles* and *shadow reckoning*, which he may have learned from the Egyptians.

The pyramid of height H has a square base, so the distance from its centre is half the base ($\frac{1}{2}$b). He measured the shadow of the pyramid (s), the shadow of the pole (p) and the height of the pole (h). Thales made an equation by comparing the ratio of the sides of the two similar triangles:

$$\frac{H}{\frac{1}{2}b + s} = \frac{h}{p} \quad \text{so} \quad H = \frac{h(\frac{1}{2}b + s)}{p}$$

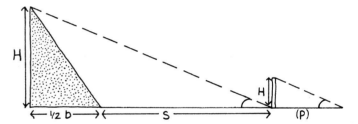

As he knew the lengths of h, b, s and p Thales was able to calculate the height of the pyramid (137 m or 450 ft.) He also used this method to work out the distance of ships from the coast.

This photograph of Egypt's best-known pyramids was taken from the river Nile. The Great Pyramid, measured by Thales, is on the left.

Moebius and his Merry Band

Once upon a time there was a Caliph who lived in Baghdad. Like all caliphs he had a beautiful daughter. All the Eastern princes wanted to marry her, but the Caliph was a bit choosy. He wanted a son-in-law who was a mathematician and good at solving problems. So he set the princes a task and promised that, whoever solved the problem, would be allowed to visit the palace.

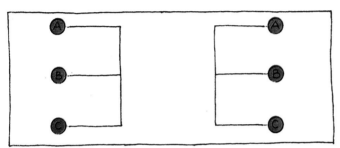

The problem was to join similar letters in the diagram to each other by drawing lines – A to A, B to B and C to C. The lines must not cross each other or any other lines. Can you solve the problem and would *you* have been able to visit the Caliph's palace?

August Ferdinand Moebius (of Möbius) was a famous German mathematician who lived from 1790 to 1868. He was a pupil of *Gauss*, who was one of the greatest mathematicians who ever lived. In 1858 Moebius discovered something which fascinated mathematicians and helped to start a new branch of geometry.

Some Experiments

You can do for yourself these experiments which Moebius did all those years ago. You will need a pair of scissors, some paste (unless you use gummed paper of sticky tape), 5 strips of paper, or sticky tape, 30 cm long and 3 cm wide (or about 12 in. by 1 in.).

All good mathematicians keep a record of their results. If you want to do the same, make a copy of this table and complete it as you do each experiment.

Expt. No.	(A) BEFORE CUTTING		Where the strip was cut	(B) WHAT HAPPENED AFTER CUTTING
	Number of half twists	Number of edges and surfaces		
1st	0		half	
2nd	1		half	
3rd	1		third	
4th	2		half	
5th	2		third	

Before you start, think about this. Everybody knows that a piece of paper has two surfaces, one on the front and one on the back. Everybody also knows that a piece of paper has a number of edges. But supposing everybody is wrong ...

1st Experiment
1. Take a strip and label the angles A, B, C, D.
2. Draw a red line along the strip on both sides.
3. Stick A on the back of D and B on the back of C.
4. Complete the table at (A). How many edges and surfaces does the strip have?
5. Cut along the red line.
6. Complete the table at (B).

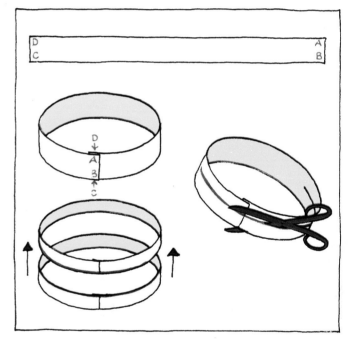

2nd Experiment
1. Repeat the 1st experiment, but this time give the strip a *half-twist* before sticking *A on C and B on D*.
2. Draw a red line on the surface of the strip half-way between the edges. What do you notice?
3. Make a X anywhere on the edge of the strip. Run your finger round the edge until it returns to the X. What do you notice? Complete (A).
4. Cut along the red line.
5. Complete part (B) of the table.

What you, and Moebius, discovered was that it is possible to make a strip with ONE *surface and* ONE

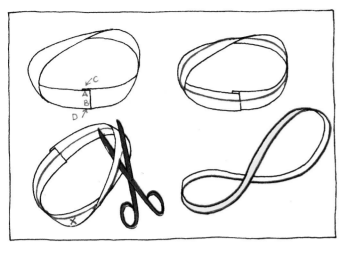

edge. This plaything for mathematicians is called the Moebius strip or band. Perhaps some day someone will train a flea to walk from any point on the strip to any other point without crossing an edge!

Now have some more fun with the rest of these strange twists and cuts.

3rd Experiment

1. Repeat the first instruction of the 2nd experiment. Complete (A).
2. Draw a red line on the surface of the strip but this time *one third* of the way from one edge. Continue drawing the line until it meets itself.
3. Cut along the line *carefully*.
4. Complete the table at (B).

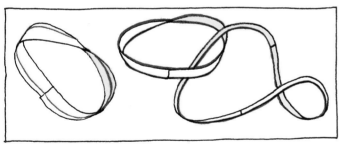

4th Experiment

1. Make *two* half twists in the strip and stick. Complete (A).
2. Draw a red line *half way* from the edge and cut along it.
3. Complete the table at (B).

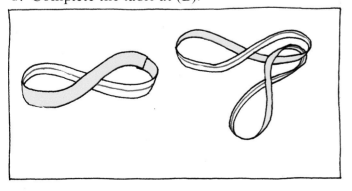

5th Experiment

1. Repeat instruction No. 1 of the last experiment.
2. Draw a red line *one third* of the way from one edge and cut along it.
3. Complete the table.

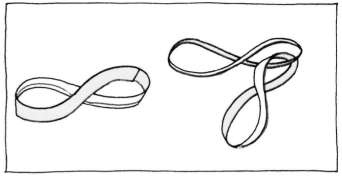

Compare your results with these:

| Expt. No. | (A) BEFORE CUTTING | | Where the strip was cut | (B) WHAT HAPPENED AFTER CUTTING |
	Number of half twists	Number of edges and surfaces		
1st	0	2	half	2 loops
2nd	1	1	half	1 loop, 2 twists
3rd	1	1	third	2 interlocking loops
4th	2	2	half	2 interlocking loops
5th	2	2	third	2 interlocking loops

The Caliph's Daughter

The Caliph's daughter has not been forgotten. The princes found the problem quite easy. Did you? Here are some solutions.

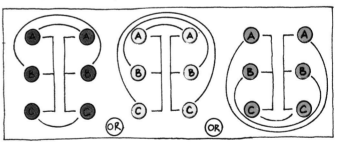

Unfortunately, the Caliph set the princes a rather more difficult problem and it is possible that his daughter never did marry. In this problem the diagram has been changed but the task is still the same – to join the letters which are similar without crossing lines. Put the problem on a Moebius strip and see what happens. Give the strip a half twist and stick A, B and C to A^1, B^1 and C^1. Draw lines all the way round the strip.

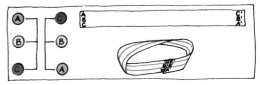

115

Euler and his Networks

Euler was a famous Swiss mathematician who was born at Basle in 1707. His full name was Léonard or Leonhard Euler (pronounced OILER). He was a very great scholar who studied astronomy, eastern languages, medicine, physics and religion. He studied so hard that he lost the use of his right eye when he was 28. Thirty years later he lost the sight of the other eye, but he carried on working until the day of his death in 1783.

At the beginning of this century a scientific society in Switzerland began to publish his works. Many years later about 50 large volumes had been printed, but the task was never completed. It has been said that Euler discovered more facts about mathematics than any other person. He studied many branches of the subject. Algebra, geometry, new work on numbers and applied mathematics were only a few of them. His work on friendly numbers has already been mentioned on page 65. He also gave his name to Euler's formula which connects the edges, faces and vertices of solids. One of the things for which he is best remembered is his founding of a new branch of mathematics called *topology*.

Topology is an interesting subject to learn about because it contains a lot of tricks and puzzles. It also asks unusual questions such as:

How many colours are needed on a map?

What does the inside of a football look like?

How can you take off a waistcoat without removing a jacket?

The subject does have a serious side as well. It is used to solve practical problems in transport and industry. It is part of advanced work in mathematics and is a great help in our space age.

Topology is rather like geometry except that it has no measurements. It has lines, points and figures and deals more with place and position than with size and shape. In this subject figures are allowed to change their sizes and shapes. Topology is interested in what changes and what stays the same when figures are stretched or bent. It is sometimes called *rubber-sheet geometry*.

Stretching and Bending

Try to find a piece of rubber such as a balloon or an old inner tube to do experiments A and B. These will show you how figures can be *distorted* in topology.

As the balloon goes down, the clown's face changes shape.

A 1. Draw a line AB on the sheet of rubber.

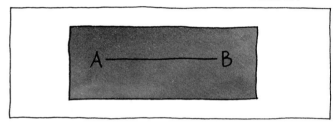

   2. With a friend bend it or stretch it but do not tear it.

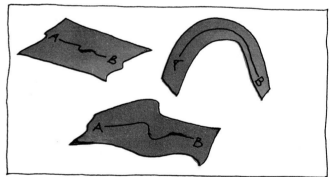

   3. Think about what has changed and what has stayed the same. You will have seen that AB does not remain a straight line. AB becomes longer and the path from A to B becomes crooked. Yet AB does not cross itself and still remains a path. In topology a path like AB is called *arc* AB even though it may be straight or curved.

B 1. Draw a figure, such as a circle, rectangle or triangle, on the sheet of rubber. Put a dot inside the figure.

116

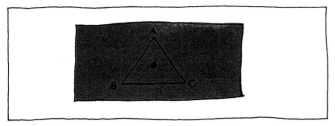

2. Now notice what happens when you bend and stretch the sheet. No matter how the sheet is distorted, the figure ABC still has an inside and an outside. The dot stays inside the figure and the order of the points A, B, C does not alter.

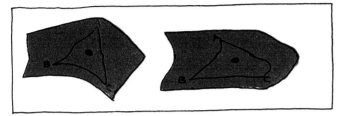

The Bridge Problem

Koenigsberg was once German but is now Russian. Through the city runs the River Pregel, which has two islands in the middle. The islands are joined to each other and to the river banks by seven bridges.

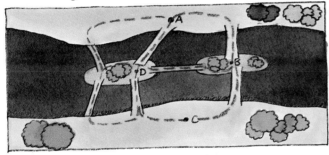

Two hundred years ago the people of Koenigsberg began to ask each other a question. They wondered if it was possible to take their Sunday walk in such a way that they would cross *each* bridge once only. Can you solve their problem?

A man who could, and did, was Léonard Euler. He was at that time serving at the court of the Russian Empress and learned about the problem of the seven bridges. He thought about it and drew a diagram to help him. Euler soon came up with the solution: it was *not* possible for the citzens of Koenigsberg to arrange their walk so that they could cross every bridge once.

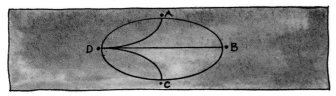

Euler's Network

When Euler drew his diagram of the seven bridges two things happened. He invented *networks* and founded topology. In his network, each arc represented a bridge and the points A, B, C and D were the *vertices*. So the arcs (bridges) could only be travelled *once* although the vertices could be passed through more than once. Euler counted the number of arcs to the vertices. He found that the number of arcs to vertices A, B, C and D were all odd numbers, so he called the vertices *odd*. Euler discovered that, as more than two vertices in the network were odd, it was not possible to cross the bridges in one journey. He also discovered other important laws for *traversing*, or crossing, networks. These laws are used when networks are drawn to represent roads between towns, railways connecting underground stations, shipping and air routes, and other links.

Networks

You can perhaps re-discover some of Euler's laws for yourself as you draw these networks.

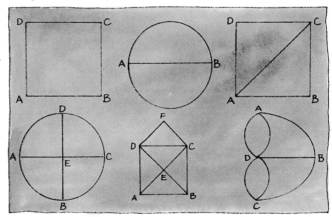

Copy this table and complete it. Remember that a vertex is *odd* if it has an odd number of arcs to it, and *even* if it has an even number of arcs to it. The end column is answered by asking yourself if you can draw the arcs only *once* and without lifting your pencil from the paper. What do you notice about (vi)?

Network	Number of ODD vertices	Number of EVEN vertices	If the network can be traced (yes or no)
(i) (ii) (iii) (iv) (v) (vi)			

117

Regions

A network divides a plane (flat) surface into pieces or *regions*. In the diagram (i) has one region because it is an *open* network, but (ii) has 2 regions and (iii) has 4 regions. This is because the *outside* region has to be included in a *closed* network.

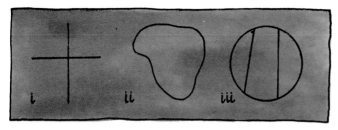

Examine the figures in the diagram below. Then write in the table the numbers of regions (or faces), vertices and arcs (or edges). Leave the last column blank for the moment.

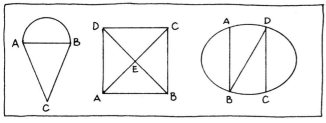

Network	Number of regions or faces (F)	Number of vertices (V)	Number of arcs or edges (E)	F + V − E = ?
(i)				
(ii)				
(iii)				

Do you remember Euler's discovery which connects the faces, edges and vertices of solids? It was $F + V - E = 2$. Now complete the last column of the table.

The Map Problem

This problem is about networks and regions. When maps are drawn, countries bordering each other must have different colours. How many different colours are needed to make a map? Up to now it has been possible to colour maps by using only *four* different colours. Yet no mathematician has been able to prove that four are enough for all maps. Here is a chance for *you* to become famous. However, in the meantime perhaps you can copy these imaginary maps so that bordering countries each have a different colour. The first is drawn for you.

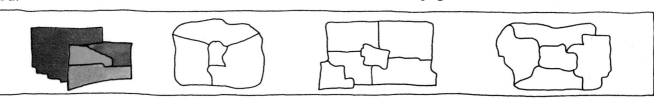

The Ring Puzzle

Connect three key rings as in the diagram.

What happens when you remove *one* ring?

All Tied Up

Tie a piece of string loosely round each of your wrists. Tie a second piece to the wrists of your friend so that you are looped together.

Can you separate yourselves without cutting the string, taking it off your wrists or untying the knots?

The Services Problem

These houses on a new estate have to be supplied with gas, water and electricity. The snag is that no pipes or wire must cross each other. Is it possible?

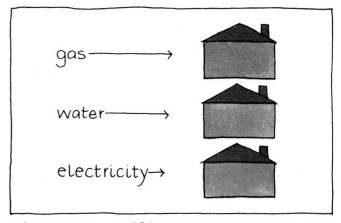

Answers on page 136.

118

Bears and Babies

Nicholas Alkemade, a 21-year-old flight sergeant, had an amazing escape on 23rd March, 1944. He jumped without a parachute from a burning bomber over Germany and fell about 5500 m (18 000 ft.). His fall was broken by a fir tree and he landed on a deep bank of snow. Mr. Alkemade lived to tell the story, but he was very lucky indeed. Yet a mouse could fall to the earth from a great height and survive quite easily. Why is this?

The harvest mouse is very small. It weighs between 4 and 10 grams ($2\frac{1}{2}$ and $5\frac{3}{4}$ ounces) and measures about 13.5 cm (5 ins.) from tip to tail. It has to spend most of its time eating because it must eat half its bodyweight every day. Yet humans can manage quite well by eating only one fiftieth of their weight daily. Why the difference?

Babies need to be wrapped up warmly during the first weeks of their lives. Like mice they would not live long in a cold climate. Yet polar bears actually enjoy splashing in icy rivers and eating cold fish, even though they wear fur coats. How do you account for that?

Small and Large Bodies
Obviously the difference has something to do with the size of little and large creatures. More particularly, it is about the *volume* and *surface area* of their bodies. It would be very difficult to measure the actual bodies of small and large animals in order to compare them. What is possible, however, is to measure some big and little solid objects. The task is to compare the surface area and volume of four cubes.

To Find the Surface Area of Cubes
1. Make a net of a cube whose edge is 1 cm long.

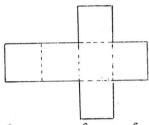

2. What is the area of one face in square centimetres (cm²)?
3. How many faces has the cube?
4. What is the area of *all* the faces?
5. Make a note of the surface area of a cube of edge 1 cm.
6. Make nets of cubes 2 cm, 3 cm and 4 cm long.
7. What is the surface area of these cubes?

To Find the Volume of the Cubes
1. Fold along the dotted lines of the nets.
2. Make the cube shapes. There is no need to stick them together.
3. What is the volume of the smallest cube in cubic centimetres (cm³)?
4. What are the volumes of the other cubes?

Make a table to show what you have found out. Do your answers agree with the information in this table?

Edge of cube cm	Surface area of cube cm²	Volume of cube cm³
1	6	1
2	24	8
3	54	27
4	96	64

Comparing the Area and Volume

Notice in the table how the surface areas and volumes grow at different rates. To compare this rate of growth we have to divide the surface area by the volume. This *ratio* is shown in the last column.

Edge of cube cm	Surface area of cube cm²	Volume of cube cm³	Ratio of units of area to units of volume	
1	6	1	$\frac{6}{1}$ or	6:1
2	24	8	$\frac{24}{8}$ or	3:1
3	54	27	$\frac{54}{27}$ or	2:1
4	96	64	$\frac{96}{64}$ or	1·5:1

Notice how the ratio of the units or area to the units of volume *decrease* from 6:1 to 1·5:1 in a very short time. Perhaps you can calculate the ratios for still larger cubes and see how the ratios continue to decrease. This ratio of the areas to the volumes of cubes can be plotted on a graph to show the decrease.

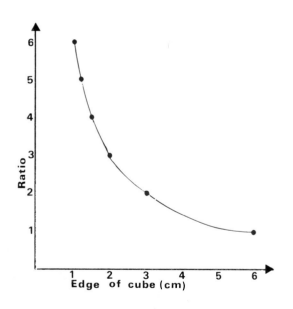

Areas and Volumes of Creatures

This decrease in the ratio of the units of surface areas and volumes is amazing. The cube with an edge 1 cm long has four times as much area to volume ratio as the cube of edge 4 cm long. This happens with living creatures as well as with cubes. It is of great importance because it means that small animals have more area of skin for each unit of volume than larger ones. Mice and other small animals therefore lose their body heat rapidly. Polar bears have a large volume to produce heat and a smaller surface to lose it and so can live quite happily in a cold climate. Babies lose heat from their bodies very quickly and must be kept warm.

A mouse which has to replace its heat fast really needs more food, for its size, than an elephant.

What about the mouse without a parachute? The mouse's body has more surface area, compared to its weight, than a human's. If a mouse fell, this surface area would act as a parachute and allow it to float to earth more slowly. People without parachutes would not have enough surface area to balance their weight. They would, therefore, fall faster. You will have noticed that, when doing free falls, parachutists spread their arms and legs when leaving the aircraft. This is to make more surface area until they are ready to pull the parachute cord.

How to Measure Your Skin Area

Hospitals estimate that the total skin area of a person's body is 100 times greater than the area of one side of the hand. To find your surface area:

1. Draw round your hand on a sheet of squared paper. This outline will show the front of your hand, with the fingers closed, to the wrist.
2. Put a tick inside the squares, or more than half squares, enclosed by the outline. Ignore the rest of the squares.
3. Count the number of squares with ticks inside.
4. This is the area of your hand in the square units you are using.
5. Multiply this area by 100 to find the total skin area of your body.

Example: Area of hand = 100 cm²
              Total skin area = 100 cm² × 100
                              = 10 000 cm² or 1 m²

The skin of an adult spread out flat covers about 2 m² (20 sq. ft.) and weighs 3 kg or about $6\frac{1}{2}$ lbs.

How to Measure Your Volume

Seven-tenths of our body is water, so our *density* is almost the same as that of water. As the weight of 1 litre of water is 1 kg, it is possible to find the volume of our bodies. (The weight of a gallon of water is 10 lbs.)

Example:

    Weight of body = 50 kg
    Volume of body = 50 litres, which takes
                     up 50 cubic decimetres
                   = 1000 cm³ × 50
                   = 50000 cm³

Find your weight on bathroom scales and calculate *your* volume.

The *ratio* will be the units of surface area divided by the units of volume.

Example: $\dfrac{10000}{50000} = \dfrac{1}{5}$ or 1:5

What is *your* ratio? How many cm² of skin have you for every litre of you? Are you bear or baby, man or mouse?

Sky divers plunging earthward spread their arms and legs to increase their surface area and give themselves more control.

Strong and Beautiful Shapes

Architects in ancient Greece were the people who directed the building work. Over the years, ways of building changed as better methods were discovered. The builders of Stonehenge erected massive pillars with heavy stones on top. Egyptians built their temples in the same way. Romans used semicircular *arches*. Eight hundred years ago a new Gothic style developed with pointed arches and tall, graceful buildings.

A section through a Gothic church, showing the arches and how the building was supported by buttresses.

In modern times, *rectangular* blocks are built on rock or piles driven into the earth. *Architecture* is the art of designing buildings. In their plans, architects try to follow two ideas. A building must be attractive and it must serve the purpose for which it is built. Of course, a building has to be *strong* so that it will not fall down in a storm.

Civil engineers design and build roads, harbours and bridges. These too must be attractive and serve their purpose. The history of bridges is interesting. The earliest ones must have been fallen logs across a stream. The first *girder* bridges were made of tree trunks. The length of a span from one support to another depended on how long and strong the trunks were. Later, steel girders made possible much longer bridges. They were strengthened by *struts* and were supported on stone piers.

The Romans discovered that *stone arches* could be used. These were fine for short bridges with a central pier but were too heavy to bridge wide stretches of river. In modern times, steel girders have made much longer arched bridges possible. The Sydney Harbour Bridge has the roadway slung underneath and not on top of the arch. The Forth Railway Bridge is a *cantilever type*. This has arms which come out in opposite directions to balance one side with the other. The road is hung below cables which are anchored into rock at each end. Architects and civil engineers depend on arches and triangles to make their creations strong.

The Golden Gate suspension bridge at the entrance to San Francisco bay. The two massive steel cables which support the bridge are nearly a metre in diameter. You can see many strong triangles in the picture.

Strong Arches

Some bridges of ancient Rome are still standing. They were built using an arch shape strong enough to bear the weight above. Wedge-shaped stones were put side by side to form a curve. The downward force of gravity made the sides of the arch spread out. This outward *thrust* had to be balanced by buttresses. These are heavy masses of stone which make the arch a safe and strong structure.

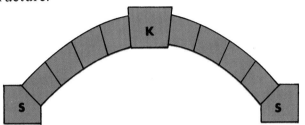

K is the keystone at the top of the arch. S are the stones that take the pressure. There are different kinds of arches. From left to right these are Semicircular (Roman), Horseshoe (Moorish), and Lancet (Medieval).

The Romans used arches for their city gates and triumphal monuments. The French Arc de Triomphe in Paris is an arch started by Napoleon in memory of his troops.

Arches can be semicircular, horseshoe or lancet (pointed). Some arches today are made of reinforced concrete to support bridges. They do not have arch stones but the idea is similar to the one used in the old arch bridges.

Rigid Triangles

When polygons are made of geometry strips they can easily be pushed out of shape, even when they are screwed tightly together. Squares become rhombuses and rectangles turn into parallelograms. Other regular polygons quickly lose their shape and could not possibly be used for constructions.

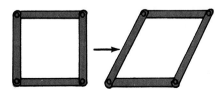

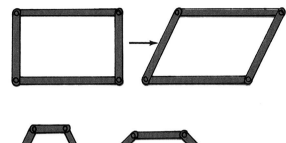

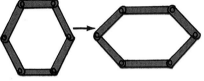

The triangle is the only shape that remains *rigid*. The other polygons have to be made rigid by using struts to change them into shapes made up of triangles.

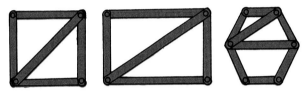

In this way, five-barred gates and lattice fencing make strong shapes. Builders and engineers use this *rigidity* to erect girders, bridges and electricity pylons.

If this five-barred gate had no diagonals it would fall apart. The triangles give it strength.

A Beautiful Shape

Architects do not only have to make buildings secure. They have to make them pleasing to the eye as well. Not all rectangles, for example, look right. Some appear too fat, while others seem too long and narrow. It has been agreed that there is one rectangle which has exactly the right proportions. Johannes Kepler, a famous astronomer and mathematician, described the rectangle as a jewel. Leonardo da Vinci, one of the greatest geniuses of all time, said that the rectangle had divine proportions. Last century it was renamed the *golden rectangle*.

Cutting Out a Golden Rectangle

1. Find a postcard, an index card 125 by 75 mm (5 in. by 3 in.), or a sheet of paper 33 cm by 20 cm (13 in. by 8 in.)
2. Fold one corner over to form a square.
3. Cut off the square.
4. Shapes (a) and (d) are almost the shapes of golden rectangles.

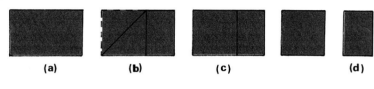

(a)　　(b)　　(c)　　(d)

The Golden Ratio

In the diagram, ABCD represents a golden rectangle.

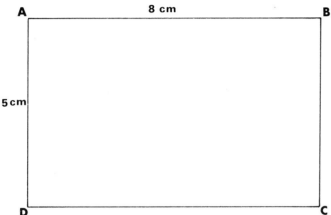

A　　　8 cm　　　B

5 cm

D　　　　　　　C

$AB = 8\,cm;\ AD = 5\,cm;\ \dfrac{AB}{AD} = \dfrac{8}{5} = 1\cdot6$

The ratio of AB to AD is 1·6:1

The sides of a golden rectangle are such that the smaller one, AD, is to the larger one, AB, as the larger one, AB, is to the sum of both AB and AD. AD:AB as AB:AB + AD.

$AB + AD = 13\,cm;\ \dfrac{AB + AD}{AB} = \dfrac{13}{8} = 1\cdot6$

(approximately)

This ratio is nearer 1·62 and is called the *golden ratio*.

Constructing a Golden Rectangle

The Greeks had a simple way of drawing a golden rectangle.

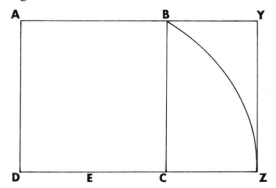

A　　　　B　　Y

D　　E　　C　　Z

1. Draw a square ABCD.
2. From the midpoint (E) of DC draw an arc from B to Z.
3. Complete the golden rectangle AYZD.
4. Measure AY and AB. What is the ratio?
5. Do you notice anything interesting about rectangle BYZC?

Making More Golden Rectangles

A golden rectangle can be made into a square and another golden rectangle. In the diagram the rectangle BYZC is also golden. This can be continued again and again. When one square is cut from a golden rectangle, another square can be cut from this to leave another golden rectangle, and so on.

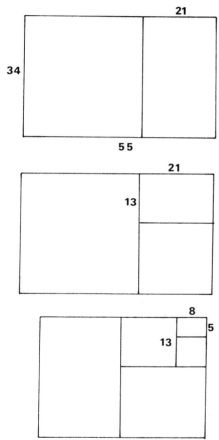

In the diagram the rectangles were 55 by 34, 34 by 21, 21 by 13, 13 by 8, 8 by 5, . . . Where have you seen these numbers before?

Do you remember Fibonacci fractions from page 66? The set of numbers was, 1, 1, 2, 3, 5, 8, 13, 21, 34, 55 . . .

The set of fractions was $\frac{1}{2}, \frac{2}{3}, \frac{3}{5}, \frac{5}{8}, \frac{8}{13}, \frac{13}{21}, \frac{21}{34}, \frac{34}{55}, \ldots$

When the ratios of sides are taken:

$\frac{1}{1} = 1, \frac{2}{1} = 2, \frac{3}{2} = 1\cdot5, \frac{5}{3} = 1\cdot66, \frac{8}{5} = 1\cdot6, \frac{13}{8} = 1\cdot625,$
$\frac{21}{13} = 1\cdot62, \frac{34}{21} = 1\cdot62, \frac{55}{34} = 1\cdot62, \ldots$

The ratios of the sides approach more and more to the golden ratio.

Fun Maths

Parties have changed greatly over the years. They have much more music and dancing in them these days. At one time people entertained themselves with pencil-and-paper games and brainteasers. Even now it is not unusual for families to show each other tricks and stunts.

Many problems are based on mathematics. On pages 38 and 40 there were puzzles with numbers. On these pages the tricks are mostly from other branches of mathematics such as algebra, geometry and topology. Although the games are meant to entertain, they will, at the same time, use some mathematical ideas. The notes on page 137 explain how the tricks are done and the reasoning behind them. Sometimes tricks are based on some false information, so be on the look-out for this.

The L-shaped Farm

Many problems are about rich people who die and leave something to their family with strange conditions in the will. In this one a farmer died and left his farm equally to his four sons. The snag was that the farm had an awkward shape. It was in three sections which could not be altered. How was the farm divided so that each son had a quarter?

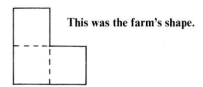

This was the farm's shape.

Twenty-one Cards

Count out 21 cards from a pack. Deal them out face upwards in three columns, beginning at the left hand side each time, until there are seven rows. Ask a friend to choose a card by *remembering* but not touching it. Then ask your friend to tell you which column it is in. Pick up the cards in order in *columns*, putting the column with the card in it between the other two columns. Put out the cards again in three columns of seven rows and again ask your friend to tell you what column the card is in. Again sandwich that column of cards between the other two columns. Repeat this a third time in the same way. After you have picked up the cards for the third time, turn them over so that the faces are not seen. You will be able to deal the cards one at a time in front of your friend and turn over the chosen card.

Find the Square

Draw a square of side 8 units on a piece of paper or card and then draw inside it 64 small squares. Now divide up the square into 2 triangles and 2 trapezia as shown.

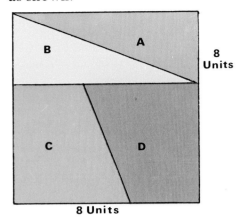

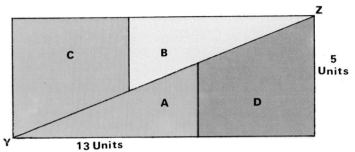

Cut out the four figures and re-arrange them to form a rectangle.

The area of the square = 8 × 8 = 64 square units.

The area of the rectangle = 13 × 5 = 65 square units

Where did the 65th square come from?

Dots on a Domino

Ask your friend to chose any domino from the pack. Give him or her the following instructions. (The one shown is an example.)

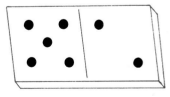

Multiply the large number by 5	5 × 5 = 25
Add 8	25 + 8 = 33
Multiply by 2	33 × 2 = 66
Add the smaller number on the domino	66 + 2 = 68
Ask your friend for that number	68
Subtract 16	68 − 16 = 52
The two numbers on the domino are	5 and 2

A Horse, a Horse ...

If you think that this is another story about a man who died and left a will, you are mistaken. It is about a *woman* who died and left a will. Lady Porter was a racehorse owner until she died. In her will she left 17 horses to her three daughters. To the eldest she left a half of the string, to the middle daughter a third and to the youngest one a ninth. Mr. McKane, the family solicitor, was worried for a moment. Then he had a bright idea. How did he solve the problem?

Codes and Ciphers

There are different ways of sending messages. Codes are all kinds of way of sending secrets and a word, letter or sign can stand for other words or sentences. A *cipher* has one symbol for every letter. For example, XZY can stand for CAB when the first letter of the alphabet represents the last letter. (A = Z, B = Y, C = X, etc.) Ciphers are very old. The Spartans wound a belt in a spiral around a stick, wrote a message along its length and unwound the belt. The message could only be read by someone who had a stick of the same size.

Here is a simple cipher using numerals. Can you solve it?

$$632 + 632 = 5271$$

Networks

Here are 12 vertices.

Can you connect them by 5 straight lines without lifting your pencil, to make an open network? (i)
Can you connect them by 5 straight lines, without lifting your pencil, making a closed network? You end on the first vertex, without crossing any vertex twice. The lines may cross. (ii)

A Cross Square

Draw a shape like this on a piece of card and cut it out. The problem is to make 4 straight cuts so as to divide the cross into 5 pieces which can be re-assembled to form a square.

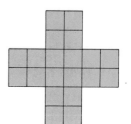

Where do you Live?

Have you ever written your school address out in full? It could be something like this:

Room 12, Loggerheads School, Wood Lane, Timber, Lumbershire, Lathland, Yewrope, Northern Hemisphere, Earth, The Universe.

It looks like a full addresss, but there is still something missing. It doesn't say where the pupil is in Room 12. Even a position such as *near the door* or *at the front* is not exact enough. The address has to be where two lines meet so that a position can be mapped exactly.

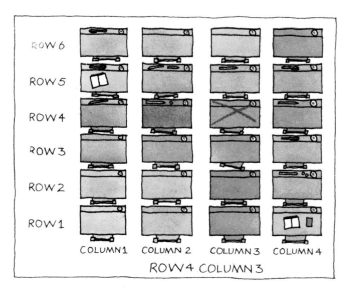

Theatre seats have a number in a row so that patrons can be shown quickly to their exact place. Modern cities are often built in blocks or roads so that it is possible to say exactly where a certain street and avenue meet.

A point on a map is fixed exactly where grid lines meet.

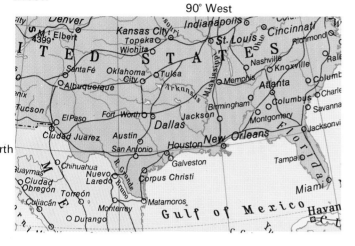

On this map we can place the town of New Orleans exactly by finding 30° North and 90° West.

The discovery of this way of describing an exact position was part of the work of a famous Frenchman. René Descartes (pronounced DAY-CART) was born in Touraine. In his youth he was a soldier in the armies of two noblemen and he travelled in many countries. He had money left to him by his family and by some people who were interested in his future. Because of this, he did not have to earn a living but was able to spend his life studying. From the age of 32 Descartes lived in the Netherlands and led a quiet life with his books. Queen Christina of Sweden heard of his work and invited him to her country. It was there that he died at the age of 54.

Descartes was a thinker and scientist who has been called the Father of Modern Mathematics.

Many people say that René Descartes was the father of modern philosophy.

He is famous for his invention which links geometry and algebra. Until the 1600s these two subjects had grown separately. Greek mathematicians had solved problems in geometry by drawing diagrams. Descartes went a step further and showed that equations in algebra, and diagrams in geometry, can be linked. In 1637 he published a book which started new thinking in mathematics.

Cartesian Geometry

Cartesian Geometry uses Descartes' name to describe this idea. He showed that lines can be drawn to represent equations, and equations can be written to describe lines. Descartes' work is of great practical use because it helps to solve problems. Scientists and engineers make up equations to describe curves when they are designing ships, aircraft and space satellites. What follows is a simplified explanation of some of Descartes' ideas.

Graphs are, of course, ways of showing information as a picture. A line graph has two arms called *axes* (AX-EES). The horizontal *axis* is called x and the vertical axis is y. These axes have arrows at the ends to show that they go on and on. Numbers are spaced along the axes, which meet at zero.

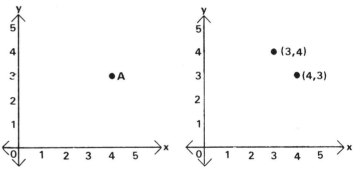

Point A has been placed on the graph. It is 4 places along the x axis and 3 places up the y axis. Point A is where 4 places along and 3 places up meet. This point is called an *address*. The address of point A is (4, 3).

Coordinates are distances from the two axes. (4, 3) are the coordinates of point A. The numbers (4, 3) are in a certain *order*. The 4 is first because it is along the x axis. The 3 is second because it is up the y axis. (4, 3) is an *ordered pair*. (4, 3) is different from (3, 4).

127

Graph of an Equation

An equation is like a balance. The values of the numbers on one side balance the values of the numbers on the other side. The equation $y = 2x$ means that the value of y is equal to twice the value of x. So, if x is 1, y will be 2. A table can be made to show the values of x and y.

When $x = 0$	1	2	3	4	5	6
then $y = 0$	2	4	6	8	10	12

These are the ordered pairs (0, 0), (1, 2), (2, 4), (3, 6), (4, 8), (5, 10), (6, 12).
The ordered pairs are plotted on a graph. It is part of the graph of $y = 2x$.

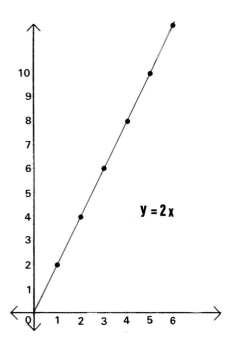

Descartes' discovery enabled mathematicians to draw equations as sets of ordered pairs.

Kinds of Graph

Lines which solve equations are sometimes straight and sometimes curved. This graph shows part of the line $y = x + 3$.

x	0	1	2	3	4	5
y	3	4	5	6	7	8

Each pair of numbers in the table are coordinates for points on the line. The coordinates are (0, 3), (1, 4), (2, 5), (3, 6), (4, 7), (5, 8). The equation $y = x + 3$ describes the set of ordered pairs. The *straight line* graph solves the equation.

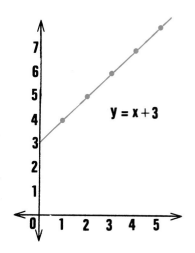

The next graph shows part of the line $y = x^2$.

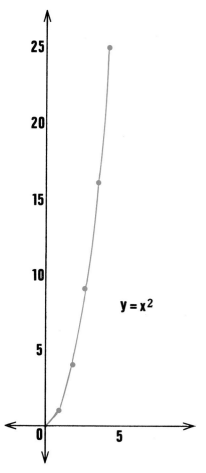

x	0	1	2	3	4	5
y	0	1	4	9	16	25

The coordinates are (0, 0), (1, 1), (2, 4), (3, 9) (4, 16), (5, 25). The equation $y = x^2$ describes the set of ordered pairs. This graph is a curved line which shows the link between the area of a square and one of its sides. From the graph it is possible to find the area of squares whose sides are up to 5 units long.

128

Calendar Curiosities

Julius Caesar divided the year into 12 months of 30 and 31 days, except for February, which had only 29 days. Every fourth year, February had 30 days. This calendar was used for 1500 years until Pope Gregory made it more accurate.

A year is the amount of time it takes for the Earth to make a complete revolution round the Sun. People have tried to measure this period of time perfectly because the calendar must fit the seasons. Julius Caesar's old calendar was a little bit out, so over the years the Easter celebrations in the Roman Church were moving away from the spring equinox. Pope Gregory XIII decided to put the matter right, so he ordered that the day after 4th October 1582 should become the 15th October. This Gregorian calendar, as it was called, also made sure the error would not occur again. It was arranged that century years should not be leap years unless they could be divided by 400.

At this time, England had broken away from the Roman Catholic Church and so refused to follow the Pope's edict. The Gregorian calendar was not adopted by the British Government until 1752. The British were still using the Julian calendar and were 11 days behind the rest of Europe. However, it was decreed that the day after 2nd September 1752 should be 14th September. This upset many people who thought that their lives had been shortened. "Give us our eleven days!" they cried.

The Gregorian Calendar

The Gregorian calendar is very accurate. The difference between its year and the Sun's year is about 25 seconds. This difference will increase by just over half a second every 100 years because the solar year is becoming shorter. In 4316, the Gregorian year will be one day in front of the Sun's year.

What Day Was It?

Do you know on what *day* you were born? Here is a way of finding out the day or any day on which famous events took place. This method deals with the days on any date from 15th September 1753 to the end of the year 2199.

Example: On what day was 8th March 1918?
(1) Take the last 2 digits of the year   19 18
(2) Divide (1) by 4 and ignore
    remainder: $18 \div 4 = 4$
(3) Take the key number of the month
    (from the table below)   4

Key numbers of the month			
January	1	June	5
January (leap year)	0	July	0
February	4	August	3
February (leap year)	3	September	6
March	4	October	1
April	0	November	4
May	2	December	6

(4) Take the key number of the century
    (table below)   0

Key numbers of the centuries	
1700s	4
1800s	2
1900s	0
2000s	6
2100s	4

(5) Take the day   8
(6) Add (1), (2), (3), (4) and (5)
    $18 + 4 + 4 + 0 + 8$ $= 34$
(7) Divide (6) by 7 $\frac{34}{7} = 4$ remainder 6
(8) The *remainder* gives the day of the
    month from the table below   *Friday*

Days of the week	
0	Saturday
1	Sunday
2	Monday
3	Tuesday
4	Wednesday
5	Thursday
6	Friday

So 8th March 1918 was a Friday.

When you have worked out the day of your birth, is this verse true about you?

Monday's child is fair of face,
Tuesday's child is full of grace,
Wednesday's child is full of woe,
Thursday's child has far to go,
Friday's child is loving and giving,
Saturday's child works hard for a living,
But the child that is born on the Sabbath day
Is bonny and blithe and good and gay.

Famous Days

4 July 1776 Declaration of Independence
3 September 1939, World War II started
7 May 1945, Germany surrendered to the Allies
2 September 1945, end of World War II
12 April 1961, first manned space flight
20 July 1969, first man landed on the Moon
On what days did these events take place?

The Hebrew Calendar

The Hebrew calendar started 3760 years and 3 months before the Christian era began. To find the year in the Hebrew calendar one has to add 3760 to the date in the Gregorian calendar. The month will not be exactly right as the Hebrew year starts in the autumn.

When is Easter Sunday?

There are certain days, such as Christmas, which fall on the same date each year. Easter Day is not one of them. It is a movable feast. In A.D. 325 it was decided that Easter Day should be on the first Sunday after the full moon which was on or after the spring equinox. This is the day when the Sun is halfway between being nearest to the Earth in midsummer and farthest from it in midwinter. The equinox is on 21st March, so Easter always falls between 22nd March and 25th April.

Prayer books have in them tables to find Easter Day by using Golden Numbers and Sunday letters. The mathematician Karl Friedrich Gauss, who taught Moebius, discovered a formula for finding dates of Easter Days from 1582 to the year 2000. The numbers 24 in (5) and 5 in (10) are the special ones to use from 1900 to the year 2000.

The Easter full moon comes (d) days after 21st March. Easter day is the $(22 + d + e)$ of March or the $(d + e - 9)$ of April.

In 1985, Easter Day could not have been in March because $22 + 15 + 1 = 38$, which is impossible. So, in 1985 Easter Day must have been $15 + 1 - 9$, or 7th April.

A Calendar Trick

Look at a month on a calendar and ask your friend to choose any week of seven days.

JUNE				
Monday		3	10	17	24
Tuesday		4	11	18	25
Wednesday		5	12	19	26
Thursday		6	13	20	27
Friday		7	14	21	28
Saturday	1	8	15	22	29
Sunday	2	9	16	23	30

1. Ask your friend what is the number of the first day of the week.   10
2. Tell your friend to add all the numbers of that week (10 to 16).   91
3. Interrupt your friend to give the result, which you obtained by adding 3 to the first date and multiplying by 7 $13 \times 7 = 91$

Example: To find the date for Easter Day in 1985:
1. Divide the year by 4 $\frac{1985}{4} = 496$ rem. 1 (a)
2. Divide the year by 7 $\frac{1985}{7} = 283$ rem. 4 (b)
3. Divide the year by 19 $\frac{1985}{19} = 104$ rem. 9 (c)
4. Multiply the *remainder* in (3) by 19 $9 \times 19 = 171$
5. Add 24 to (4) $171 + 24 = 195$
6. Divide (5) by 30 $\frac{195}{30} = 6$ rem. 15 (d)
7. Multiply the remainder in (1) by 2 $1 \times 2 = 2$
8. Multiply the remainder in (2) by 4 $4 \times 4 = 16$
9. Multiply the remainder in (6) by 6 $15 \times 6 = 90$
10. Add 5 to (7), (8) and (9) $5 + 2 + 16 + 90 = 113$
11. Divide (10) by 7 $\frac{113}{7} = 16$ rem. 1 (e)

Toilet Roll Maths

There is a great amount of mathematics to be learned from ordinary things. A teacher once wanted to show to the class that maths can be found in unlikely places. The pupils were divided into groups and each group was given a task. The groups were each given a *toilet roll* which had this information written on the wrapper:

> 2-ply roll
> 240 sheets
> 11·1 cm × 13·9 cm
> Total area 3·7 sq. m
> Minimum roll length 31·8 m

The pupils were allowed to use calculators and a reference library. This is what they wrote. The task is given first in each case.

Task 1: Describe the roll. What is its mass and length?

The roll is in the shape of a cylinder 11·2 cm high. The paper is wound round a cardboard tube which is also in the shape of a cylinder. The roll has a *mass* of about 140 grams.

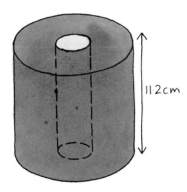

We found the *length of paper* in the roll in two ways.

1. We multiplied the length of one sheet by the numbers of sheets. We took this information from the wrapper.
   Length of 1 sheet = 13·9 cm
   Number of sheets = 240
   Length of the role = 13·9 × 240
   = 3336 cm
   = 33·36 metres

2. We unwound the roll and tried to measure its length. We found this very difficult. So we folded the paper into 10 lengths of 24 sheets. 24 sheets made a length of about 3·2 m, so 240 sheets would be about 32 m long. The wrapper on the roll gives the *minimum* length of the roll as 31·8 m and we agree with that.

Task 2: Find the diameter, radius and circumference of the roll.

The diameter of the roll was found by putting it between two books. The diameter is 11·5 cm.
The radius is a half of the diameter. The radius is 5·75 cm.

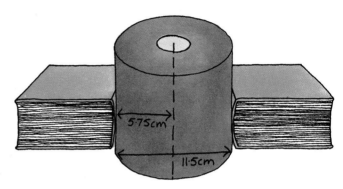

The circumference of the roll can be found in two ways:
1. by winding a tape measure round it. The circumferences is about 36 cm.
2. by using the formula C = 2πr
   = 2 × 3·14 × 5·75 cm
   = 36·11 or about 36 cm

Task 3: What is the shape, length, width and mass of one sheet of toilet paper? What is the area of all the paper?

A sheet of the paper is rectangular in shape. A rectangle is a parallelogram with one right angle. This means that *all* the angles are 90° each.

The wrapper says that each sheet of paper is 13·9 cm long and 11·1 cm wide. When we measured it we thought it was 13·8 cm long and 11·2 cm wide.

Their area would be 13·9 × 11·1 cm
   = 154·29 square centimetres
   = about 154 cm²

Our area would be 13·8 × 11·2
   = 154·56 square centimetres
   = about 155 cm²

Their total area of the paper
   = 154·29 cm² × 240
   = 37029·6 cm²
   = 3·7 m² (approximately

Our total area would be
   154·56 cm² × 240
   = 37094·4 cm²
   = 3·7 m² (approximately)

The wrapper says it is 3·7 m², so we agree with the area.

The mass of a sheet of paper cannot be measured on any balance scale we have. We found the mass of one sheet of paper by calculation. The roll of paper has a mass of 140 grams. There are 240 sheets in a roll. So the mass of one sheet

$$= \frac{140g}{240}$$

$$= 0.58 \text{ or approximately } 0.6\,g$$

This is the mass of 2 drawing pins.

Task 4: Find the diameter, radius and circumference of the cardboard tube.

The cardboard tube is cylindrical. The cylinder has a perpendicular surface with a circle at both ends. *Its diameter* is 4·4 cm or 44 mm. We put the circular end of the tube on millimetre squared paper and measured its width.

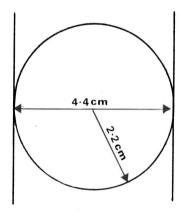

Its radius is $\frac{4·4}{2}$ cm, which is 2·2 cm or 22 mm.
Its circumference is πd or 2πr

C = 3·14 × 4·4 cm	C = 2 × 3·14 × 22 mm
= 13·816 cm	= 138·16 mm
= about 13·8 cm	= about 138 mm

Task 5: Find the volume of the cardboard tube and its surface area.

The volume of the tube is the amount of space it takes up. To find its volume we had to find the area of the circular top and multiply it by the height of the tube.

The area of the circle is πr²
The volume of the tube is πr²h

$$= 3.14 × 2.2\,cm × 2.2\,cm × 11.1\,cm$$
$$= 168.69336 \text{ cubic centimetres}$$
$$= \text{about } 168.7\,cm^3$$

The surface area of the tube is found by multiplying the circumference of the tube by its height. This is like cutting the tube and finding the area of a rectangle.

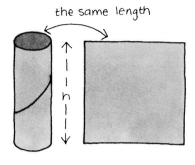

the same length

$$A = Ch$$
$$= 36\,cm × 11.1\,cm$$
$$= 399.6 \text{ square centimetres}$$
$$= \text{about } 400\,cm^2$$

Task 6: Annulus is the Latin word for a ring. In mathematics an annulus is the region between two concentric circles. These are circles which have the same centre. Look at the top of a toilet roll. Can you find the area of the annulus?

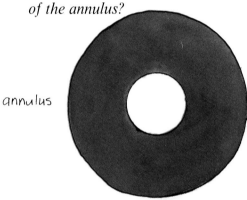

annulus

The annulus is the place where the paper is. To find its area we subtracted the area of the top of the tube from the area of the top of the toilet roll.

Area of top of roll = πr²
$$= 3.14 × 5.75\,cm × 5.75\,cm$$
$$= 103.8\,cm^2 \text{ (approximately)}$$

Area of hole
$$= 3.14 × 2.2\,cm × 2.2\,cm$$
$$= 15.1976 \text{ square centimetres}$$
$$= 15.2\,cm^2 \text{ (approximately)}$$

Area of annulus
$$= 103.8\,cm^2 - 15.2\,cm^2$$
$$= 88.6\,cm^2$$

Task 7: What is the volume of paper in the roll?
To find the volume of paper we decided to subtract the volume of the tube from the volume of the roll.

Volume of roll
$$= πr^2h$$
$$= 3.14 × 5.75\,cm × 5.75\,cm$$
$$\quad × 11.1\,cm$$
$$= 1152.36 \text{ cubic centimetres}$$
$$= \text{about } 1152\,cm^3$$

Volume of tube $= 3.14 \times 2.2\,\text{cm} \times 2.2\,\text{cm} \times$
$\qquad\qquad\quad 11.1\,\text{cm}$
$\qquad\qquad = \text{about } 169\,\text{cm}^3$
Volume of paper $= 1152\,\text{cm}^3 - 169\,\text{cm}^3$
$\qquad\qquad\quad = 983\,\text{cm}^3 \text{ approximately}$

Task 8: The spiral on the outside of the cardboard tube has a special name. It is a helix (pronounced HEE-LICKS). Look up the word in the dictionary and write about it. Where else would you find helical spirals?

A helix is a spiral. It is a curve on a cylinder, cone and sphere. It goes round and round these shapes at the same angle.

You will find a helix on a corkscrew or the thread of a screw. Some molluscs such as the snail have a helix on their shells.

Task 9: If you were to cut along the helix of the cardboard tube what figure would you find? Cut along the line and write what you have discovered.

We thought it might be a diamond shape, but when we cut it out it was a parallelogram.

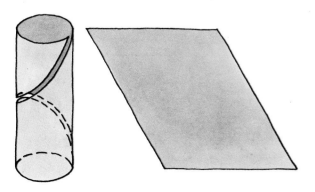

Chances

What are the *chances* of your doing well in your next exam? Will you *probably* play for your team in a match soon? Are you *likely* to come into a fortune during the next ten years? Is it *possible* that you will meet a famous person this year? Is your favourite team *certain* to win, lose of draw on Saturday? What are the *odds* against having an accident playing tennis?

You may think that nobody knows the answers to questions like those. Or you may think that the answers depend on luck or on other things. In fact, it is possible to work out mathematically the chances of most events happening. The branches which deal with chance are *statistics* and *probability*. Statisticians work out the chances of fires breaking out or burglaries occurring. They advise insurance companies on what rates to charge. They also know how long people are expected to live when they give advice about pensions. Many people have to *predict* what is likely to happen in the future and use probability to help them. Probability is just as accurate as any other branch of mathematics.

Galileo Galilei (1564–1642) is well known for his work on gravity and for insisting that the Earth goes round the Sun. He is also famous for being a professor of mathematics at the University of Pisa at the young age of 25. During that time, some gamblers asked Galileo why throwing three dice gives a total of 10 more often than a total of 9. This must have been the birth of the study of probability. Many mathematicians have developed it since in order to predict events.

Galileo was one of the greatest scientists of all time. He made important discoveries in physics, astronomy and mathematics.

One of them was *Blaise Pascal*, who lived about the same time as Galileo. Pascal's name crops up in many branches of mathematics. At the age of 16 he was famous for his work on curves and conic sections. He was interested in projective geometry. He invented a calculating machine when he was 19 because he became bored by adding long columns of figures in his father's office. In 1654, one of his friends called de Mere sent him a problem. It was this: how often will two sixes come up if two dice are thrown 24 times; This started Pascal off on his study of probability.

Tossing coins explains how probability works. A coin has two sides: a head (H) and a tail (T). If a coin is tossed a number of times it is likely to come down heads and tails an equal number of times. The more times a coin is tossed the more likely it is that the number of heads and tails is equal.

This is what will happen when coins are tossed:

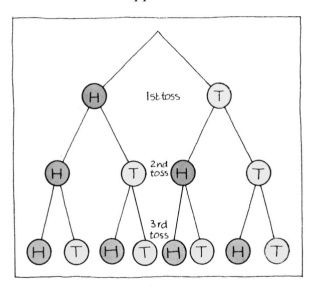

1. When a coin is tossed *once*, the result is H or T.
2. When a coin is tossed *twice*, there are 4 possible results: HH, HT, TH and TT. As HT is the same as TH, the chances are:
   1 in 4 of throwing HH
   2 in 4 of throwing HT
   1 in 4 of throwing TT
3. When a coin is tossed *three times*, there are 8 possible results: HHH, HHT, HTH, HTT, THH, THT, TTH, TTT. (HHT, HTH, THH are the same, and HTT, THT, TTH are the same.)
   So the chances are:
   1 in 8 of throwing HHH
   3 in 8 of throwing HHT
   3 in 8 of throwing HTT
   1 in 8 of throwing TTT

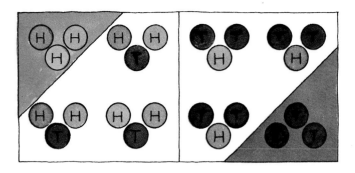

Pascal's Triangle

Pascal's Triangle (page 69) is also his probability triangle.

To find the probability of tossing 4 coins, the fourth line is used, the fifth for 5 coins, and so on.

By using the triangle it is possible to see that:

(a) the chance of getting 6 heads when tossing 6 coins is 1 in 64 $\frac{1}{64}$;
(b) the chance of having four tails when tossing 4 coins is 1 in 16 or $\frac{1}{16}$;
(c) the chance of getting 4 heads and one tail when tossing 5 coins is 5 in 32 or $\frac{5}{32}$.

The probability of events is shown by a fraction between 0 and 1. Here are some examples of a scale. On it, something certain to happen is 1 and something which cannot possibly happen is 0.

All living things die	1
A coin will come down heads	$\frac{1}{2}$
A team will win (it could win, lose or draw)	$\frac{1}{3}$
A card drawn from a pack will be a heart	$\frac{1}{4}$
A 6 will be thrown in dice	$\frac{1}{6}$
A fellow pupil can jump a height of 3 metres	0

Calculating the Chances

Working out the probability of something happening is both interesting and important. The following information is needed:

1. The number of ways in which the event can happen   (n)
2. The number of ways it can fail   (f)
3. The number of ways it can succeed (s)

A thing can either succeed or fail, so the possible ways an event can happen is f + s.

This is also the same as (n), so n = f + s.

The probability (P) of something happening is the number of successful results (s) divided by the number of possible results (n).

So $P = \dfrac{s}{n}$

Example: What is the possibility of throwing a number on a dice greater than 2?

Number of successful events possible (throwing 3, 4, 5, 6) = 4 (s).

Number of failures possible (throwing 1 or 2) = 2 (f)

$$P = \frac{s}{n} = \frac{4}{2+4} = \frac{4}{6} = \frac{2}{3} \text{ or 2 in 3}$$

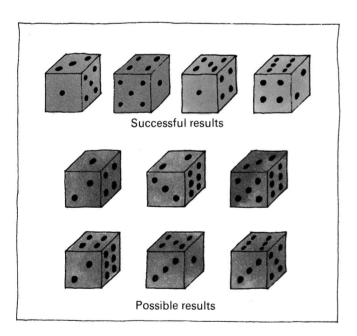

Successful results

Possible results

Combinations

How many ways are there of arranging 6 books on a shelf? In how many ways can the letters of the word CLASSROOM be arranged? What are the possible groupings of 8 people round a table? What are the chances of winning a fortune on the football pools? These are all questions connected with an area of probability called *permutation*. This is the number of combinations of the order of things or numbers.

Imagine the number of ways of arranging the letters of the alphabet in order to crack a code.

Letter	Combinations	Number
A	A	1
A, B	AB, BA	2
A, B, C	ABC, ACB, BAC BCA, CAB, CBA	6
A, B, C, D	ABCD, ABDC, ACDB ACBD, ADBC, ADCB BACD, BADC, BCDA BCAD, BDAC, BDCA CABD, CADB, CBAD CBDA, CDAB, CDBA DABC, DACB, DCAB DCBA, DBAC, DBCA	24

This could be very tedious, but fortunately there is an easy way of finding the pattern of permutations.

For one element the permutation is	1
For two elements it is	$1 \times 2 = 2$
For three it is	$1 \times 2 \times 3 = 6$
For four it is	$1 \times 2 \times 3 \times 4 = 24$

To save writing these products, the permutation is represented by a *factorial* number. This is shown as a numeral followed by an exclamation mark.

$2! = 1 \times 2 = 2; \ 3! = 1 \times 2 \times 3 = 6;$
$4! = 1 \times 2 \times 3 \times 4 = 24$

The number of ways of arranging 6 books on a shelf is 6!, which is 720. The letters of CLASSROOM can be arranged in 9! or 362 880 different ways. Factorials increase rapidly in value. The number of permutations of the 26 letters of the alphabet is 26! or

403 290 000 000 000 000 000 000 000

What do you suppose are the chances of guessing correctly the result of more than 30 football matches which can finish as a home win, or an away win, or a draw? No wonder mathematicians choose the exclamation mark to express factorials!

Answers

1. 3   2. 6
3. 9   4. 40
5. 4   6. 6
7. x − 5 years   8. John is 10, Mary is 15
9. 2y years   10. Tom is 8, Jane is 16

Page 80
A = 17   B = 35   C = 78

Page 86
1. 188·4 cm   2. 1232 m   3. 44 cm

Page 87/88
1. 616 m²   2. 38·5 cm²   3. 1386 m²

Page 100
The lily covered half the pond on the 29th day.

Page 103
(a) Chair, table, wardrobe, chest of drawers, sideboard, stool are six of many things likely to belong to a set of furniture.

Page 104
(b) You may be an element of these sets: children, girls, boys, pupils, students, humans, stamp-collectors, scouts, and many others.
(c) {domestic animals} or {cats, dogs, gerbils, budgerigars, ...}
This set will contain any tame animals living with people.
(d) 4 ε{square numbers} The number will be one of the set of 1, 4, 9, 16, 25, ...
(e) 5εN
(f) Empty

Page 105
(g) (i) parallelogram, rhombus, square, rect angle.
    (ii) triangle, quadrilateral, pentagon, hexagon, heptagon, octagon, nonagon, decagon, etc.
    (iii) tetrahedron, hexahedron, octahedron, dodecahedron, icosahedron.
(h) The children are over 1½ metres tall and weigh more than 40 kg.
(i) A ⊂ D ⊂ ∪
(j) They are eleven-year-olds who play a musical instrument and like games

(k)
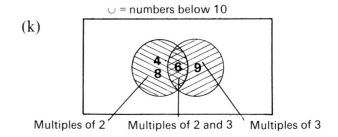
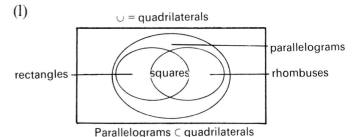
∪ = numbers below 10

Multiples of 2   Multiples of 2 and 3   Multiples of 3

(l)
∪ = quadrilaterals

rectangles — squares — rhombuses
parallelograms

Parallelograms ⊂ quadrilaterals

(m)
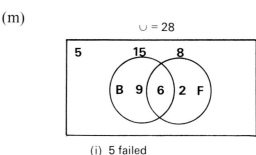
∪ = 28
5   15   8
B 9   6   2 F

(i) 5 failed
(ii) 9 passed in Biology only
(iii) 2 passed *only* in French

Page 117
Networks

Network	Number of ODD vertices	Number of EVEN vertices	If the network can be traced (yes or no)
(i)	0	4	yes
(ii)	2	0	yes
(iii)	2	2	yes
(iv)	4	1	no
(v)	2	4	yes
(vi)	4	0	no

Number (vi) is the network for the Koenigsberg bridges.

Page 118
Regions

Network	Number of regions or faces (F)	Number of vertices (V)	Number of arcs or edges (E)	F + V − E = ?
(i)	3	3	4	2
(ii)	5	5	8	2
(iii)	5	4	7	2

The Map Problem Each map can be completed by using only 4 colours.

The Ring Puzzle When one ring is removed, the other two are freed as well.

All Tied Up Loop your string under your friend's wrist loop. Pull your loop over your friend's hand to free yourself.

The Services Problem This cannot be solved.

Page 125

The L-shaped Farm The solution was to make another L-shape which took a quarter off each of the three squares. Perhaps the lawyer was good at geometry.

Twenty-one Cards When you deal the cards finally in front of your friend, the chosen card is the 11th. This is really an example of sorting, as is shown by the diagrams. After the first cut, the chosen card will be in the red area; after the second cut it will be in the blue area; and after the third cut it is always the 11th card.

If chosen card	Positions will be after		
is number...	1st cut	2nd cut	deal
1 to 3	8	10	11
4 to 6	9	10	11
7 to 9	10	10	11
10 to 12	11	11	11
13 to 15	12	11	11
16 to 18	13	12	11
19 to 21	14	12	11

Set of 21 cards
1 2 3
4 5 6
7 8 9
10 11 12
13 14 15
16 17 18
19 20 21

Find the Square There never was a 65th square. The line YZ which separates C and B from A and D is not really straight. In fact, there is a gap between the two areas in the shape of a very flat parallelogram whose area is exactlty one square.

Line YZ is really this shape, much exaggerated here

Incidentally, if your square were 16 units by 16 units, there would be 4 extra squares to look for.

Dots on a Domino Algebra can help with this one. The larger number can be called x.

Multiply x by 5	$= 5x$
Add 8	$= 5x + 8$
Multiply by 2	$= 10x + 16$
Add the smaller number	$= 10x + 18$
Subtract 16	$= 10x + 2$

$10x + 2$ must be a number with two digits. $10x$ is in the tens column and the second number is 2.

Page 126

A Horse, a Horse Mr. McKane solved the problem by using his knowledge of fractions, and with an inflatable horse he always carried around with him! This is how he worked it out:

$\frac{1}{2} + \frac{1}{3} + \frac{1}{9} = \frac{9}{18} + \frac{6}{18} + \frac{2}{18} = \frac{17}{18}$

$\frac{17}{18}$ is $\frac{1}{18}$ short of $\frac{18}{18}$, which is 1

He blew up his inflatable horse and put it in the paddock with the other 17. He then divided up the horses as follows:

The eldest daughter had $\frac{1}{2}$ of 18, which is 9 horses.

The middle one had $\frac{1}{3}$ of 18, which is 6 horses. The youngest one had $\frac{1}{9}$ of 18, which is 2 horses.

$9 + 6 + 2 = 17$

Mr. McKane took his inflatable horse, let the air out of it and put it back in his pocket. And everybody lived happily ever after.

Codes and Ciphers $632 + 632 = 5271$
Two + two = four

Networks

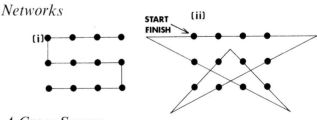

A Cross Square

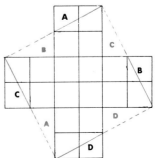

Index

Page numbers in *italics (123)* refer to illustrations.

A

Abacus 28, *28*
Acute angle 79, 94, *94*
Adding machine 29
Addition 31, 32, 53, 55, 91
Address 126, 127
Adjacent angle 94, *94*
A'h-mosè 12
Algebra 31, 62–63, *62–63*, 71, 103, 127
Alkemade, Nicholas 119
Alphabet 62
Alpha Centauri 98
Alternative angle 94, *94*
Amoeba 98
Amphora 24
Angle 31, 73, 74, *74*, 79. 93–95, *93–95*, 97
Anglo-Saxons *see* Saxons
Animal size 119, 120
Annulus 132, *132*
Apothecaries' system 19
Appian Way *15*
Applied mathematics 101
Aquarius *41*
Arabs *13*, 14, 30, *30*, 49, 62, 65
Arc 72, 85
Arc de Triomphe 123
Arch 122, 123, *123*
Archimedes 45, 71, 86
Architect 101, 122, 123
Architecture 26, *26*, 122
Area 27, 31, 80, 82, 87, 119–120, 131, 132
Aries *41*
Arithmetic 8, 32–35, *32–35*, 91–92, *91–92*
Arm balance *18*
Art 106–107, *106–107*
Associative law 91
Astrolabe 111
Astrology 41
Astronomy 20, 111
Atomic energy 62
Atoms 45
Avoirdupois system 19
Axes 127, *127*
Axioms 72
Aztec Sun Stone *59*

B

Babylonians 13, *13*, 18, 20, *21*
Balance 18, *18*
Banking 11, 23, 44, *44*
Bar graph 60, *60*
Barter 18, 22
Bases 55–56, *55*, 56, 83
Bean plant growth *59*
Bee cell 97, *97*, 108
Bhaskara 49
Bible 42
Binary system 57–58, *57–58*
Bisecting 73

Bissaker, Robert 29
Block graph 60, *60*
Body 119, 120
Body measures 16, 89–90, *89–90*
Boole, George 103
Braces 104
Brahmins 42
Brick-laying 94, *94*, 96, *96*, 101
Bridge 122–123, *122–123*
Bridge-crossing problem 117, *117*
Britannia coin *23*
Broken line graph 61, *61*
Building 26, *26*, 101, *101*, 122, *122*, 123
Bull's head weight *18*
Buttress *122*, 123

C

Caesar, Julius 21
Calculating machine 29
Calculator 29, 54, 57
Calendar 20, 41, 129, 130
Caliph's puzzle 114, *114*, 115
Cancer *41*
Candle clock *19*, 21
Cantilever bridge 122
Cantor, Georg 103
Capacity 24, 27
Capricorn *41*
Cardinal numbers 65, *65*
Card tricks 125
Carroll, Lewis 32
Cartesian geometry 127
Cave paintings 10, *10*, 59
Cell 98
Centilitre 25, 31
Centimetre 16, 17, 19, *25*, 31
Chance 133
Chart 59–61, *59–61*
Cheops pyramid 113, *113*
Chess 98, *98*
Chinese 22, 23, 28, *28*, 39; numerals 12, *12*
Chord 85
Christmas Carol, A (Dickens) 8
Chronometer 21
Cipher 126
Circle 20, 27, 31, *38*, 40, *40*, 72, 85–88, *85–88*, 108, 112, *112*
Circle words 85
Circumference 31, 72, 85, 86, 131, 132
Civil engineer 122
Clay tablet 13, *13*
Clerical work 8
Clock *13*, 21
Code 126
Code card 57–58, *57–58*
Coin 22, *22*, 23
Coin tossing 134, *134*
Columbus, Christopher 78
Column graph 60, *60*
Combinations *see* Permutation
Commerce 8, 109
Commutative law 91
Compass *21*
Compasses 72
Composite numbers 48
Computer 9, 29, 57, 59, *59*, 103
Concentric circle 132
Cone 75, 85, *85*, 88, *88*, 133
Containers 24–25, *24–25*

Contractor 101
Cooking spoon *24*, 25
Coordinates 127, 128
Corresponding angle 94, *94*
Count-down 44
Counting 10–11, *10–11*, 28, 32, 43, 44, 55–56, *55–56*
Counting tablet 28
Courage symbol 30
Crachit, Bob 8, *8*
Crane 102
Crossing roads 36, *37*
Cross square 126
Crystal 108
Cube 24, 25, 26, *26*, 27, 31, 70–71, *70–71*, 108, 119, 120
Cubic centimetre *25*
Cubic numbers 71
Cubit measurement 16, 90
Cuboid 26, 27, *27*
Curve *see* Circle
Cylinder 75, 85, *85*, 131, 132, 133

D

da Vinci, Leonardo 123
Day 20, 21, 129
Decagon 79
Decilitre 31
Decimal fractions 53–54
Decimal point 53, *53*
Decimal system 52, *52*, 55, *55*
Decimetre 27, *25*, 31
Definite numbers *see* Finite numbers
Degree 21, 31, 95, *95*
Denominator 44, 50, 53
Desargues, Gérard 108
Descartes, René 71, 127, 128
Diameter 31, 85, 86, *86*, 131, 132
Dice throwing 133, 134, 135
Die 23
Digit 16, *17*, 33, 38, 55, 56
Digital watch 21
Digit measurement 16
Dipstick 24
Directed numbers 44
Distance measurement 17
Division 29, 31, 32, 35, 51
Division bonds 35
Dodecahedron 77, *77*
Domestic machinery 102, *102*
Domino trick 125
Drink 24
Drinking vessel 24
Dumb-bell nebula *52*
Dustboard 13, 14, 28

E

Earth 41, 78, 133
Easter Day 130
Education 8
Edward I of England 16
Egg-timer 21
Egyptians: art 106; numbers 12, *12*, *13*, 44, 49, 59; measurement 16, *18*, 20, *20*, 21, 72, 93; weights 18
Einstein, Albert 62, *62*
Electron 45
Elements of a set *see* Members of a set
Elizabeth I of England 19
Ellipse 88, *88*, 108
Empty set *see* Null set

English bond 96, *96*
English measurement 16
Equals sign 31, 62
Equation 62, 63, *63*, 127, 128
Equilateral triangle 72, 97, *97*
Equivalence 50
Eratosthenes 46
Estimating 36–37, *36–37*
Euclid 48, 65, 72
Euler, Léonard 65, 71, 103, 116–117, 118
Euler's formula 71
Even numbers 64
Exponents *see* Index

F
Factorial number 135
Factor trees 48
Falling 119, 120
Fates 42
Fathom 89, *89*
Fibonacci numbers 66, 108
Figurate numbers 67–69, *67–69*
Finger counting 11
Finger measurement 16
Finite numbers 45
Finite sets 104
Firkin 24
Five-barred gate 123, *123*
Five-grouping 13
Flat *see* Plane shapes
Flat, musical 109
Flemish bond 96, *97*
Floor area 27
Foot 16, 31
Force 101, *101*
Foretelling with stars 41
Formula 62
Forth Railway Bridge 122
Fractions 39, 44, 49–51, 53
Fractions words 50
Free-falling 120, *121*
Frequency 109
Friendly numbers 65
Fun maths 38, 114–115, 125, 126
Furies 42

G
Galilei, Galileo 133, *133*
Gallon 24
Games 125
Gauss, Karl Friedrich 114, 130
Gemini *41*
Geo-board 80
Geometrical shapes 75
Geometry 31, 65, 72–73, *72–73*, 93, 108, 113, 127
Geometry set 72, *73*
Girder bridge 122
Gods 41, 42
Gold 22
Golden numbers 41, 130
Golden ratio 124
Golden rectangle 123–124
Goliath 16, *16*, 18
Good Luck symbol 30
Gothic style 122
Graces, three 42

Gram 19, 31
Graph 43, 59–61, *59–61*, 99, *99*, *120*, 127, *127*, 128, *128*
Graphics 59, *59*
Gravity 101
Greek arithmetic 67
Greeks 22, *22*, 28, 41, 42, 45, 72, 113, 124, 127; alphabet 62, *62*; measurement 16, 21; numbers 30, *30*, 46, 65, 67
Gregory, Pope 21, 129
Gregorian calendar 129
Grid lines *127*
Grouping division 35
Grouping numerals 11, 12
Guessing numbers 36, *36*, 39
Gunter, Edmund 29

H
Harpies 42
Harvest mouse 119
Hectare 31
Height 26, 31
Helix 133, *133*
Heptagon 79
Hexagon 69, 79, 97, *97*, 108
Hexagonal numbers 69
Hexahedra 70, 71
Hindu-Arabic numerals 14, 15
Hindus 42, 49
Histogram 60, *60*
Hogshead 24
Honeycomb 97, *97*, 108
Horizontal graph 60, *60*
Hour-glass 21
House building 101, *101*
Household appliances 102, *102*
House service puzzle 118, *118*
Hundred 14, 38
Hundredths 45, *53*

I
Icosahedron 77
Imperial System 19, 50
Improper fractions 50
Inch 16, 31
Inclined plane 102
Index 99
Indian numerals 14
Industry 9, 101, 109, 127
Infinite numbers 45, 67
Infinite sets 104
Integers 44
Irrational numbers 45
Isosceles trapezium 82, *82*
Isosceles triangle 79

J
Jar 24
Julian calendar 129
Jupiter 42

K
Kepler, Johannes 123
Kilderkin 24
Kilogram 19, 31, 56, *56*, 58, *58*
Kilometre 17, 31
Kite 82, *82*
Koenigsberg, Russia 117

L
Land measurement 72
Lantern clock *13*
Large numbers 45, 65
Latin 15
Lattice 74, *74*
Lattice fencing 123, *123*
Laws of Thought, The (Boole) 103
Leibnitz, Gottfried Wilhelm von 57
Length measurement 16–17, *16–17*, 26, 27, 31, 65, 131
Leo *41*
Leonardo da Vinci *see* da Vinci
Leonardo of Pisa *see* Fibonacci
Libra 19, *41*
Lifting tackle 102
Light-years *52*
Line bisecting 73
Line drawing 72, *72*
Line graph 127, *127*
Line numbering 43, 45
Lion weight *19*
Liquid measure 24–25, *24–25*
Litre 24, *25*, 27, 31
Lloyds of London 41
Load 101, *101*
Logarithms 100, *100*
Logic 9, 103
Long division 35
Lo Shu 39
Lucky numbers 41, 42
Lutine Bell 41
Lydian coinage 22

M
Machinery 28–29, *28–29*, 101, 102
Magic circle 40
Magic number 38, 41, 42
Magic squares 39
Map 118, *118*, 126, *127*
Mass 18, 19, 131, 132
Mathematics 8–9, *8–9*, 30–31, *31*, 101, *101*, 106–109, *106–109* *see also* Algebra, Arithmetic, Geometry, Modern Maths
Mayans 11
Measurements 37, 65, 89, *89*, 93; capacity 24, *24–25*; decimal notation 53; house furnishing 102; length 16–17, *16–17*; liquid 24–25, *24–25*; size and shape 26, 27; time 20–21, *20–21*
Medicine spoon 25
Members of a set 103
Merchants' measures 17, 19
Meter 102
Metre 16, 17, 27, 31
Metric system 19, 24, 50, 54, 90
Mile 17
Mileage meter 29
Millilitre 25
Millimetre 17, 31
Million 39, 45
Minting machine 23
Minus symbol 31, 44
Minute symbol 31
Mixed numbers 50
Möbius *see* Moebius, August Ferdinand
Mock Turtle 32
Modern Maths 8, 103, 127
Moebius, August Ferdinand 114

Moebius strip 115
Mollusc *133*
Mondrian, Piet 106
Money 22–23, *22–23*
Month 20
Moon 20
Mosaic 96, *96*
Mouse 119, 120
Multiplication 29, 33, 51, 62; bonds 35; law for 91, 92; sign 31, *31*; square 29, 33
Music 109, *109*

N

Nail board *see* Geo-board
Napier, John 28, *28*, 100
Napier's bones 28, *28*
Natural numbers 43
Nature 108, *108*
Nebula *52*
Negative numbers 44
Neptune 42
Networks 117–118, *117–118*, 126
New Maths *see* Modern Maths
Noah's Ark 16
Nonagon 79
Norman tally stick *11*
Nose tapping 11, *11*
Notch-cutting *see* Tally stick
Notre Dame Cathedral, Paris 26, *26*
Nought *see* Zero
Null set 104
Number: bonds 32; estimating 36–37, *36–37*; large and small 43–45; magical 41; patterns 8, 38–40, *38–40*, 46, 67–69, *67–69*; power 98–100, *98–100*; prime 46; symbols 30, *31*; system 12, 28, 32, 44; various 64–66, *64–66*; words 15
Numerals 12–13, *12–13*, 15, 38, 52, 56, 57
Numerator 44, 50, 53

O

Oblong 81, *81*
Obtuse angle 80
Octahedron 76, *77*
Octave 109
Octagon 79, 97, *97*
Octo numerals 55–56, *55*
Odd numbers 64, *64*, 68
Odometer 29
One-for-one counting 10
One hundred *see* Hundred
Orbit 88, *88*
Ordered pairs 127, 128
Ordinal numbers 65, *65*
Oughtred, William 29, 31
Ounce 19
Overweight sign 31, *31*

P

Pace 17
Palm measurement 16
Paper money 22
Papyrus 12, *12*, 18, *18*
Parabola 88, *88*
Parachuting 119, 120
Parallel lines 31, 74, *74*
Parallelogram 31, 81, 82, *82*, 83, 133 *133*

Parliament, Houses of 11
Parthenon 26, *26*
Pascal, Blaise 29, 134
Pascal's triangle 69, *69*, 134
Patterns 8, *9*, 38–40, *38–40*, 46, 67, *67*, 67–69, *67–69*, 96–97, *96–97*
Peace symbol 30
Pendulum 21
Pentagon 42, 77, *77*, 79
Pentagonal numbers 69
Pentateuch 42
Percentage symbol 31
Perfect number 42, 65, *65*
Perimeter 62, 80, 82
Permutation 135
Perpendicular bisector 73
Persians 22
Perspective 107
Petrol tank 24
Petrol tanker 24
Phrygian coin *22*
pi 30, 86
Piano keys 109, *109*
Picture graph (pictogram, pictograph) 61, *61*
Picture writing 10, *10*, 18, 59
Pie graph 61, *61*
Pint 24
Pipe, measurement 24
Pisces *41*
Plane shapes 78–83, *78–83*
Plato 76
Platonic polyhedra 76
Plumb-line 94, *94*, 101
Plus symbol 31
Pluto 41, 42
Polar bear 119, 120
Polygon 67, 76, *76*, 79, 83–84, *83–84*, 86, 97, *97*, 123
Polygonal numbers 67
Polyhedra 70, 71, 76, *76*, 108
Positive numbers 44
Pottery 24
Pound 19
Power 71, 98–100, *98–100*
Prediction 133
Pregel, river 117
Prime numbers 46–48
Prism 76
Prison cell *11*
Probability 133–135
Projective geometry 108
Proper fractions 50
Protractor 72, 73
Pure mathematics 101
Pure numbers 64
Puzzles 38, 114–115, 125, 126
Pyramids 102, 113, *113*
Pythagoras 41, 65, 76, 94, 109, 111

Q

Quadrilaterals 42, 79, 81, *81*, 82
Quart 24

R

Radius 31, 85, 131, 132
Ratio 50, 112, 120
Rational numbers 44, 45
Ratio of elegance 90
Rectangle 27, *27*, 31, 62, *62*, 74, *74*, 80, 81, *81*, 82, 123, 124

Rectangular numbers 46
Reflex angle 94, *94*
Regions 118
Reinforced concrete 123
Rhombus 82, *82*, 83, *83*
Right angle 73, 93–94, *93–94*
Rigid triangle 123
Ring puzzle 118
Road crossing 36, *37*
Road junction *9*
Road sign 30, *30*
Romans 15, *15*, 17, 22, *23*, 24, 28, 41, 71, 96, *96*, 122, 123; measurement 16, 18, 19, *19*, 20, 21; numerals 13, *13*, 30, *30*
Rotation *see* Angle
Roundabout number 38, 54
Round numbers 37

S

Saint Basil's Church, Moscow 26, *26*
St. Peter's Square, Rome *36*
Sand-clock 21, *21*
Satellite 88, *88*
Saxons 19, 21, 24
Scale, musical 109
Scale drawing 111
Scalene triangle 79
Scales 18
Schooling *see* Education
S'choty 28
Science 109, 127; symbols 30
Score 11
Scorpio *41*
Scribe 12
Scrooge, Ebenezer 8
Second symbol 31
Sector 85
Seki Kowa 40
Semicircle 85
Senses 42
Sequence 67
Sets 34, 45, 103–105, *103–105*, 106
Set square 74, *74*
Shadow reckoning 112, 113, *113*
Shakespeare, William 89
Shape patterns 96–97, *96–97*
Shapes 8, *9*, 26–27, *26–27*, 30, *59*, 67–69, *67–69*, 108, *108*, 112, *112*
Sharing division 35
Sharp, musical 109
Shekel 18
Shipping 8
Short division 35
Short measure 17, 19
Sieve of Eratosthenes 46
Signs 30, *30*, 44
Silver 22
Similar triangles 112, *112*, 113
Sixty-counting 13
Size 26–27, *26–27*, 119–120
Skin 120
Slide-rule 29, *29*, 100
Small numbers 45
Solar year 129
Solids 26, *26*, 75–77, *75–77*
Soroban 28
Sound counting 11
Space figures 75
Span measurement 16
Spiral 108, 133

Spirit-level 94, 101
Sporting events 54, *54*
Spring equinox 129, 130
Square 46, 63, *63*, 71, 81, *81*, 82, 96,
    96, 112, *112*
Square centimetre 31
Square metre 27, 31
Square numbers *9*, 42, 68, 69
Square yard 27
Standard measures 17, 19, 24
Star-making *42*
Star of David 42
Stater coin *22*
Statistics 133
Steel girder 122
Steelyard 19, *19*
Stellate numbers 69
Stevin, Simon 52
Stick measurement 16
Straight angle 94, *94*
Street planning 126
Stretcher bond 96, *96*
String puzzle 118
Studying mathematics 8, 9
Suan pan 28
Subdividing numbers 45
Subset 105
Subtraction 29, 31, 32, 34, 51, 53, 55
Sun 20, 41, 45, 133
Sundial 20, 21, *21*
Sunflower 108, *109*
Supplementary angle 94, *94*
Surface area 27, 119, 120, 132
Surveying 101, *101*, 110, 111, 112,
    112
Sydney Harbour Bridge 122
Sydney Opera House *9*
Symbols 30, 31, 42, 43, 44, 49, 53,
    59, 126

T

Talent 18
Tallier 11

Tally stick 11, *11*
Tangent 85
Tankard 24
Taurus *41*
Ten-counting 11, 13, 55
Ten numerals 52
Tenths 45, *53*
Terms 50
Tessellation 96–97, *96–97*
Tetrahedron 76, *76*, 108
Thales 113
Theodolite 101, *101*, 111, 112
Thousandths 45, 53
Three-dimensional shapes (3-D) 26,
    75, *75*
Three Rs 32
Through the Looking Glass (Carroll)
    32
Tiling 96, *96*
Time 20–21, *20–21*
Timetable *32*
Toe counting 11
Tone 109
Tonne 31
Topology 116–118
Trade 8, 18, 19
Trapezium 82, *82*, 83
Trapezoid 82
Triangle 27, 31, 72, 78–80, *78–80*, 94,
    110–113, *110–113*, 123
Triangular numbers *9*, 67–68, 69
Triangulation 111, *111*
Tricks *see* Fun maths
Trigon 110
Trigonometry 110–111, *110–111*
Trinity 42
Troy system 19
Two-dimensional shapes (2-D) 27,
    27, 78, *78*

U

Uncia 19
Underweight sign 31, *31*
Underworld 41, 42

United Nations Building *26*
Universal set 105

V

Vanishing point 107, *108*
Venn, Rev. John 103
Venn diagrams 103, 105
Vertex 71, *71*, 93, *93*, 97, *97*, 117,
    117, 126
Vertical graph 60, *60*
Vertical angle 95, *95*
Vibration 109
Virgo *41*
Volume 26, *26*, 27, 31, 71, 119–120,
    132

W

Wall calendar 10, *11*
Wallpapering 102, *102*
Watch 21
Water 24
Water-clock *19*, 21
Weather chart 44
Week days 21
Weighing 18–19, *18–19*, 23, 54, 56,
    56, 58, *58*
Weightlessness 19
Wheelbarrow 101, *101*
Whole number 32, 43, 44, 49, 51, 53,
    103
Width 26, 27, 31
Wine 24, *25*
Words for numbers 15

Y

Yard 17, 27
Year 20, 129
Yih King 39

Z

Zero 14, 43, 44, 45, 53
Zodiac signs *41*

Acknowledgements

Pages: 8 Hodder & Stoughton, 9 top Taylor Woodrow, bottom Australia News & Information Bureau, 10 bottom Royal Airforce Museum, Hendon, 11 Mansel, 12 & 13 Michael Holford, 17 Italian Tourist Office, 18 top Salter Industrial Measurement Ltd, middle Avery Ltd, bottom Fotomas, 19 top Fotomas, bottom British Museum, 21 top Science Museum, bottom left Sonia Halliday, bottom right Michael Holford, 22 middle British Museum, bottom Michael Holford, 23 top British Museum, middle British Tourist Authority, bottom Scala, 24 British Museum, 26 top Michael Holford, left Zefa, middle Michael Holford, right Zefa, 28 top Scottish National Portrait Gallery, bottom Michael Holford, 32 British Airports Authority, 36 & 37 to Zefa, 37 bottom Barker & Dobson Ltd, 45 V. Fleming/D. Parker: Science Photo Library, 49 Zefa, 52 Hale Laboratories, 54 SSIH Equipment UK Ltd, 59 top Zefa, bottom Moving Picture Company, 72 Helix Ltd, 75 Zefa, 85 Colorsport, 89 top Nasa, 91 J. Allan Cash, 93 Zefa, 96 Peter Clayton, 101 top Sir Robert McAlpine & Sons Ltd, bottom Ordnance Survey, 103 Mansell, 108 & 109 Zefa, 106 Zefa, 107 top Tate Gallery, London, bottom Scala, 113 Robert Harding, 116 Denise Gardner/T. E. Davey, 121 Tony Stone Associates, 122 Zefa, 127 Mansell, 129 British Museum, 133 Mansell.

Picture Research by Penny J. Warn.

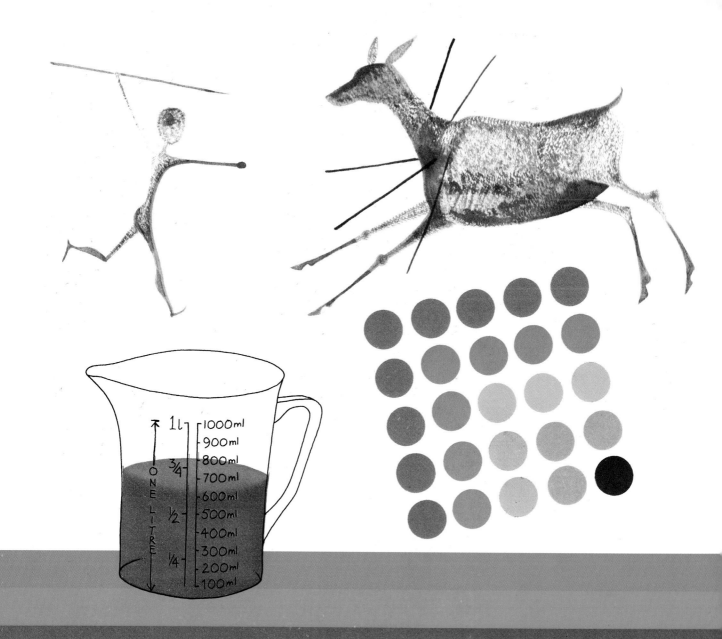